Human Trafficking

Emerging Legal Issues and Applications

Edited By
Nora M. Cronin
Kimberly A. Ellis

Contributors

Peter W. Blair, Jr.
Robin Boyle Laisure
Melissa L. Breger
Nicole Campion
Felicity Gerry, QC
Gonzalo Martinez de Vedia

Bryanne Perlanski
Fiona McLeod, SC
Julia Muraszkiewicz
Alan W. Scheflin
Catarina Sjölin, LL.M.
Niovi Vavoula, LL.M.

Lawyers & Judges Publishing Company, Inc.

Tucson, Arizona

 **Lawyers & Judges
Publishing Company, Inc.**
P.O. Box 30040 • Tucson, AZ 85751-0040
(520) 323-1500 • FAX (520) 323-0055
e-mail: sales@lawyersandjudges.com
www.lawyersandjudges.com

Library of Congress Cataloging-in-Publication Data

Library of Congress Cataloging-in-Publication Data

Names: Cronin, Nora M., editor. | Ellis, Kimberly A., editor. | Blair, Peter W., Jr.
Title: Human trafficking : emerging legal issues and applications / edited by Nora M. Cronin, Kimberly A. Ellis ; contributors, Peter W. Blair, Jr. [and eleven others].
Description: Tucson, Arizona : Lawyers & Judges Publishing Company, [2016] | Includes bibliographical references and index.
Identifiers: LCCN 2016046982| ISBN 9781936360222 (hardcover : alk. paper) | ISBN 1936360225 (hardcover : alk. paper)
Subjects: LCSH: Human trafficking--Law and legislation. | Human trafficking--Law and legislation--United States. | Human trafficking--Law and legislation--Australia.
Classification: LCC K5297 .H8595 2016 | DDC 345/.02551--dc23
LC record available at https://lccn.loc.gov/2016046982

ISBN 13: 978-1-936360-22-2
ISBN 10: 1-936360-22-5

Printed in the United States of America
10 9 8 7 6 5 4 3 2 1

Dedication

We gratefully acknowledge the victims of trafficking who have come forward to tell their stories, and we dedicate this work to those who have yet to come out of the shadows.

Contents

PART I:
HUMAN TRAFFICKING IN CONTEXT

PART II:
DIGITAL ASPECTS IN IDENTIFYING AND INVESTIGATING
THE HUMAN TRAFFICKING CASE

Chapter 5: Using Digital Technologies to Combat Human Trafficking:
Privacy Implications **111**
By Felicity Gerry QC, Julia Muraszkiewicz, LL.M., and Niovi Vavoula, LL.M.

Chapter 6: Human Trafficking in the Dark:
Sex Trafficking on the Dark Web **135**
By Bryanne Perlanski

PART III:
SPECIAL ISSUES

PART IV:
ADDITIONAL LEGAL APPLICATIONS FOR TRAFFICKING LAWS

Foreword

Alicia Ouellette

Although it exists largely in the shadows, human trafficking—the acquisition and forced exploitation of men, women, and children—is a worldwide problem. From the streets of New York to Australia, Europe, Asia, South America, and Africa, humans prey upon men, women, and children for profit, sex, forced marriages, forced labor, domestic servitude, and other forms of slavery.

The numbers alone are staggering. Globally, the International Labour Organization estimates that at least 20.9 million people are victims of forced labor, that some 44 percent these are trafficking victims, and that 4.5 million are subject to forced sexual exploitation. Seventy-five percent of underage sex trafficking victims report having been advertised or sold online. The average age of entry into the sex trade in America is 12–14 years old. By some reports, 3,287 people are sold or kidnapped and forced into slavery every day, and the price paid for the average human sold into slavery is $100. Human trafficking is thought to be the second-largest source of illegal income worldwide, second only to drug trafficking. In a 2014 report, the Urban Institute estimated that the underground sex economy in the United States ranged from $39.9 million in Denver, Colorado, to $290 million in Atlanta, Georgia.

Trafficking in persons is a criminal act and a violation of the human rights of its victims. Its effects on victims are catastrophic. Yet, it is often the victims who find themselves caught in criminal prosecutions for prostitution, drug offenses, and immigration offenses. Prosecuting the traffickers remains challenging. While the number of prosecutions of traffickers is increasing, most convictions still take place in a few countries, and the number of victims continues to increase.

Human Trafficking: Emerging Legal Issues and Applications tackles the complex, multi-dimensional issues that arise as governments and activists across the world mobilize to assist victims and combat the practice of modern day slavery. The book proceeds in five parts. Part I puts human trafficking in context, starting with Gonzalo Martinez de Vedia's exploration of U.S. responses to labor trafficking. Next, Felicity Gerry demonstrates the complexity of recognizing human trafficking victims in cases involving the drug trade, arguing for a proactive, intentional approach by criminal attorneys. Nicole Campion argues that creative legal approaches to human trafficking, such as New York's specialized courts, ensure that child and adult victims who are arrested for crimes such as prostitution receive favorable and appropriate treatment. Finally, Fiona McLeod assesses the Australian response and enforcement efforts identifying gaps in redress for trafficking victims.

Part II explores the role of technology in identifying and investigating cases of human trafficking. Felicity Gerry, Julia Muraszkiewicz, and Niovi Vavoula highlight the potential privacy implications of digital tracking, data collection, unmanned aircraft, and biometrics when used as tools for combatting trafficking. Bryanne Perlanski details how the Dark Web, an anonymous cyber location, has changed the practice of trafficking, allowing traffickers to stay ahead of and out of sight of law enforcement.

Part III explores special legal considerations raised by human trafficking. Nora Cronin and Alan Scheflin present Alan's cutting-edge new Social Influence Model (SIM) as a tool for lawyers to get evidence of undue influence before the court. Melissa Breger challenges practitioners and judges to address the rehabilitation needs of traumatized, sex-trafficked children through therapeutic foster care. Next, Julia Muraskiewicz tackles the thorny problem of identifying trafficking victims and explores the European framework for identification. Felicity Gerry and Catarina Sjolin focus on the impact of trafficking on women and girls, and the concomitant challenges of achieving gender equality.

Part IV explores new applications of trafficking law with Robin Boyle Laisure's chapter comparing cults and human trafficking. Specifically, Laisure argues that cult leaders share important traits with traffickers, inflicting similar exploitative, manipulative harm on victims, and, given these similarities, that trafficking laws may be useful to capture and prosecute cult leaders.

Finally, the Appendices detail U.S. anti-trafficking law. In a fascinating comparison, Peter Blair, Jr. first contrasts U.S. federal law governing sex trafficking with the laws of several states. He then contrasts the jurisdictions' approaches to labor trafficking laws.

As a whole, this volume immerses the reader in the complex and heartbreaking problem of human trafficking. At the same time, it offers practical and tested approaches from around the globe, presenting readers with legal and societal tools that could go a long way toward stopping perpetrators, identifying and empowering victims and potential victims, and, perhaps most urgently, restoring the dignity, health, and wellbeing to trafficking victims throughout the globe.

— Alicia Ouellette
President & Dean
Albany Law School

Preface

Kimberly Ellis

When human trafficking began appearing on my newsfeed with increasing frequency, I started to wonder what kind of tools were out there to help lawyers and other practitioners working on the ground with victims. I noticed that, while plenty of research and anecdotal materials exist on the topic, there was a need for information and guidance specifically geared for the practitioner.

I wanted to create a book that would do something tangible to help those who were vulnerable to or victimized by human trafficking, and who didn't have the power to help themselves. I began reaching out to human trafficking experts around the world, seeking contributions that would inspire and inform practitioners across jurisdictions.

Nora Cronin, a former senior prosecutor practicing in New York, had recently convened a Continuing Legal Education program on human trafficking for the New York State Bar Association. When I found out that she had a background in writing and journalism, I approached Nora and invited her to be my co-author on this project.

A year later, our collaboration has resulted in what we think will be a powerful tool for seasoned and new lawyers alike, as well as judges, social workers, law enforcement, policy-makers, and academics.

This book has been written to assist those who fight at all levels to eradicate and prevent human trafficking, and those who work with the victims whose lives have been darkened by this crime.

Every care has been taken to ensure the accuracy of the cases and legislation cited in this book. Because of the ever-evolving nature of human trafficking and the laws designed to address it, we, of course, encourage you to verify that all laws are current at the time you use them in your practice.

Additionally, our contributors come from around the world and, as such, some of the spellings and word usage in their chapters will reflect the writing practices of their respective countries.

We hope you find this book to be useful in the work that you do to set right the wrongs of human trafficking.

—Kimberly Ellis, Co-Editor

Acknowledgments

Nora Cronin: I gratefully acknowledge the efforts of all of our contributors who have worked tirelessly to bring this book together, and the efforts of my co-editor Kim Ellis for introducing me to contributors many hours out of my time zone who have taught me so much in this process. I also thank Raymond Brescia at Albany Law School for his assistance in helping me find contributors affiliated with that institution, as well as my alma matter, St. John's University School of Law, for helping me find Robin's chapter. I also acknowledge St. John's relatively successful efforts to shape me into a disciplined and thoughtful attorney, and for giving me the opportunity to make lifelong friends who are an endless source of inspiration, a shoulder to cry on, and constantly challenge me to be my best self.

Thank you. *–Nora*

Kimberly Ellis: First and foremost, I thank Dmitri and Rosella—the two shining suns of my life—for your support and patience during the writing of this book. I could not have done this without you. I would like to thank my co-editor, Nora Cronin, for joining me in this endeavor and contributing her expertise and round-the-clock teamwork. A big thank you to Alicia Ouellette for writing the thoughtful Foreword to this book, and to all our contributors, who so graciously shared their knowledge through this work—it has been a privilege to work with each of you. A special note of gratitude to Roslyn Petelin of the University of Queensland Writing, Editing, and Publishing Program, for her guidance and support. Thanks to Melissa Curley and Scott Downman, also of the University of Queensland, for taking the time to chat with me about your work. I would like to thank Steve Weintraub and Raphael Bressel, Esq., of Lawyers & Judges Publishing, Inc. for believing in this project. Thank you to my dear friend, Christine Beck-Millan, Esq., for your encouragement and enthusiasm when this book was still a twinkle in my eye. Thank you to Jim Hecht for our interest and for putting me in touch with Nicole. Thanks to my family for their support. Finally, I acknowledge the suffering of the millions of trafficked and exploited men, women, and children around the world, and the tireless efforts of those who work to help them. This book is for you. *–Kim*

Introduction

Human Trafficking: Modern Criminals Profiting from Exploitation

I first became interested in human trafficking while still in college. I was just dipping my toes into the pool of gender issues and human rights, but not really understanding or able to comprehend the myriad of forces that go into creating a trafficking victim, or why trafficking as an industry is a profitable one, and one that draws criminals to it because it is a low-risk, high-profit crime. Interestingly, and perhaps disappointingly, despite this initial familiarity with the idea of exploitation and criminal profit in my young adult years, I do not recall focusing on this issue again until the end of my time as a trial attorney at the Brooklyn District Attorney's Office.

I was working on a case with another assistant district attorney who was prosecuting a homicide in one of the housing projects in the Bedford-Stuyvesant section of Brooklyn[1]. The victim in the case was a teenage boy who was riding his bicycle and was caught in the crossfire of a drive-by shooting. Tragically, this fact pattern is an all-too familiar case to a city prosecutor, but upon closer examination of the motivation behind the shooting, a new type of story began to emerge that I had yet to consider as an attorney, but had considered the motivations and systemic failures that give rise to the type of crime from the time I was a young adult—it was time to re-educate myself.

The shooter in this case was in a rival gang with the intended target, who had begun to profit from bringing drugs acquired in New York City to the neighboring state of Vermont, and selling the drugs at a high mark-up to college students in that state. The key to getting into that market was befriending the women at the institution; the gang members making them believe that they were their boyfriends through manipulation. Based on what I learned, the women, who were mostly young, middle-to-upper-middle-class, and white, were thrilled to be associated with men whom they considered to be status symbols, mostly because

---

1. For purposes of this introduction, the specific facts, names, and institutions involved in this case are spoken of in general terms.

they differed from the men at college and had fancy cars, expensive sneakers, and gave the women "street cred" in rural Vermont. The women were then relatively unperturbed when asked to sell drugs for these men, and turned over all the profits to the gangs. The profits, for their part, skyrocketed, the gangs got rich, and eventually it lead to a shooting on the streets of Brooklyn over turf that existed hundreds of miles away.

Gang members eventually became uninterested in the risk of running drugs out of the city every weekend, and began to discover their profits would be much higher if, instead, they just sold women. Using the same manipulation and intimidation tactics from the case in Vermont, women would be brought down to the city from the suburbs north and east of the city, or recruited locally, where they would be forced to have sex with gang members, friends of the gang members, and eventually complete strangers. These facts and developments shocked me, but I as I learned more about the subject, I discovered that this story, while typical of a trafficking case in the moral bankruptcy of the traffickers and their devaluation of human life for their own financial gains, is not necessarily typical in its fact pattern. In fact, one of the most frightening things about the crime of human trafficking is that there is no "typical victim." The only trait that trafficking victims have in common is that they are vulnerable in some way, and traffickers are aware that these vulnerabilities make them exploitable.

Unfortunately, many victims are vulnerable because they represent those who may already be on the fringes of the communities in which they live—immigrants, youth, women, LGBTQ-identified, those with non-conforming gender expressions, and minority populations. Mistrust of authority figures and "systems," even if those systems include dedicated and sensitive social workers, is rampant. These dynamics allow traffickers to come to their intended targets under the guise of a friendly face, promising their victims that "they are the only ones who can understand" and "want to help." A trust relationship is built, and then traffickers betray that trust by using this relationship to have their victims engage in illegal activity that benefits the trafficker. Even in the cases where the behavior is legal, such as in labor trafficking cases involving farm work or domestic service, the circumstances surrounding the work is such that it is clear that a victim would not have engaged in the work if they were truly given an option.

Interestingly, although there is no typical victim, traffickers are really all the same. Similar to the gang members from the case in Brooklyn, they are expert manipulators, keen to exploit weaknesses or needs they perceive their victims as having, which is why trafficking as a crime should shock the conscience of us all. My hope is that once we are cognizant of these dark forces at work in our world, we can begin to innovate and make space for change.

Because there is so much work ahead of us in the anti-trafficking community, this book is meant to be both a primer on topics relevant to the modern human trafficking case, as well as a point of departure for further discussion. We hope that future trafficking prosecutions, as well as legislation and reforms designed to assist victims, create more case law and standard practice over time.

We include topics that are relevant to emerging trends in human trafficking—including use of the Internet, the Dark Web, and judicial innovations such as New York State's Human Trafficking Intervention Courts. As the chapters within this book demonstrate, technology has profoundly affected the ability of traffickers not only to recruit victims, but also to make their business of selling these victims more profitable. As the high-stakes crime unfolds, victims often find themselves before courts in place of the traffickers, and our chapter on New York State's Human Trafficking Intervention Courts explains how one jurisdiction has recognized that, within the law, there are individuals who are brought into criminal courts as defendants who deserve to be recognized as victims.

In addition, we introduce lawyers to a new concept that may become the next tool for getting evidence of undue influence admitted into court: the Social Influence Model. Alan W. Scheflin and I make use of the Social Influence Model he created in 2015 to help trafficking victims in the three contexts in which they may enter the courtroom: as civil plaintiffs for restitution, as witnesses in a case against their trafficker, or as defendants in their own criminal cases.

We also include a primer on labor trafficking, as this topic is often overshadowed by sex trafficking, both in terms of public understanding and arrests and prosecutions of perpetrators.

Although, as is pointed out elsewhere in the book, trafficking disproportionately affects women because of their often already-marginalized places in the societies from which they are trafficked, as well as the consequences that women face as a result of being trafficked, Gonzalo Martinez de Vedia cites a statistic in his chapter that only 55% of overall victims of trafficking overall are female. Men are victims of trafficking as well, but their victimization is often difficult to detect. Labor trafficking is one area where additional male victims may be identified, although this crime is often overlooked both by the public and by law enforcement when taking steps to combat human trafficking. Hopefully, evaluating the circumstances surrounding the cases discussed in our labor trafficking chapter will give practitioners the tools they need to identify a labor trafficking case, and to respond to the legal and social service needs of the victims.

There is also a robust analysis of trafficking's place against a larger backdrop of international human rights issues, including the case of Mary Jane Veloso, who was rescued before she was put to death by firing squad in Indonesia thanks to the legal work of our contributor Felicity Gerry, QC, who discusses the case in her chapter. This case demonstrates the urgent need to see those who are trafficked as victims and rightly put criminal responsibility back onto the shoulders of those who seek to traffic them for profit.

Practitioners who have developed an expertise in human trafficking laws often find themselves in high demand for more information, and because of that—and for comparative purposes for further advocacy—we have included two charts in the Appendices of this book that compare the current penal codes on sex and labor trafficking within selected states and the U.S. federal law. In terms of international human rights law, there are chapters in this book that deal specifically with Australian law on the topic, as well as E.U. and international protocols that are still relatively new in terms of international norms. This can make this topic exciting, but due to the serious nature of the crimes being perpetrated, also put great responsibility on the practitioner to understand the global landscape of the laws they are upholding.

In the final section of the book, we use the ideas set forth by trafficking laws themselves for legal innovation. Robin Boyle Laisure offers an application of human trafficking statutes to assist prosecutors in another challenging area—bringing leaders of cults to justice. Cult leaders are similar to traffickers in that they seek out vulnerable victims, many of whom are alienated even from their own family, and often fall prey to clever manipulation by leaders who offer them a chance to have their needs of social acceptance met. Often this leads to the trafficker overcoming the victim's free will, and the victim then engaging in criminal behavior where only the trafficker profits, or in some cases, the goals of the cult leader are advanced.

There is an uphill climb in stopping worldwide human trafficking, and lawyers, judges, and advocates need tools to educate themselves, juries, and the public regarding this emerging threat to human rights. We hope you will find the information within these pages to be a resource to help you achieve the goal of educating yourself so you can continue to assist others. Best of luck, and know that every contributor to this publication is with you as we continue to fight for justice.

— Nora M. Cronin
Co-Editor

Part I
Human Trafficking in Context

Chapter 1

Labor Trafficking: The *Garcia* Case and Beyond[1]

By Gonzalo Martinez de Vedia

Early in the summer of 2002, when farm owners across the United States were bracing for a difficult harvest under the hottest and driest conditions since the Dust Bowl, federal prosecutors delivered the industry another blow by way of a criminal complaint in the rural Western District of New York.[2] Maria Garcia and five associates—a group of contractors among the thousands who each year deliver farm hands to labor-intensive crops across the country—was indicted on a slew of crimes, including the unusual charge of "forced labor,"[3] a form of human trafficking.

Though often used interchangeably with the term "human smuggling," a felony to which the northern border of New York is no stranger, the legal definition of trafficking in persons refers to the exploitation of a person through force, fraud, or coercion, and does not require transportation.[4] Rather than a violation of a nation's borders, human trafficking is the criminal abuse of a person for profit. Human smugglers offer willing customers a service; for human traffickers, people themselves are the commodity.

National media outlets soon picked up on this seemingly anachronistic story, reminiscent of the days of chattel slavery. According to the complaint, Garcia, a U.S. citizen from Texas, had recruited dozens of undocumented Mexican men and boys in Arizona with promises of gainful employment. With the help of her son, husband, and several others, she packed the would-be workers into vans with seats removed so as to fit as many as 30 of them at a time. Told to stay quiet behind blacked-out, meshed windows, the immigrants rode over 2,000 miles across nine states to isolated labor camps in Western New York.

Upon arrival, they learned their true predicament: The drive had ostensibly cost each of them between $1,000 and $1,800, a debt they would have to repay the Garcias one minimum-wage hour at a time, toiling in vegetable fields sun-up to sun-down under armed threat. Their paychecks would also have to cover rent and utilities for the squalid, overcrowded trailers that would double as the site of their false imprisonment. The scheme left the workers with virtually no pay, so the Garcias found another method to motivate the crew: "If we didn't work harder," said one of the men, "they would lock us in a small truck for a month without feeding us."[5]

A Farmworker Legal Services (FLSNY) attorney, Dan Werner, who would go on to represent the workers in a civil suit, likened the end of the ordeal to that of "slaves escaping before the Civil War." After sneaking out in the middle of the night, he recalled, the workers "slept in a forest, near some railroad tracks, with people out looking for them."[6] Rather than charge a violation of the 13th Amendment prohibition of slavery (famously ratified in 1865 after the U.S. Civil War) however, federal prosecutors of the *Garcia* case made first use in the continental U.S. of labor trafficking provisions established less than two years earlier by the Victims of Trafficking and Violence Prevention Act of 2000 (TVPA), a landmark bill hailed by Congress as its answer to modern forms of slavery.

The agricultural industry, deeply reliant on farm labor contractors, would follow the case closely, from its unexpected start that summer in the federal courthouses of Buffalo, to Garcia's guilty plea to a violation of U.S.C. Title 18, § 1589 (forced labor), through to her sentencing to 46 months and order of mandatory restitution to the victims. Perhaps with more alarm still, industry observers also witnessed the extension of civil liability beyond the Garcia family to the many farm-owning "grower defendants" who benefitted from their services. Taken together, the criminal and civil prosecutions of all involved could have seemed to announce that the TVPA had opened a new avenue for justice across the U.S. for victims of the worst types of workplace abuse.

This chapter is a consideration of U.S. responses to trafficked labor as they stand today, over a decade since the pioneering prosecutions of *U.S. v. Garcia et. al.*, and *Javier Hernandez v. Maria Garcia-Botello*.[7] Despite the relative success of the Garcia plaintiffs at the turn of the century, uses of labor trafficking provisions in the law have since become a rarity, rather than an industry-shifting, criminal enterprise-threatening recurrence.

Further, the umbrella human trafficking conventions set by the TVPA have instead predominantly served to intercept and disrupt criminal activity that exclusively relates to commercial sex and sexual exploitation, addressing other types of human trafficking crimes mostly just in theory. Despite indications that labor trafficking remains prevalent in U.S. agriculture and several other low-wage industries, workers such as the plaintiffs in *Garcia* are all too often left alone to find their own justice when they fall prey to exploiters. This blind spot in the U.S. response to human trafficking only widens in consideration of new transnational trends, such as the recent increase in entry to the U.S. of unaccompanied minors from Central America, which have left new generations of immigrants more vulnerable to these types of crime than ever.

Finally, this chapter questions the overall effectiveness of federal criminal justice responses to labor trafficking in addressing the forces that drive such types of exploitation. Rather, a more localized and holistic approach may better serve to address the problem.

1.1 The TVPA as a Sex-Trafficking-Driven Umbrella Law

In many circles, *Garcia*'s 2002 application of the TVPA in the agricultural expanses of Western New York came as a surprise. The political context in which President Clinton signed the bill into law was far removed from that which once greeted Lincoln's Emancipation Proclamation. At the beginning of the 21st century, public awareness around the issue of slavery had long shifted away from American farms towards a more complex narrative of transnational criminal enterprises trading in persons for exploitation in a range of private industries, particularly commercial sex.

In line with the concurrently drafted United Nations Palermo Protocol to Prevent, Suppress and Punish Trafficking in Persons, the TVPA encompassed all forms of trafficking. However, in a telling introductory clause, its authors memorialized their expectation that when it came to "this contemporary manifestation of slavery," the victims would be "predominantly women and children,"[8] a demographic disproportionately affected by sex trafficking.

Global estimates indeed place the percentage of overall trafficking victims who are female at 55 percent—a true, if slight majority. Children make up just over a quarter.[9] The past 15 years of application of the TVPA by law enforcement and prosecutors, however, suggests its architects may not have only been pointing to this numerical fact in their introductory qualification, but also signaling a broader moral prioritization that deems sex trafficking of women, particularly young women and girls, a more urgent and prevalent problem than exploitation for labor.

In a country where 92% of constituents believe human trafficking victims "are almost always female,"[10] the political coalitions necessary to sustain the now four-time reauthorization of this anti-trafficking law would have to respond first and foremost to that public perception, real or imagined. Accordingly, the last of these TVPA iterations passed Congress as an amendment to the 2013 Violence Against Women Act.[11] Likewise, New York State's version of the law, the most recent enhancement of which was enacted in January of 2016, met Governor Cuomo's pen as part of a Women's Equality Agenda.[12] Although this embedding of trafficking legislation within women's rights campaigns has proven politically strategic, such framing also inadvertently perpetuates the public image of trafficking as a one-gender issue.

At all jurisdictional levels, application of trafficking statutes strongly reflects this single-track outlook. Federal authorities report that out of 257 trafficking cases pursued for prosecution under the TVPA in the last recorded 12-month period, more than 95% (248) exclusively concerned the trade of sex.[13] Records in Albany reveal an even heavier bias towards such cases within New York: Of the 42 convictions obtained in the nine-year history of the State's trafficking law, all but one involved commercial sex.[14] That low ratio, 2.4%, sets New York in line with all other states: Of the 479 cases researchers recently found to have ever been charged under state-level trafficking law, only 11 (2.3%) cited a law specific to labor trafficking.[15]

These numbers from law enforcement and prosecutors stand in sharp contrast to the caseloads of another pillar of the U.S. response to trafficking in persons: The broad network of federally-funded service providers for whom the identification by law enforcement of a trafficking victim is just the start of the work. Grant monitors for one of the two major funding streams for these services report that the majority of cases their grantees encounter are of labor trafficking—which affects all genders more evenly—in addition to a significant percentage with elements of both sexual and non-sexual exploitation.[16] Individual victim-serving agencies corroborate that national tendency in their own numbers: One of the largest New York legal services providers reported that labor trafficking cases made up 60% of their overall trafficking caseload.[17]

A side-by-side comparison of such metrics from the law enforcement and services sectors reveals a tiered response to human trafficking across the United States. Whereas trafficking crimes involving mostly younger women and girls for sexual exploitation trigger both service provision and prosecutions, the type of trafficking that exploits mostly foreign nationals of all ages and genders for manual labor is often identified and addressed by service providers, but elicits little to no response from federal investigators and prosecutors.

Although researchers have shown that boys and LGTBQ youth make up an under-identified portion of sex trafficking cases,[18] these prosecutions have almost invariably involved women and girls.

1.2 Harvest of Shame

A nationwide study of service provider records reveals that labor trafficking is most common in specific types of high-risk workplaces. Not surprisingly, the low-wage industries of domestic service and care giving, restaurants, hospitality and agriculture topped the list. Of these, agriculture served as the venue for exploitation in nearly a fifth of the cases.[19]

These are uneasy statistics for New York, where agriculture brought in more than $7 billion in gross receipts in 2014, making it the state's number one industry. Unwilling to use these proceeds to provide wages and conditions attractive to local workers, the 10,345 New York farms that hire outside help have turned to more pliant, economically desperate workers from as far as Mexico, Central America and the Caribbean. Within this increasingly consolidated industry, only 1,429 (14%) of the state's agricultural operations require more than ten workers. It is that highest-earning tier of New York farms that most relies on the state's 60,944 farmworkers.[20]

Collectively, these employers only sponsor about nine percent of the statewide agricultural workforce through the H2-A Guestworker Program,[21] the only legal means to procure foreign labor for work on farms in the United States. The vast majority of the overall industry instead relies on registered or informal labor contractors such as Garcia to source their hired help. The largest farms in particular, whose infrastructure often includes on-site, barrack-style farm labor camps, pay top dollar to this sprawling network of brokers, who secure a constant flow of workers to harvest crops during narrow, unpredictable time windows or to staff 24-hour, 365-days-a-year milking rotations. Indeed, the dairy industry—New York State's top agricultural sector—must rely on informal referral networks to procure foreign labor, since seasonal visas, by definition, cannot meet their year-round demands.

The work of these contractors does not end with a successful job placement. It is often these same facilitators who help finance the journeys of immigrants from impoverished, violence-ridden communities to the work camps, and who manage them afterwards as crew bosses. As the U.S. government continues to pour billions of dollars into militarizing its southern border, the cost of all northward journeys has steadily increased, pushing more immigrants to indebt themselves to smuggling networks.

As a result, a growing norm for new arrivals to U.S. agriculture is to spend their first months or years working off a debt to "coyotes" (hired border-crossing guides), transporters, and labor brokers who walk a fine line between smuggling and trafficking. To secure the repayment of these often-exorbitant fees, smugglers may confiscate documents, threaten violence, firing or deportation, or simply apply unreasonable interest rates on the loan principals, turning smuggling into a form of trafficking defined in U.S. law as "debt bondage."[22] Unlike a time when indentured servants tended Britain's colonial farms throughout North America for a fixed period of time, victims of this type of crime face indeterminate years of exploitation under coercive creditors as a rite of passage into the U.S. labor force.

---

22 U.S.C. § 7102 (5): Debt bondage

The term "debt bondage" means the status or condition of a debtor arising from a pledge by the debtor of his or her personal services or of those of a person under his or her control as a security for debt, if the value of those services as reasonably assessed is not applied toward the liquidation of the debt or the length and nature of those services are not respectively limited and defined.

Debt brokers and labor contractors are in constant and direct contact with New York's farmworkers by design. They provide a layer of deniability between the workforce and the end recipients of trafficked labor—the land-owning employers. Although litigators have at times succeeded in naming such parties liable as "joint employers" alongside their contractors, criminal justice responses to labor trafficking have largely ignored the complicity of deeper-pocket farm employers, fixating on their hired brokers instead.

As in *Garcia*, these crew bosses are often second-generation immigrants or even former low-wage workers, who provide farms with easy access to a known workforce, often from their own hometowns in Latin America. The agricultural industry's version of low-level management, they stand a rung above hand-harvesters and milkers, earning themselves a higher pay that depends on their ability to extract efficient, compliant labor from their fellow immigrants or former colleagues. Insofar as they employ coercive tactics to achieve production goals, the middlemen often assume complete and sole liability for the criminal activity. These "mayordomos," as workers know them, are easily dispensable, allowing farmers to avoid legal ramifications in case of an outside inquiry.

The liability buffer created by this labor contracting system leaves farmworkers at constant and ubiquitous risk of extreme forms of exploitation under unafraid, unscrupulous employers who act with impunity. A survey of the unauthorized Spanish-speaking farmworker population in San Diego County, California, revealed that 31% of the workforce had at some point experienced violations that meet the legal standard for human trafficking.[23] Another study administered a few states down the East Coast migrant stream from New York, in North Carolina, found that one in five farmworkers in that area had experienced some form of trafficking, with significant numbers reporting deception and lies (21%), restriction and deprivation (15%), and even threats to physical integrity (12%).[24]

While the prevalence of the first two categories warns of increasing sophistication within farm labor trafficking schemes, involving bait-and-switch job offers, debt repayments and psychological manipulation, the mere existence of the third is a sobering reminder that current farm labor standards for auditing and enforcement are weak enough to allow recurring cases where employers simply force their workers through actual or threatened physical harm.

If such surveys warn that low-wage industries have persisted in extracting labor through force, fraud and coercion from marginalized, vulnerable and criminalized sectors of society, any expansion of said populations has only served to exacerbate the trend. In recent years, heightened gang violence and political instability in El Salvador, Guatemala, and Honduras has resulted in a surge of unaccompanied minors fleeing northward for safety. U.S. Customs and Border Protection (CBP) apprehended a record 68,541 of these youth in 2014, designated "unaccompanied alien children" (UACs).[25] This figure dropped to 39,970 in 2015, only to rise again, already standing at 48,311 as of July 30, 2016.[26]

Once processed by CBP, the Office of Refugee and Resettlement (ORR), an agency within the Department of Health and Human Services, is tasked with finding appropriate homes for the UACs pending the resolution of their immigration proceedings. In 2014, at the height of (and reportedly overwhelmed by) the spike in UAC arrivals, ORR placed several such Guatemalan teenagers as young as 14 with sponsors in Marion, Ohio, who in turn forced them to work on egg farms. In the federal prosecution that followed, *U.S. v. Castillo-Serrano et. al.*,[27] officials charged the crew leaders with labor trafficking, but, as in *U.S. v. Garcia*, failed to hold any of the farm owners accountable.

The *Castillo-Serrano* plaintiffs were just several of 635 UACs released to sponsors in the entire state of Ohio in 2014. By comparison, New York State received 5,955 UACs over that same period.[28] As the Ohio case revealed, improvised custody arrangements, thin support networks, and economic stress have rendered this new generation of young immigrants uniquely vulnerable to forced and coerced labor. The next section of this chapter will consider that, despite the statistical likelihood that some of the thousands of UACs placed in New York have ended up in situations comparable to that in *Castillo-Serrano*, officials in the more agricultural areas of the State may be the least likely to identify or respond to such abuses.

Manner and Means of the Conspiracy (*U.S. vs. Castillo-Serrano et. al. Indictment*)

It was part of the conspiracy that the Defendants:

- [...] submitted false and fraudulent Applications to ORR in which they represented themselves and their associates to immigration officials as the minor victims' relatives and family friends, in order to have the minor victims released to the Defendants' custody. In doing so, the Defendants and their associates affirmed that the victims would go to school and be protected from abuse.
- [...] focused their recruitment efforts on individuals under the age of 18, believing them to be easier to bring successfully into the country, easier to control, and harder workers.
- [...] obtained deeds to real property from the victims' families to secure the victims' debts for being smuggled into the United States, and that the Defendants retained the deeds to those properties if any portion of the smuggling debts were unpaid or any dispute between the parties remained.

1.3 Governmental Abdication

From the view of the federal government buildings around Niagara Square in downtown Buffalo, New York, the past 15 years have made the *Garcia* case seem more an historical anomaly than a watershed moment. Federal officials have since inquired into only a handful of labor trafficking cases. Yet even when these rare probes into low-wage industries have led to the certification of victims of forced labor, referrals to social services, and even the granting of federal immigration status reserved for victims of trafficking—the T visa—criminal charges often fall short of the TVPA, instead focusing on employers' "harboring" or "transporting of illegal aliens."

By taking this approach, officials send a problematic message to the un-documented community—that their irregular immigration status may be of more interest to the government than their victimization. Hesitant to apply a trafficking lens to the worst abuses taking place in farms, restaurants, and other businesses, officials in rural New York have joined a national trend[29] of reserving use of the all-encompassing TVPA only to address sexual exploitation.

For the Western District of New York (WDNY) specifically, anti-trafficking work for the past decade has predominantly involved disrupting the activities of sex traffickers its two urban hubs, Buffalo and Rochester. Those efforts alone generated so many trafficking cases in 2015 as to make theirs the District with the most prosecutions of that type in the entire country—a distinction made more dramaticn considering the relatively low population of its area compared to other jurisdictions.

WDNY's record of combatting such types of abuse is notable in its own right, and speaks to the effectiveness of their federally funded Enhanced Collaborative Model Anti-Trafficking Task Force. But it also begs the question of why, in a district home to some of the country's largest employers of vulnerable farmworkers—and given the known prevalence of forced labor in comparably agricultural areas—none have had their rights vindicated under trafficking laws in the WDNY courts since *Garcia*.

The Enhanced Collaborative Task Force Model

The U.S. Department of Justice (DOJ), through funding authorized by the Trafficking Victims Protection Act, has supported 48 regional Anti-Trafficking Task Forces since 2004. As of FY2015, DOJ was actively funding 20 of these collaborations, which provide matching grants to a service provider and law enforcement sponsor through, respectively, the Office of Victims of Crime (OVC) and the Bureau of Justice Assistance. Although these groups only cover part of the country, DOJ encourages all jurisdictions to adopt the Enhanced Collaborative Task Force Model. An e-guide to the creation and administration of such task forces is available online, through OVC's Training and Technical Assistance Center, at https://www.ovcttac.gov/taskforceguide/eguide/.

Asked point-blank about this dearth of labor-related cases on live television, the current United States Attorney for this District (at the time of publication), William J. Hochul, Jr., offered a telling theory:

> From what I've seen, from my vantage point, it is very difficult to conduct an investigation when agriculture workers, who may be here for two to five days during a harvest time, are involved. By the time law enforcement would even get a lead that there are potential undocumented workers who are being held against their will and then mobilize the resources to conduct the investigations, those workers may in fact have already moved on to the next community.[30]

Though the remarks were intended to explain the relative challenge of investigating labor trafficking cases, Hochul instead revealed his seeming unfamiliarity with the tens of thousands of migrant workers who each year harvest the crops of Western New York for months—not days—at a time. Further, the presidentially appointed prosecutor appeared to suggest that the transience of the victim population in question hampers the ability of federal enforcement agents to serve them, despite the fact that many of the sex trafficking cases his office success-fully and plentifully prosecutes involve the constant shuffling of victims across cities and states.

A consideration of the political context within which Hochul directs this office yields reasons to believe his single-track response to human trafficking crimes is more complex than mere ignorance of any one-victim population. In Western New York, as with all other rural areas in the State, the business side of the agricultural industry figures much more prominently in politics than the priorities of the agricultural workforce. Whereas one contingent enjoys vigorous advocacy at all levels of government by the Farm Bureau, the other does not have as much as the right to collective bargaining as a protected activity under the National Labor Relations Act (farm and domestic workers were excluded from such protections in a deal with Southern Democrats in the 1930s). Even if New York's farmworkers were to overcome the risk of firing to form political associations such as California's United Farm Workers or North Carolina's Farm Labor Organizing Committee, these groups would hold less political sway than established actors such as the Farm Bureau. For one, the irregular immigration status and relative transience of farm workers severely impair their strength at the polls.

Given this political context, the average town hall discussion of agriculture is much more likely to focus on the concerns of the business side than to take into account challenges facing the sector's workforce. At one such gathering in 2012, for example, in Appleton, New York, two towns down the Lake Ontario shoreline from fields where the *Garcia* plaintiffs once labored in debt bondage, the Congressional Representative for New York's 26th District (who happens to be Hochul's wife) provided assurances that it was her "priority to listen to the concerns of our family farms and streamline services to make their businesses run more efficiently." The owner of a nearby vineyard and member of the Niag-ara County Farm Bureau, in attendance that day, reiterated that focus, expressing gratitude that her elected representative seemed aware of "the various rules and regulations that limit our flexibility to conduct our businesses."[31]

Although the farm owner's comments that day were in specific reference to legislative proposals, this political imperative presumably extends to any govern-ment oversight—regulatory or enforcement-related. Insofar as Hochul must set his prosecutorial priorities within that political environment, it is clear he would face more than a practical challenge in aiming investigative resources towards the labor camps of the biggest employers and landowners in his district.

Whether the factors keeping Hochul's office from the area's farm labor camps have been practical or political, the outcomes speak for themselves: Of the 12 cases that earned WDNY its number-one place in trafficking prosecutions for 2015, none involved farm labor abuses, or trafficking charges in any industry other than sex work. Indeed, not a single trafficking prosecution during Hochul's tenure so far has involved labor trafficking—an unlikely state of affairs for the district that once pioneered the application of labor trafficking law to agriculture at the dawn of the TVPA.

1.4 *Garcia*: Emblem of a System

Even if WDNY were to reprioritize forced labor alongside other types of trafficking prosecutions, the shift would only address one element of a broader, systemic issue. As much as the farming industry may prefer to believe Garcia was a rogue actor among an otherwise above-board status quo, a comparison of her behavior to the current standards for agricultural labor brokering suggests the main difference between her and many other contractors still staffing New York's farms may simply be that she was caught. Far from an anomaly, Maria Garcia, until the date of her indictment, appeared as one of hundreds of labor contractors legally registered with the New York State Department of Labor.

Indeed, a criminal-justice-only approach to labor trafficking might serve more to validate than transform the industries that benefit from forced labor. By casting the precious few middlemen who are each year named in federal complaints charging forced and coerced labor as "bad apple" perpetrators, the U.S. justice system suggests that such instances are manageable ruptures in an otherwise accountable system, rather than predictable expressions of no-questions-asked supply chains, where consumers and middlemen simply demand the best quality product and services for the lowest possible price. By that standard, the pushing of workers into maximum productivity through human trafficking is not a failing of the current system, but rather its purest achievement.

1.5 Promising Practices

For their part, U.S. Attorney Hochul and the WDNY Anti-Trafficking Task Force recently convened a subgroup solely dedicated to the identification and prosecution of labor trafficking. This new committee, one of the first of its kind in the country, is led by the Worker Justice Center of New York (WJCNY), which, under its previous existence as FLSNY, and in tandem with Hochul's predecessors, once helped Garcia's victims escape indentured servitude.

One of the WJCNY staff involved in that extraction, Renan Salgado, coordinates the group, which includes prosecutors, law enforcement agencies, and service providers. His hope is to remind officials that although labor trafficking cases follow a different pattern than sex trafficking and its "low-hanging" evidentiary trails on, for example, web-based escort sites, they follow a pattern nonetheless—one more obvious and common than is widely accepted. "There is a mentality that these are difficult cases, which leads to a reluctance to dedicate resources," he says. "We are out to change that."

The latest data and recommendations from the highest levels of U.S. government seem to support that push, and point to NGOs such as WJCNY as crucial partners in creating that shift. The 2015 Assessment of U.S. Government Activities to Combat Trafficking in Persons by the Attorney General's Office, for example, recommends an increase in "targeted training and outreach efforts with partners who can help identify potential labor trafficking victims."[32] Unburdened by some of the political considerations that may keep government officials from high-risk workplaces, and able to approach potentially undocumented trafficking victims without bearing a badge—the mere sight of which is to many undocumented immigrants synonymous with immigration enforcement—NGOs stand to make greater headway into marginalized communities where pockets of labor trafficking persist.

If and until these new partnerships lead to an overhaul in federal responses to labor trafficking, state and local actors have stepped in to fill the void. As of 2011, state-level prosecutions overtook the federal response to trafficking by way of total cases prosecuted. The gap has only widened since.[33] One local government partly responsible for this increase, Alameda County, outside of San Francisco, credits part of its progress against the issue to assigning an Assistant District Attorney to solely focus on the intricacies of labor trafficking cases.

In New York, where no such county-level prosecutorial position exists to hone in on high-risk workplaces, leadership has instead come out of Albany: The Governor's office recently convened an Exploited Worker Task Force it credits with recovering millions of dollars of back wages and damages from hundreds of businesses.[34] Although the initiative has so far focused on civil penalties and health and safety matters, is also represents a rare advance of the State into its riskiest industries, which in turn will lead to more contact between officials and those segments of the New York State workforce that labors under force, fraud, or coercion.

If the 15 years since federal officials first handled the *Garcia* case are any indication, state officials may have to think beyond prosecutions towards comprehensive services, peer-to-peer prevention programs, and industry-wide regulation to secure that the next round of labor trafficking cases it identifies might be the last.

FY2015 Federal Labor Trafficking Prosecutions

Although the U.S. Government reported nine criminal labor trafficking prosecutions for FY2015, advocates have only been able to find records for six such cases. By contrast, survivors of labor trafficking brought ten civil suits against their exploiters during the same period. See following tables.

Federal Criminal Forced Labor Cases Filed in FY 2015 Under Trafficking Statutes (Chapter 77, Title 18)

Case name	Docket number & jurisdiction	Date of indictment	Status (as of 6/5/16)
US v. Alvarado McTague et. al.	14-cr-00055 (W.D.Va.)	12/4/14	Ongoing.
US v. Andres et. al.	14-cr-1461 (D.Az.)	11/5/14	D pled guilty; restitution not ordered.
US v. Castillo-Serrano et. al.	15-cr-00024 (N.D.Oh.)	1/14/15	Ongoing.
US v. Clark (Esthela)	15-cr-00093 (M.D.Fla.)	6/24/15	Ongoing.
US v. Drayton	15-cr-2 (M.D.N.C.)	1/5/15	D pled guilty; restitution not ordered.
US v. Homoud et. al.	15-cr-00391 (W.D.Tex.)	6/3/15	Both Ds pled guilty; restitution ordered in the amount of $120,000 (Ds jointly and severally liable).

(Source: The Human Trafficking Pro Bono Legal Center, criminal and civil federal trafficking databases, www.htprobono.org.)

Federal Civil Forced Labor Cases Filed in FY 2015 Under 18 USC § 1595 (Civil Trafficking Statute)

Case name	Docket number & jurisdiction	Date of indictment	Status (as of 6/5/16)
Arma v. Prakoso	14-cv-03113 (D. Md.)	10/2/14	Dismissed (voluntarily).
Menocal v. GEO Group, Inc.	14-cv-02887 (D. Colo.)	10/22/14	Ongoing.
Lipenga v. Kambalame	14-cv-03980 (D. Md.)	12/29/14	Ongoing.
Ouedraogo v. Bonkoungou	15-cv-01345 (S.D.N.Y.)	2/24/15	Dismissed (voluntarily).
Chun v. Kim	15-cv-01154 (N.D. Ga.)	4/14/15	Settled in the amount of $30,000.
C.G.B. v. Santa Lucia	15-cv-03401 (D.N.J.)	5/15/15	Ongoing.
Cruz-Cruz v. McKenzie Farms	15-cv-00157 (E.D. Ky.)	5/28/15	Ongoing.
Gutierrez-Morales v. Planck	15-cv-00158 (E.D. Ky.)	5/28/15	Ongoing.
Juarez v. Standard Drywall, Inc.	15-cv-00105 (D. Wy.)	7/7/15	Ongoing.
Adhikari v. KBR	15-cv-01248 (E.D. Va.)	9/28/15	Ongoing.

(Source: The Human Trafficking Pro Bono Legal Center, criminal and civil federal trafficking databases, www.htprobono.org.)

Endnotes

1. An earlier version of this chapter originally appears in de Vedia, *Blind Eyes to Trafficked Labor in Western New York*, 102 Voices of Mexico (2016).

2. Department of Justice, "Six Indicted in Conspiracy for Trafficking and Holding Migrant Workers in Conditions of Forced Labor in Western New York," June 19, 2002.

3. 18 U.S.C. § 1589.

4. 18 U.S.C. § 1589.

5. Steven Greenhouse, "Migrant Camp Laborers Face Forced Labor Charges," N.Y. Times, June 21, 2002.

6. Dan Herbeck, "Contractor Gets 46 Months in Prison for 'Despicable' Abuse of Farm Labor," The Buffalo News, May 27, 2005.

7. *U.S. vs. Garcia et. al* (WDNY) 02-CV-0523(S)(Sr); 02 Civ. 0523(S)(Sr); 02-CV-523S.

8. Public Law 106-386.

9. International Labor Organization, "2012 Global Estimate of Forced Labour," June 2012.

10. Vanessa Bouche, Amy Farrell, & Dana Wittmer, "Identifying Effective Counter-Trafficking Programs and Practices in the U.S.: Legislative, Legal, and Public Opinion Strategies that Work," National Institute of Justice, 2016.

11. Public Law 113-4.

12. New York State Governor's Office, "Governor Cuomo Signs Legislation to Protect and Further Women's Equality in New York State," October 21, 2015 (https://www.governor.ny.gov/news/governor-cuomo-signs-legislation-protect-and-further-women-s-equality-new-york-state).

13. U.S. State Department, "Trafficking in Persons Report," June 2016.

14. New York State Division of Criminal Justice Services, 2015.

15. Vanessa Bouche, Amy Farrell, & Dana Wittmer, "Identifying Effective Counter-Trafficking Programs and Practices in the U.S.: Legislative, Legal, and Public Opinion Strategies that Work," National Institute of Justice, 2016.

16. Banks, Duren, and Tracey Kyckelhahn, "Characteristics of Suspected Human Trafficking Incidents, 2008– 2010," US Department of Justice, 2011.

17. City Bar Justice Center, "Measuring the Impact of Legal Services on Human Trafficking Survivors, 2016" (http://www2.nycbar.org/citybarjusticecenter/images/stories/pdfs/the-impact-of-legal-services-on-human-trafficking-survivors.pdf).

18. Curtis, Ric, et. al., "The Commercial Sexual Exploitation of Children in New York City," John Jay College of Criminal Justice, September 2008.

19. Owens, Colleen, et. al., "Understanding the Organization, Operation, and Victimization Process of Labor Trafficking in the United States," Urban Institute, October 21, 2014.

20. U.S. Department of Agriculture, "Census of Agriculture," 2012 (http://www.agcensus.usda.gov/Publications/2012/Full_Report/Volume_1,_Chapter_2_County_Level/New_York/).

21. U.S. Department of Labor, Office of Foreign Labor Certification, "H-2A Temporary Agricultural Labor Certification Program – Selected Statistics, 2015" (https://www.foreignlaborcert.doleta.gov/pdf/H-2A_Selected_Statistics_FY_2015_Q4.pdf).

22. 22 U.S.C. § 7102 (5).

23. Zhang, Sheldon X., "Looking for a Hidden Population: Trafficking of Migrant Laborers in San Diego County," U.S. Department of Justice, November 2012.

24. Barrick, Kelle, et. al., "Indicators of Labor Trafficking Among North Carolina Migrant Farmworkers," U.S. Department of Justice, November 2013.

25. 6 U.S.C. § 279(g)(2).

26. U.S. Customs and Border Protection, "United States Border Patrol Southwest Family Unit Subject and Unaccompanied Alien Children Apprehen-

sions Fiscal Year 2016" (https://www.cbp.gov/newsroom/stats/southwest-border-unaccompanied-children/fy-2016).

27. *U.S. vs. Castillo-Serrano, et. al.*, 3:15CR0024 (OHND 2015).

28. U.S. Department of Health and Human Services, Administration for Children and Families, Office of Refugee Resettlement. "Unaccompanied Children Released to Sponsors By State," August 25, 2016 (http://www.acf.hhs.gov/orr/programs/ucs/state-by-state-uc-placed-sponsors).

29. Febrey, Annick, "Reevaluating the Trafficking Victims Protection Act," *The Hill*, March 31, 2016.

30. Biandudi Hofer, Helene, "Human Trafficking In Monroe County", *WXXI News*, September 25, 2014 (http://wxxinews.org/post/watch-human-trafficking-monroe-county-need-know-special).

31. Hochul, Kathy, Press Release: "Niagara County Farmers Meet With Hochul to Share Concerns," April 23, 2012 (http://votesmart.org/public-statement/689974/niagara-county-farmers-meet-with-hochul-to-share-concerns#.V7kuqpMrJE4).

32. U.S. Department of Justice, "Attorney General's Annual Report to Congress and Assessment of U.S. Government Activities to Combat Trafficking in Persons," 2015.

33. Vanessa Bouche, Amy Farrell, & Dana Wittmer, "Identifying Effective Counter-Trafficking Programs and Practices in the U.S.: Legislative, Legal, and Public Opinion Strategies that Work," National Institute of Justice, 2016.

34. New York State Governor's Office, "Employers to Repay Nearly $4 Million in Back Wages and Damages to More Than 7,500 Workers," July 20, 2016 (http://www.governor.ny.gov/news/governor-cuomo-announces-employers-repay-nearly-4-million-back-wages-and-damages-more-7500).

Chapter 2

Human Trafficking in the Drug Trade:

Lessons for Attorneys from the *Mary Jane Veloso* Case

By Felicity Gerry, QC

Synopsis
2.1 Human Trafficking
2.2 Drug Trafficking
2.3 Identifying Victims
2.4 Non-Punishment
2.5 An Attorney's Role
2.6 Conclusion
Endnotes

A Human Trafficking Victim on Death Row

In April 2015, two Australian citizens and several from other countries were executed in Indonesia after being convicted of drug-trafficking offences. At the last minute, on the same death row, Filipina maid Mary Jane Veloso was reprieved. The single mother had also been convicted of drug-trafficking offences. However, she had always maintained that she had been deceived into carrying the drugs in a suitcase provided to her as part of her recruitment to work abroad. Shortly before she was due to be executed, human trafficking mechanisms were invoked by her attorneys in the Philippines.[1] There was a public campaign about her human trafficking status, and the arrest of her recruiters in Manila led to a high-profile discussion between the presidents of the two countries. Her recruiters were charged with both human trafficking and illegal recruitment. At the time of writing, Mary Jane Veloso still awaits her fate on death row. This dramatic case highlights the issue of human trafficking in the drug trade.

In 2016, the Philippines was the third-most-common country of origin for federally certified trafficking victims, according to the latest version of the U.S. Department of State's Trafficking in Persons Report.[2] Even though Mary Jane Veloso was not trafficked into the U.S., lessons can be learned from her case in relation to the approach to human trafficking in the U.S. that go beyond the use of overseas Filipina workers, to the need for systemic change in criminal justice towards those trafficked to commit crime.

It is estimated that 14,500 to 17,500 people, primarily women and children, are trafficked to the U.S. annually.[3] The Trafficking Victims Protection Act of 2000 (TVPA) enhances pre-existing criminal penalties, affords protections to trafficking victims, and makes available certain benefits and services to victims of severe forms of trafficking.[4] The FBI, under its human trafficking program, investigates human trafficking cases falling under the following investigative areas:

- *Domestic Sex Trafficking of Adults:* When persons are compelled to engage in commercial sex acts through means of force, fraud, and/or coercion
- *Sex Trafficking of International Adults and Children:* When foreign nationals, both adult and juveniles, are compelled to engage in commercial sex acts with a nexus to the United States through force, fraud, and/or coercion. (Note: Matters of domestic juvenile sex trafficking are handled by the FBI's Violent Crimes against Children Section.)
- *Forced Labor:* When persons, domestic or foreign nationals, are compelled to work in some service or industry through force or coercion
- *Domestic Servitude:* When persons, domestic or foreign nationals, are compelled to engage in domestic work for families or households, through means of force or coercion.[5]

There is little focus on human trafficking in the drug trade. Fifty percent (95,800) of sentenced inmates in U.S federal prison are serving time for drug offenses.[6] Taking Mary Jane Veloso's case as the focus, this chapter explores some of the issues that can arise for attorneys in the complex cross-section of human trafficking and drug trafficking.[7]

DJ's Story

At the age of 14, DJ was sold by her mother to a trafficker who forced her into prostitution and labor. When her traffickers realized she held an American passport, they began using her as a mule to traffic drugs across international borders. She was forced at one stage to swallow 86 balloons filled with drugs and was taken to the airport. DJ's "master" stayed by her side and threatened to kill her if she said anything to anyone. DJ witnessed a fellow victim collapse and die when a balloon she had swallowed disintegrated in her body. The flight attendants were unhelpful at this time, as they appeared to have the impression that DJ was drunk. DJ eventually managed to escape her traffickers, and was able to seek assistance and mentoring from the Tronie Foundation's Global Survivor Leadership Program. Her hope is that by sharing her story she can be a voice for other victims who are still being trafficked.[8]

2.1 Human Trafficking

Human trafficking is a highly lucrative industry that extends to all corners of the globe. The phrases "human trafficking," "slavery," and "forced labor" are often used interchangeably and can have different effects in terms of ownership and control, but the core issue is the exploitation of people for profit and power.[9] Developed countries have become the destination for slaves plucked from source countries, and people are also trafficked within their own states. These are generally the impoverished, the unempowered, the uneducated and the dispossessed, and largely women and girls, particularly in the context of sexual exploitation.

The potential profits from human exploitation are huge. The 2014 International Labor Office report (the ILO report), "Profits and Poverty," estimated that 20.9 million men, women and children are in forced labor globally, trafficked for labor and sexual exploitation or held in slavery like conditions,[10] and concluded that the victims are a "vast nation of men, women and children... virtually invisible, hidden behind a wall of coercion, threats and economic exploitation." Socioeconomic factors include lack of education and literacy, poverty and other wealth and income shocks, all of which need to be addressed to empower people to avoid exploitation.[11]

This chapter is an introduction to what criminal attorneys can do to identify victims and divert them from prosecution or argue for reduced punishments, together with an overview of corporate responsibility, thus highlighting how attorneys in all spheres can contribute to the global effort to end slavery. It is axiomatic that developing the role of attorneys in this context would require debate and professional guidance.

There are distinctions in definition between slavery, servitude, forced labor, sexual exploitation and human trafficking: The 1926 Slavery Convention defines slavery as "the status or condition of a person over whom any or all of the powers attaching to the right of ownership are exercised."[12] The 1930 Forced Labor Convention defines forced labor as "All work or service which is exacted from any person under the menace of any penalty and for which the said person has not offered himself voluntarily."[13] Forced labor therefore includes practices such as slavery.

The 1999 ILO Worst Forms of Child Labor Convention defines "worst forms of child labor" to include "all forms of slavery or practices similar to slavery, such as the sale and trafficking of children, debt bondage and serfdom and forced or compulsory labor, including forced or compulsory recruitment of children for use in armed conflict." In the context of the drug trade, there could be aspects of all these mechanisms. So, for the purposes of this chapter, there is a focus on the movement and control of people best reflected by the international acceptance of human trafficking as a global phenomenon.

The 2005 Convention on Action Against Trafficking in Human Beings (The Trafficking Protocol)[14] has been signed and ratified by most countries. It defines human trafficking as follows:

Trafficking in persons shall mean the recruitment, transportation, transfer, harbouring or receipt of persons, by means of the threat or use of force or other forms of coercion, of abduction, of fraud, of deception, of abuse of power or of a position of vulnerability or of the giving or receiving of payments or benefits to achieve the consent of a person having control over another person, for the purpose of exploitation. Exploitation shall include, at a minimum, the exploitation of the prostitution of others or other forms of sexual exploitation, forced labor or services, slavery or practices similar to slavery, servitude or removal of organs.[15]

The ILO Committee of Experts on the Application of Conventions and Recommendations (CEACR) has provided guidance on the scope of the definition of forced labor, stressing that it encompasses trafficking in persons for the purposes of labor and sexual exploitation as defined by the Palermo Protocol. This guidance supplements the UN Convention Against Transnational Organised Crime (2000) criminalising trafficking in persons whether it occurs within countries or across borders, and whether or not conducted by organised crime networks.[16]

Human trafficking is often misunderstood due to concern over migration,[17] but trafficking is a booming and secretive industry that has been referred to as "modern slavery", as well as "the crime of the 21st Century."[18] Unsurprisingly, given the scale of human exploitation, a high degree of criminal income is generated by modern slavery—particularly in the context of the sex trade.[19] The ILO report concluded that "there is an urgent need to address the socio-economic root causes of this hugely profitable illegal practice if it is to be overcome."[20] Globalization permits trafficking groups to operate seamlessly across borders. High-volume, cross-border flows of people, money, and commodities create greater opportunities for criminals to make money. There are simply more people and situations to exploit. For this reason, only interventions at a regional or global level are likely to have any chance of succeeding. In this context, the U.S has signed and ratified the following instruments:[21]

- United Nations Convention against Transnational Organized Crime
- The Protocol to Prevent, Suppress and Punish Trafficking in Persons, Especially Women and Children, supplementing the United Nations Convention against Transnational Organized Crime
- The Protocol against the Smuggling of Migrants by Land, Sea and Air, supplementing the United Nations Convention against Transnational Organized Crime.

The U.S. Department of Justice sets out a number of provisions in the U.S. Code that target trafficking in persons, also known as involuntary servitude/slavery or forced labor. These provisions are contained in Chapter 77 of Title 18 and are sometimes referred to generally as Chapter 77 offenses. The TVPA also supplemented existing laws in the context of victim protection.[22]

While there may be an overlap on the ground between the number of trafficked victims and the number of people as controlled operatives in the drug trade, there is no legislative or policy link. It is therefore necessary to integrate national responses into international strategies. This can be done by promoting partnerships across borders and developing international networks that champion "transnational organised justice." This includes promoting regional collaborative efforts on border control, mutual legal assistance, extradition and similar efforts that require a vision that transcends national boundaries. This will help minimize the growth of "safe havens" for transnational organised crime. It also allows for cooperation in context, for example, of policing crime and migration.[23]

2.2 Drug Trafficking

Clearly, human exploitation is much more than human trafficking. In the context of drug trafficking, coerced couriers are treated severely by law enforcement as part of an illegal trade rather than approached as potential victims of human exploitation. Illegal immigrants or refugees are treated as self-interested economic migrants. However, if individuals are forced workers or sexually exploited, the fact that they may also carry drugs should not mean that they are denied protective support. The FBI services for victims includes helplines, a victim specialist, and assistance with food, medical and child care, and transportation. It is not targeted at those who may be exploited in organised crime. From a policing perspective, it is still seen very much as a "war" on drugs. U.S. drug policy remains focused on supply reduction.[24]

In her 2014 *Human Trafficking Search* blog post, "When Drug Trafficking Becomes Human Trafficking," Michelle Lillie wrote about supply and demand as follows:

> Following the economic laws of supply and demand, Latin American drug traffickers and criminal organizations have decided to increase profits by diversifying their market to include the trafficking of drugs, labor and sex. Drug cartels have been accused of using their illicit markets to traffic Central American children for the purpose of sexual exploitation in the United States. Entire towns whose economy was once funded by profits from the illicit drug trade now make their living off the procurement, trafficking and exploitation of women and children in the sex trade. San Miguel Tenacingo, a small Mexican town located just outside Mexico City is commonly known as the city that sex trafficking built where one city official estimated that 30-50 percent of the town's population are involved in the illicit sex trade. Being involved in the sex trade is not condemned; in fact it is almost encouraged. A local university interviewed young boys from San Miguel Tenacingo and found that 16 percent wanted to be a pimp when they grew up and 44 percent had friends who said they wanted to be one. (Source: http://www.humantraffickingsearch.net/wp1/when-drug-trafficking-becomes-human-trafficking).

2.3 Identifying Victims

The UNDOC Report highlights key issues and implications for response to transnational organised crime in 13 categories. These include improving victim identification systems to enable the provision of protection and support, investing in a victim-centred approach with appropriate training for law enforcement to include the vital importance of ensuring the protection of victims, encouraging intelligence-led approaches to include transnational cooperative criminal intelligence structures, and better regional criminal justice coordination.[25]

What this also requires is a re-think of attitude away from the traditional view of "illegal immigrants" or "drug traffickers" in order to differentiate between traffickers and victims. Identification (as with any crime) is vital since progress will never be made unless efforts are made to separately identify bosses from workers, perpetrators from victims, conspirators from pawns, terrorists from cannon fodder. Attorneys are not specifically mentioned in either the ILO report or the UNDOC report but they can play a key role. Where there is criminal, cross-border, terrorist, or suspect financial activity, attorneys are almost inevitably connected to the potential solution, perhaps more than any other stakeholder.

In the UK, the Crown Prosecution Service in England and Wales has issued guidelines to be applied in relation to decisions to prosecute human trafficking victims for criminal offending.[26] What is recognised is the need to identify and divert victims rather than prosecute, largely as a result of the application of the non-punishment provisions of the Trafficking Protocol via the common law doctrine of abuse of process. This places a duty on prosecutors to indict suspects on credible evidence but to divert victims into suitable support, thus maximising potential witness evidence.

It is notable that in one study of human trafficking prosecutions in the U.S., in 49 percent of the cases, victims testified at the grand jury hearing. Only 11 percent of cases involved the victim testifying at the disposition, and less than half (40 percent) involved the victim testifying at trial. In 31 percent of the cases, restitution was paid to the victim; prosecutors sought forfeit of assets or property in 46 percent of the cases.[27]

There are clearly issues of victim engagement, and data is limited on the opportunities at least offered to drug couriers for protection or witness assistance. So, it seems that opportunities to expose and prevent transnational organised crime are lost. There are 1.2 million attorneys in the U.S.[28] This equates to approximately 1 attorney per 300 citizens.[29] Subject to a recognition of attorney-client privilege and suitable protective measures for those victims who engage with investigators, attorneys could be a valuable resource for combatting human trafficking in the commercial and criminal sectors.

For criminal attorneys, it is an opportunity not so much to assist the State but to achieve a favourable outcome for a client. In Mary Jane Veloso's case, human trafficking referral mechanisms were pursued by her attorneys, giving details of her exploitation by recruiters of overseas workers and leading to a prosecution of those recruiters based on her evidence and the evidence of others who had been recruited. The evidence gathered for those proceedings is likely to be valuable in demonstrating her own status as a victim of human trafficking from the Phillipines, to enable at least a review of Mary Jane's death sentence.

Marcela's Story

In his 2013 *Time* magazine article, "The Mexican Drug Cartels' Other Business: Sex Trafficking," Ioan Grillo wrote about a victim named Marcela. Marcela was 16 when she met her trafficker, who posed as a wealthy businessman and asked her to marry him. He took her instead to a part of Mexico City known for its high level of prostitution, kept her in a hotel room, and forced her to have sex with up to 40 men per day. The customers paid $15 each to Marcela's trafficker and his accomplices. She escaped a week later when law enforcement raided the hotel, and testified against her traffickers despite their threats. The perpetrators received prison sentences.

2.4 Non-Punishment

Accurate victim identification is vital for the effective investigation of the trafficking crime, as well as to ensure effective protection of victims' rights, including non-punishment of victims for offences caused or directly linked with their being trafficked. It becomes all the more important in the context of international drug trafficking that those who are coerced are separated from those who volunteer. The Trafficking Protocol contains a non–punishment provision:

> **Article 26—Non-punishment provision**
> Each Party shall, in accordance with the basic principles of its legal system, provide for the possibility of not imposing penalties on victims for their involvement in unlawful activities, to the extent that they have been compelled to do so.

Article 10 of the UNODC Model Law Against Trafficking in Persons provides for "Non-liability [non-punishment] [non-prosecution] of victims of trafficking in persons,"[30] which includes not subjecting victims to criminal procedures, particularly children. The recommended principle is that states should ensure that "Trafficked persons shall not be detained, charged or prosecuted for the illegality of their entry into or residence in countries of transit and destination, or for their involvement in unlawful activities to the extent that such involvement is a direct consequence of their situation as trafficked persons." This has been implemented, for example, in England and Wales through the Modern Slavery Act, which provides for complete defences for those coerced into committing certain offences.[31]

Putting aside pre-conceived notions of criminal liability, the modern approach to slavery must involve non-prosecution or non-punishment; that is, not to prosecute even clear criminal offending that occurs due to exploitation. For any prosecution authority that has to balance the public interest in prosecuting or not, these are issues that ought to be taken into account.

In a sense, it does not matter if the Trafficking Protocol has not been ratified in a particular country. It is a matter of common sense. If the scourge of human trafficking is to be tackled, in the right case, it ought to be possible to argue that a trafficked individual should not be prosecuted at all, or that they should not be punished. With or without the Protocol, this is a simple solution that attorneys and judges can achieve that will have even greater effect with the right support services in place.

At ground level, someone suspected of committing a criminal offence might also be an exploited victim. European cases have dealt with the factual need to identify an individual's status as a victim on credible evidence.[32] Any jurisdiction would require the same. On an evidentiary basis, this can mean more than testimony; it can also require following up and tracking histories.

2.5 An Attorney's Role

The American Bar Association (ABA) Task Force on Human Trafficking has started a campaign to bring awareness to this issue. The ABA created the short film *Voices for Victims: Attorneys Against Human Trafficking* to "highlight the role that attorneys play in representing victims of human trafficking and some legal measures that can be employed to help facilitate the enforcement of anti-human trafficking laws." To accompany the film, there is a toolkit designed to "assist state, county, city, and local bar associations in hosting events and panel discussions regarding human trafficking as a means to raise public awareness."[33]

ABA toolkit for legal professionals

The ABA Taskforce on Human Trafficking has created a helpful toolkit, *Voices for Victims: Lawyers Against Human Trafficking Tool Kit for Bar Associations*.

The toolkit lists helpful resources for those whose work brings them into contact with the issues around human trafficking. This includes:

- Judges who may preside over cases with human trafficking issues in criminal court, juvenile court, civil court and family court
- Prosecutors who work with victims in criminal cases and face challenges in building cases against traffickers, working with traumatized victims, and interacting with victims who have often been

previously treated as criminals and have a fear of law enforcement
- Defense attorneys who work with human trafficking victims who have been accused of crimes, often prostitution
- Immigration attorneys who work with victims applying for visas
- Family law attorneys who represent victims applying for restraining orders or child custody orders
- Social workers who assist trafficking victims in accessing services
- Psychologist and mental health providers who address impacts of trauma on a victim's ability to recall information and testify in court
- Law enforcement personnel who encounter victims and perpetrators of human trafficking
- Local legislators who promulgate laws to address the harms of human trafficking

The *Toolkit* is available on the ABA's website.

For those victims apprehended committing crime (national or transnational), if such evidence is sensitively gathered at an early stage, prosecutors can give consideration to the question of whether to proceed with prosecuting a suspect who might be a victim of trafficking, particularly where the suspect has been compelled or coerced to commit a criminal offence as a direct consequence of being trafficked. The T visa (Nonimmigrant Status) issue is just one factor in what is increasingly recognised as a need for a broader approach: Prosecutors may use their discretion to choose not to proceed with criminal charges against a defendant they suspect may be a victim of trafficking, or support an application for T or U visas for those victims who lack immigration status. Furthermore, for those already convicted of crimes as a result of their being trafficked, defense attorneys may move for vacatur on those convictions. Courts in the United States are taking an increasingly broad view of the types of convictions that may be vacated.[34]

In the UK, guidance is that prosecutors should adopt a three-stage assessment:

1. Is there a reason to believe that the person has been trafficked? If so:
2. If there is clear evidence of a credible defence of duress, the case should be discontinued on evidential grounds; but
3. Even where there is no clear evidence of duress, but the offence may have been committed as a result of compulsion arising from trafficking, prosecutors should consider whether the public interest lies in proceeding to prosecute or not.[35]

The rationale for non-punishment of victims of trafficking is that, while on the face of it, a victim may have committed an offense, the reality is that the trafficked person acts without real autonomy. They have no, or limited, free will because of the degree of control exercised over them and the methods used by traffickers; consequently they are not responsible for the commission of the offence and should not therefore be considered accountable for the unlawful act committed. The vulnerable situation of the trafficked person becomes worse where the State fails to identify such a person as a victim of trafficking, as a consequence of which they may be denied their right to safety and assistance as a trafficked person and instead be treated as an ordinary criminal suspect.[36]

This requires qualified and trained officials to identify and help victims of trafficking and engaging attorneys in those duties. If evidence or information obtained supports the fact that the suspect has been trafficked and committed the offence while they were coerced, manipulated or deceived, informed consideration can be given to diverting the victim away from prosecution and into programs and safety. It requires governments to ensure support is available and attorneys to ensure the right people are diverted. Cooperation is required to ensure that those who have migrated transnationally under coercion will be sympathetically treated.

For criminal defense attorneys, a suspicion that a client might be a victim of trafficking and compelled to commit a criminal offence, as a direct consequence of being exploited, is an opportunity to identify a victim and bring relevant evidence to the prosecutor's (or investigating judge's) attention and potentially secure an acquittal, regardless of the elements of the alleged offending. There are a number of potential steps depending on the jurisdiction:

- Continue to defend on the facts and raise any relevant and available defences, such as duress
- Obtain evidence that the arrested suspect is a trafficked victim—details and circumstances—enough to engage the prosecution
- Give clear and ethical advice on the potential waiving of privilege that giving such information to law enforcement may require
- Ensure that safe systems are in place to refer the trafficked victim to local services
- Make representations about discontinuance/staying the proceedings at the point that evidence is credible that the defendant is a trafficked victim.

Even before the Modern Slavery Act, the process was well underway in England and Wales: After the UK Court of Appeal quashed the convictions of offenders who, at different stages after conviction, had been found to be victims of trafficking in human beings and to have been coerced into committing the offences.[37] The Court had the advantage of European Directive 2011/36 and previous decisions.[38]

The Court noted that the reasoning for what is effectively immunity from prosecution is that "the culpability of the victims might be significantly diminished, and sometimes effectively extinguished, not merely because of age, but because no realistic alternative was available to them but to comply with those controlling them." The Court made clear that Article 26 of The Trafficking Protocol did not prohibit the prosecution or punishment of victims of trafficking per se, but did require the prosecutor to give careful consideration as to whether public policy calls for a prosecution.

In many ways, in the context of criminal cases in any country, this approach to vulnerable suspects is not a wholly new approach; there have always been cases when there is a positive obligation not to prosecute that fundamentally engages the public interest test for any prosecution. International cooperation can be achieved by harmonising the approach of criminal justice and border systems in this regard. Importantly, the non-punishment concept was adopted in the new ILO protocol in June 2014, with 437 votes in favor. It updates the existing ILO Convention 29 on Forced Labor adopted in 1930, bringing it into the modern era to address practices such as human trafficking.[39]

2.6 Conclusion

The outcome for Mary Jane Veloso at the time of writing is unknown, but the issues her case raises are global. In the context of human exploitation, attorneys must think laterally and responsibly. Criminal attorneys, in particular, can expose and identify hidden victims, if only to act in the best interests of their vulnerable clients. Proper advice on referral mechanisms, engagement with the prosecution and some radical efforts by the courts have all demonstrated that global exploitation of people can be tackled. There is no reason why this cannot be harnessed in the context of the drug trade. The law cannot work in isolation; victims need to be supported and diverted to suitable services, and systems need to be in place to remove or block the financial incentives for those who take advantage of human exploitation. Of course, it requires law development and enforcement, but it also necessitates crime prevention. In a global market place, this requires transnational cooperation at every level—including the legal sector. If the urgency is increased by the spectre of growing international organised crime, then saving Mary Jane Veloso and trafficking victims like her becomes a global imperative.

Endnotes

1. "Saving Mary Jane: Death-row mother's last-minute rescue was thanks to Darwin lawyer" (http://www.news.com.au/lifestyle/real-life/true-stories/saving-mary-jane-deathrow-mothers-lastminute-rescue-was-thanks-to-darwin-lawyer/news-story/77c48306a13c99b3412499fe7b8042ac).

2. U.S. Department of State's Trafficking in Persons Report 2016 (http://www.state.gov/j/tip/rls/tiprpt/).

3. U.S. Department of State's Trafficking in Persons Report 2016 (http://www.state.gov/j/tip/rls/tiprpt/).

4. Victims of Trafficking and Violence Protection Act 2000 (http://www.state.gov/j/tip/laws/61124.htm).

5. FBI Human Trafficking website (https://www.fbi.gov/about-us/investigate/civilrights/human_trafficking).

6. "Prisons, Jails, and People Arrested for Drugs: Overview of Basic Data," DrugWarFacts.org website (http://www.drugwarfacts.org/cms/Prisons_and_Drugs#sthash.YxFgM55j.dpbs).

7. Taken in part from Gerry, *Let's Talk About Slaves...Human Trafficking: Exposing Hidden Victims and Criminal Profit and How Attorneys Can Help End a Global Epidemic*, 3 Griffith Journal of Law and Human Dignity 1 (2015).

8. Source: http://www.unodc.org/southasia/frontpage/2012/october/drug-mules_-swallowed-by-the-illicit-drug-trade.html.

9. There are concerns that the word "slavery" doesn't cover children exposed to hazardous work or those who are not given a fair wage, but this is probably a matter of semantics—those people have little choice, and in any event, slavery and trafficking are now commonly understood terms used interchangeably. Human exploitation is more over-arching.

10. 2014 International Labor Office report, "Profits and Poverty: The Economics of Forced Labor" (http://www.ilo.org/global/publications/ilo-bookstore/order-online/books/WCMS_243391/lang--en/index.htm).

11. 2014 International Labor Office report, "Profits and Poverty: The economics of forced labor" (http://www.ilo.org/global/publications/ilo-bookstore/order-online/books/WCMS_243391/lang--en/index.htm).

12. Slavery Convention 1926 (http://www.ohchr.org/EN/ProfessionalInterest/Pages/SlaveryConvention.aspx).

13. See note 9, above.

14. The Protocol was adopted by resolution A/RES/55/25 of 15 November 2000 at the fifty-fifth session of the General Assembly of the United Nations. In accordance with its Article 16, the Protocol was open for signature by all States and by regional economic integration organizations, provided that at least one Member State of such organization has signed the Protocol, from 12 to 15 December 2000 at the Palazzi di Giustizia in Palermo, Italy, and thereafter at United Nations Headquarters in New York until 12 December 2002.

15. The Protocol to Prevent, Suppress and Punish Trafficking in Persons, Especially Women and Children, Supplementing the UN Convention Against Transnational Organised Crime.

16. U.S Trafficking in Persons Report (http://www.humantrafficking.org/countries/united_states_of_america).

17. UNDOC Report: "Smuggling of Migrants: A Global Review" (http://www.unodc.org/documents/human-trafficking/Migrant-Smuggling/Smuggling_of_Migrants_A_Global_Review.pdf).

18. Calliste Weitenberg, "Human trafficking: A crime of the 21st century," *SBS*, Sept. 3, 2013 (http://www.sbs.com.au/news/article/2013/06/07/human-trafficking-crime-21st-century).

19. Polaris Project, "Human Trafficking: An Overview" (http://www.polarisproject.org/human-trafficking/overview).

20. 2014 International Labour Office report, "Profits and Poverty: The Economics of Forced Labour" (http://www.ilo.org/global/publications/ilo-bookstore/order-online/books/WCMS_243391/lang--en/index.htm).

21. UNODC Signatories to the United Nations Convention against Transnational Crime and its Protocols (https://www.unodc.org/unodc/en/treaties/CTOC/signatures.html).

22. US Department of Justice, "Involuntary Servitude, Forced Labor, And Sex Trafficking Statutes Enforced" (https://www.justice.gov/crt/involuntary-servitude-forced-labor-and-sex-trafficking-statutes-enforced).

23. UNODC 2009 Seminar Presentation: "Effective Criminal Justice Response to Human Trafficking" (https://www.unodc.org/indonesia/2009/11/Human-Trafficking/story.html).

24. Office of National Drug Control Policy Reducing the Supply of Illegal Drugs (https://www.ncjrs.gov/ondcppubs/publications/policy/99ndcs/iv-g.html).

25. UNDOC Report, "Transnational Organised Crime in East Asia and the Pacific: A threat Assessment" p.139 (http://www.unodc.org/documents/data-and-analysis/Studies/TOCTA_EAP_web.pdf).

26. Taken from UK CPS Legal Guidance at www.cps.co.uk.

27. "Prosecuting Human Trafficking Cases: Lessons Learned and Promising Practices" (https://www.ncjrs.gov/pdffiles1/nij/grants/223972.pdf).

28. Jeff Jacoby, "US legal bubble can't pop soon enough," *Boston Globe*, May 9, 2014 (http://www.bostonglobe.com/opinion/2014/05/09/the-attorney-bubble-pops-not-moment-too-soon/qAYzQ823qpfi4GQl2OiPZM/story.html).

29. "What Percent of the US Population do Lawyers Comprise?" (http://www.wisegeek.org/what-percent-of-the-us-population-do-lawyers-comprise.htm).

30. UNODC Model Law Against Trafficking in Persons (https://www.unodc.org/documents/human-trafficking/Model_Law_against_TIP.pdf).

31. Home Office Circular: Modern Slavery Act 2015 (https://www.gov.uk/government/uploads/system/uploads/attachment_data/file/443797/Circular_242015Final_1_.pdf).

32. *Rantsev v. Cyprus and Russia*, Application No. 25965/04 (Strasbourg, January 7, 2010) and *Case of M. and Others v. Italy and Bulgaria*, Application No. 40020/03 (July 31, 2012).

33. *Voices for Victims: Attorneys Against Human Trafficking Tool Kit for Bar Associations* (https://www.americanbar.org/content/dam/aba/multimedia/

trafficking_task_force/resources/TFHT_Toolkit/HumanTrafficking_Bar.
authcheckdam.pdf).

34. "Vacating Criminal Convictions for Trafficked Persons: A Legal Memorandum for Advocates and Legislators" (http://sexworkersproject.org/downloads/2012/20120422-memo-vacating-convictions.pdf).

35. Taken from UK CPS Legal Guidance at www.cps.co.uk.

36. Office of the Special Representative and Co-ordinator for Combatting Trafficking in Human Beings Report: "Policy and legislative recommendations towards the effective implementation of the non-punishment provision with regard to victims of trafficking" (http://www.osce.org/secretariat/101002?download=true).

37. *R v N*; *R v LE* [2012] EWCA Crim 189.

38. *R. v LM* [2010] EWCA Crim 2327, [2011] 1 Cr. App. R. 12; *R. v N* [2012] EWCA Crim 189, and [2013] Q.B. 379 applied.

39. International Labour Organization press release: "ILO adopts new Protocol to tackle modern forms of forced labor," June 11, 2014 (http://www.ilo.org/global/about-the-ilo/media-centre/press-releases/WCMS_246549/lang--en/index.htm).

Chapter 3

The New York Approach:

A Lawyer's Guide to Human Trafficking Intervention Courts

By Nicole Campion

In 2012, the International Labor Organization estimated that there are nearly 4.5 million victims of sex trafficking worldwide, hundreds of thousands of whom are within the United States borders.[1] In the United States, victims are often forced into prostitution in many different capacities, often sent by their traffickers out onto the streets in search of customers, or sent to brothels, hotels, or sometimes even people's homes.[2] For some of these victims, this could mean meeting with upwards of forty-five different men a day, with nearly all of the money they make from each going directly back to their traffickers.[3] While these young women are being abused and traumatized, their traffickers are in some cases making as much as $324,000 a year off each victim they are holding captive.[4]

Throughout their time as a trafficking victim, some of these women will face arrest for charges such as prostitution or loitering. An arrest and legal proceeding can be a traumatizing experience for an already traumatized individual, and under traditional legal systems would likely do them more harm than good. In the majority of cases across the country, these victims will be processed just as any other criminal, later being released back to the streets, and back to their traffickers. In New York, a state with one of the four-highest percentages of these human trafficking victims centered in and around New York City, the legal system is working to change the way in which victims who are arrested are handled, as part of a large initiative to fight human trafficking.[5]

New York has spent the last several years attacking human trafficking from many different angles, earning it one of the highest ratings for human trafficking laws in 2014.[6] The state has been able to accomplish this partly due to its problem-solving approach to combating trafficking, as well as being the first state to create specialized courts, and passing legislation that details how both adult and child victims arrested for crimes should be handled.[7]

3.1 The Problem: Traditional Courts and Their Harmful Effects on Trafficking Victims

For human trafficking victims arrested for any sort of crime, the arrest and resulting court proceedings can be both traumatizing and humiliating. In one Washington area courtroom, the prosecutor could be heard calling one girl arrested for prostitution by the name "a little black ho."[8] However, for a victim of trafficking, who commits these acts out of fear and force rather than by choice, being treated in this manner is even worse. After what could have been decades of trauma, abuse, and humiliation by traffickers and clients alike, victims of trafficking arrested for crimes need to be treated with an abundance of respect and care.

With the constant fear of what their traffickers would do to them should they try to escape or plead for help, most victims are quickly convicted, pay fines or spend short periods of time in jail, and are put back on the streets with their traffickers and back into the same line of work. However, it is often the case that these individuals are not committing these crimes of their own free will; they are doing so at the behest of their captors and traffickers. Their options are few and simple—do as they're told, or risk serious harm or death to themselves or their families. So, most choose to do what the trafficker asks, and continue to commit the same acts and crimes over and over again. However, being processed and treated as a criminal over and over again does nothing to treat the underlying issue causing their actions. Instead, it continues the cycle of victimization, and contributes to the reasons that these victims are not likely able to stop committing the same crimes they have been committing.

Furthermore, should these victims ever be fortunate enough to escape or be rescued from their captors, the presence of prostitution and other related charges on their records could continue to haunt them throughout the rest of their lives. Not only are they a constant reminder of what these victims had to go through, but these convictions will also be a significant roadblock in their future attempts to find decent jobs, or good housing. Even with a formal education and degrees on their resume, many employers will refuse to give jobs to women with prostitution charges, whether they were trafficking victims or not. According to former trafficking victims, they all too often hear "it's just not a good fit" from potential employers, leading these convictions to eventually "ruin their lives."[9] Many find themselves unemployed and living with friends and relatives, or back on the streets.[10]

These former victims say that not only do these convictions form a roadblock to advancement in their lives, but they can take an emotional toll as well.[11] One former victim explains that she was constantly judged or shamed because of the convictions she had while she was a victim of trafficking. She went on to explain that the constant rejection for jobs she was more than qualified for made her feel like "the shit on the bottom of your shoe."[12]

Were the court systems to have a different approach to handling trafficking victims, there is a chance that these young women would not be emerging from their lives as victims with more trauma and burdensome criminal records, but rather with all of the tools they need to begin a successful new life. In examining these issues, states like New York have begun to look for solutions outside of traditional court appearances or disposition of these cases at arraignments.

3.2 The Solution: A Problem-Solving Approach

What traditional courts do not do is seek to identify and resolve the underlying issue that is causing these individuals to commit the same acts over and over again, seemingly with no regard for the consequences. By attempting to identify and resolve the issues causing victims to commit these crimes, the courts would be able to provide them with a way out of the cycle, as well as with the services and support they need to begin a new life. With this goal in mind, lawmakers and judicial officials began to look for potential solutions for this problem, as well as new approaches to dealing with individuals who may be trafficking victims when they are arrested. In New York, it was determined that a problem-solving approach, much like the one taken in cases of domestic violence or addiction, would be the best solution.

A. What Are Problem-Solving Courts?

Over the past two decades, the United States has seen an evolution in the court system.[13] While traditional courts still remain and function in fundamentally the same manner, recent years have seen the creation and evolution of a new style of court: the problem-solving court.[14] Formed out of a need and desire to address specific problems, such as the high rate of drug use or crime recidivism, these courts target specific groups of people or specific criminal charges, and seek to do more than simply resolve a dispute between two parties or punish the wrongdoer.[15] Rather, problem-solving courts seek to dig a bit deeper into the defendant's situation and actions to determine what led them to commit the crime that they were arrested for.[16]

These specialized courts then focus on rehabilitation and treatment to attempt to treat or resolve this underlying issue in hopes that it will prevent the defendant from committing the same conduct again in the future.[17] This is done generally through rehabilitation or counseling programs created for these defendants by one of the court's many appointed service providers operating in and around the area in which the court is located. Though these courts began primarily with juvenile courts and drug courts, they have now expanded nationwide to include domestic violence, mental health, human trafficking, and many other specialized areas.

1. Essential elements of problem-solving courts

In order to achieve the fundamental goals of the problem-solving courts, each court operates around five essential elements.[18] The first of these elements is that each court provides an immediate outcome-based intervention for their defendants.[19] This intervention is achieved in many of these courts through counseling programs or other forms of treatment programs based on the issue that brought the defendant before the courts in the first place, whether it be drug abuse, domestic violence issues, or something else.

The outcome upon which the courts are focused—and upon which they assign defendants to these intervention programs—is to find and treat the root cause of the actions which led the defendant to commit the crime. In drug courts, this is generally an addiction to some form of controlled substance, while in other problem-solving courts it may be alcohol addiction, or an anger issue. Whatever the underlying problem may be, each problem-solving court will mandate the appropriate treatment or counseling necessary to remedy the problem.

The next of the five elements essential to the problem-solving courts is the provision of a non-adversarial judicial process.[20] In these courts, rather than a defense attorney on one side and a prosecutor on the other side, one attempting to free the defendant and one attempting to have them punished, the two work together to attempt to help the defendant receive treatment when it is needed. This is done in part through the third and fourth essential elements of these courts: an interdisciplinary team approach and intensive interactions between a judge and offender.[21] The courts do this by working with government and nonprofit organizations to provide defendants with counseling, treatment programs, juvenile services, and other assistance where it is deemed necessary.[22]

The judges, attorneys, and other court staff of each of the problem-solving courts are also specially trained in the issue with which that court deals in order to provide the best response and treatment needed to allow each defendant to succeed.[23] Each evaluates the cases, and works together to help the defendant through the specialized court system in order to achieve the best outcome possible. These are elements in which another stark difference between traditional courts and problem-solving courts can be seen. In a traditional court, a judge has little interaction with a defendant, and little to do with evaluating a case or defendant throughout the judicial process. There is also generally little-to-no collaboration with outside service providers or groups during a traditional trial court proceeding, whereas in the problem-solving courts, service providers and counselors are involved throughout the process.

Through the team effort of the service providers and specially trained court staff, the focus is on treating the cause of the actions—whether it be a mental health issue, substance abuse, or something else—in order to attempt to cut down on the crime rates across the nation.

The fifth and final element needed for an effective problem-solving court is a set of clearly defined rules and goals.[24] These rules and goals need to be outlined so that there is no question in each defendant's mind what they are, how they will be enforced, or the extent to which breaking the rules would be tolerated. This applies both to the court and the proceedings a defendant will go through within its doors, as well as outside of the court. This means that rules need to be put in place that govern the defendant's actions outside of court in everyday life, as well as rules that govern the mandated treatment and counseling programs. With these five elements in place, an effective problem-solving court is formed.

2. History of problem-solving courts in the United States

The problem-solving approach to combating specific types of crime is nothing new in New York, as the state currently has ten different problem-solving courts for different groups and crimes.[25] Of these, the longest-running and most well-known is the state's drug treatment courts, upon which the majority of the others have been modeled. These types of courts saw their beginnings in Miami, Florida in 1989 in response to the ever-growing crack epidemic of the 1980s.[26] As a result of the constant influx of addicts and repeat offenders, the drug treatment courts were created, in hopes that a firm intervention would help to put an end to the crack epidemic in the area. As a result of the overwhelming success of these problem-solving courts in Miami, more were created across the country.

Problem-solving courts also began to expand outside of the realm of drug offenses and into different specialized areas such as mental health, domestic violence, juvenile law, and others. In 1998, New York State joined Florida and several other states by implementing their first drug treatment court in Manhattan. These courts were created through a collaboration of officials from a wide variety of backgrounds, including prosecutors and defense attorneys, probation officers, service providers, and other personnel.[27] Now, New York's problem-solving courts, focusing on ten different areas, are all based on a similar model as these original drug courts.[28]

Over 2,300 drug treatment courts are currently in existence nationwide. These courts have been shown to reduce both relapses and recidivism rates among drug users and criminals, and have program completion rates as high as 67 percent.[29] With nearly 150 of these drug treatment courts alone statewide, many of which focus on families or juveniles, New York has become the nation's leader in creating and utilizing these types of problem-solving courts.[30]

In the first sixteen years of their operation, New York's drug treatment courts have seen 85,415 individuals pass through their doors, with an average of 67 percent of these individuals either graduating or remaining active in the program a year after entering.[31] According to the American Psychological Society, "preliminary research on the efficacy of problem-solving courts shows their clear benefits, with repeat offenses by graduates significantly reduced compared with defendants in traditional courts, helping to remove the 'revolving door' criticism often leveled at the United States legal system."[32] New York, a state with hundreds of problem-solving courts reaching thousands of people, has now expanded this successful model into the realm of human trafficking.[33]

B. New York's Human Trafficking Intervention Courts

A 2011 study from Hofstra University found that private service providers in the New York Metropolitan area came into contact with at least 11,268 survivors of trafficking in a ten-year period.[34] This is likely only a small percentage of the number of human trafficking victims actually present in the area. Human trafficking courts were created in response to this rapidly rising rates of human trafficking within the state and across the country.

More specifically, the courts, known as the Human Trafficking Intervention Courts (HTICs), were aimed at the identifying victims of trafficking who have been arrested for crimes they committed as a result of their being a victim, and helping them to receive the services they need, rather than punishing them and returning them to their traffickers. Announced as part of New York's Human Trafficking Intervention Initiative by Chief Judge Jonathan Lippman in 2013, this initiative built upon three pilot programs that had been operating within New York since the 1990s, leading to the creation of eleven total HTIC locations across New York State.[35] These courts are comprised of prosecutors, defense attorneys, and judges, all of whom are trained in how to identify and deal with the victims of trafficking.

1. Getting a client's case into New York's Human Trafficking Intervention Court

Modeled upon the earlier drug treatment and domestic violence courts previously established in New York, these courts are aimed towards those who have been arrested on low-level charges of prostitution or related offenses with the hope that, by targeting this particular group, the courts would be able to reach a large number of trafficking victims. Therefore, attorneys representing a client on charges of prostitution, loitering for the purposes of engaging in prostitution, or something similar, will likely be representing their client through the HTICs.

Typically, after arrest, a court date is set at the HTIC within two to five weeks, during which time clients are generally allowed to live at their homes without incarceration. This gives an attorney opportunities to speak to their client prior to the case beginning, in order to learn a bit more about them and begin building a relationship of trust.

It is important for an attorney to remember that a client who is a victim of human trafficking will be unlike any other client they will deal with. Practitioners report that their clients are often scared, anxious, hostile and avoidant of any discussion or questioning. One must treat these victims with great care, and work to establish a basis of trust with them prior to pushing them to answer questions regarding their status as a victim.[36] Very rarely will victims identify themselves as victims or be willing to discuss the trauma they have been through after just one meeting.[37] Understanding a client and the trauma they have faced can be crucial to ensuring the best outcome possible.

Once the scheduled court date arrives, the defendant and their attorney will appear in front of a specially trained judge and prosecutor to hear their options for proceeding with the case. Unlike in a typical court setting, where a defense attorney and prosecutor work as adversaries, here the main interest of all parties involved is what is in the best interest of the defendant. Attorneys who practice in a problem-solving court such as the human trafficking court should prepare themselves for a different style of litigation.

2. Guiding a client after entering Human Trafficking Intervention Court

When a defendant and their attorney arrive at the HTIC for their case's first court date, they will be met with an offer from the prosecutor with the District Attorney's office from the county in which the court is located. This offer will be one in which the defendant is given an opportunity, if they are willing to complete a court-mandated program, to receive an adjournment in contemplation of dismissal (ACOD) and, should they not be re-arrested for six months, a dismissal of all charges and sealing of the records. If the defendant accepts this offer, they will be referred to one of several service providers in their area, and given a start date for their sessions.

Generally, which service provider a defendant is referred to is based upon the services they are most in need of, their location, the capacity of the provider, and any language or translation services that may be necessary to allow for clear and proper communication. In New York City, these service providers include Girls Education and Mentoring Services (GEMS), and Sanctuary for Families, whose executive director, the Honorable Judy Harris Kluger, was instrumental in the creation of the HTICs.

Through these service providers, defendants are required to complete a set number of counseling sessions, generally five to six, based upon the charges and any past criminal record the defendant may have, to be completed at a pace of one per week. Should a defendant fail to attend these sessions or commit another crime during the time in which they are participating in the program, this number of sessions may increase, or they may be transferred into a different program in hopes that they would receive better assistance there.

Once the court-mandated counseling sessions are complete, generally in a two-to-four month time frame, the judge will grant the defendant an ACOD. After six months with no further arrests, the charges against the defendant are dismissed, and the record sealed. A recent study conducted from December 2013 to August 2014, which observed nearly 365 defendants in the HTICs, concluded that an average of 95.5 percent of those in these specialized courts chose to take this path by completing the program in exchange for an adjournment in contemplation of dismissal.[38]

Should a defendant decide not to accept this offer and pursue an ACOD through the completion of a program, they do have a few other options available to them.[39] The first of these options is the ability to plea to lesser charge.[40] As the majority of individuals being heard before the HTICs are charged with low-level prostitution charges, in some cases they will be given an opportunity to plea to a charge of disorderly conduct, a violation which would not appear on one's criminal record.[41] Should a defendant be eligible and choose to do this, they will generally face a small fine and be released. Similarly, defendants are given the opportunity to avoid the court-mandated programs by pleading guilty to their charges and face the short jail sentences or fines.[42] In the same study previously referenced, only nine of the 365 defendants observed chose to plea to a lesser charge or to plead guilty rather than pursuing an ACOD.[43]

Before allowing one's client to attempt to plea to a lesser charge, or to plead guilty to their current charge, there should be a serious conversation with the client laying out all of the options and consequences. Though pleading to a lesser charge that does not involve jail time and would not show on the clients criminal record may seem like a viable option, in the cases where the client is a victim of human trafficking, it is not the best option available. It does not allow the victim any form of help, or any way out of the life they are living. Rather, this option simply reduces their criminal charges, and places them right back in the hands of their traffickers. This option in most cases would better serve the traffickers waiting to get the victim back than the victim themselves.

The last option that a defendant in the HTIC will face is to reject the offer of services and face a jury trial.[44] Should a defendant choose to reject the services, the judge presiding over the case will typically urge them to reconsider, and set another follow-up court date in order to allow the defendant time to reconsider his or her decision.[45]

Typically, should a defendant reject all offers, they will proceed to a trial by jury.[46] Of the 365 defendants studied in 2013 to 2014, only two rejected their offers of services, and only one pursued a trial by jury.[47] For a victim of trafficking, a trial in front of a jury would likely only add to their trauma. They will be put in front of a room full of people, likely including their traffickers, and be forced to face evidence and descriptions of what they had done in the time leading up to their arrest. Although largely recognized to be a victim in prior appearances in the HTIC, the victim will be treated no differently than any other type of criminal defendant, and will be subject to cross-examination by the prosecutor.

C. How Can the Human Trafficking Intervention Court Help a Client?

If and when a defendant being processed through the HTIC agrees to complete the court-mandated services program in exchange for dismissal, their case is evaluated by the lawyers and judge and they are connected with a service provider in the area that best fits their needs. Here, the victim's attorney would consider all aspects of the victim's life, and what services would provide the best outcome for them.

This could include physical and medical needs, educational needs, assistance in finding a job, safe housing, translation assistance or English tutoring, and anything else that could be pertinent to an individual client's case. After taking into account all factors, the attorney may discuss with the judge and prosecutor where they feel their client would be best suited. These factors, as well as program capacities and availability, will determine which provider to pair the victim with.

Much like other problem-solving courts, the HTICs were created in an attempt to treat the root cause of the conduct that led the defendant to be arrested and charged. However, this is where we see one of the clearest differences between HTICs and courts specializing in drug abuse, mental health, or many of the other areas in which problem-solving courts may specialize. Here, the underlying cause of the defendant's actions is not an addiction to drugs, a clinical mental health issue, or a result of being young and misguided. In the HTICs, the underlying cause of the defendant's actions is often a web of coercion, force, and abuse.

Treating the problem here is not as straightforward as sending a drug addict to a treatment center, or placing youth in programs designed to put them on a path to success. Here, there is the potential for a wide array of psychological and physical traumas, as well as legal, education, and housing issues that need to be addressed in order to help solve the problem. The majority of trafficking victims, many of whom are defendants in these courts, are lured into the United States with promises of great things for them and their families. They have little-to-no education, no money, no documentation, and nowhere to go. They need counseling, protection and housing, education and job services, legal and immigration assistance, and other services, in order to help them restore their lives to one that is free of crime and victimization. As a result, the specialized human trafficking courts throughout New York State have made connections with a wide variety of service providers who are able to assist victims of all genders, ages, and races in turning their lives around.

1. Services provided through Human Trafficking Intervention Courts

The main service a defendant will receive through the HTICs, one which is generally mandated by the court, is counseling. Defendants who accept this will be assigned to a counselor from one of the court's service providers. This is done through discussion between the judge, prosecutor, service providers, and the attorney for the victim.

Attorneys representing victim-defendants should ensure that the client is aware of what each provider can offer, and that the client is being assigned to the provider that can best meet their individual needs. After this conversation and assignment, victims will be set up with an initial meeting with their counselor, who will then focus on using evidence-based, trauma-focused, cognitive-behavioral therapies to help them begin to heal.[48] This particular type of counseling is a short-term treatment method ideal for young victims exposed to repeated trauma. The treatment is implemented in a manner that encourages the victims to walk through exactly what had happened to them, so that they can put it behind them and move on—an effort aimed at reducing Post Traumatic Stress Disorder, depression, and other severe effects of the trauma.[49]

In these specialty courts, victims of trafficking are also given, through their assigned provider, a wide variety of services and assistance outside of the mandated counseling. Sanctuary and GEMS, along with many other providers statewide, frequently work with the HTICs to provide additional services such as shelter, education and job assistance, and legal help when needed.[50] Both providers have the ability to put victims in temporary safe houses and crisis shelters, as well as longer-term transitional shelters where they may remain for a designated period of time while preparing for life on their own.[51] They also assist victims in obtaining their GED or degrees, as well as teaching them basic skills and preparing them for a future career.[52]

a. The role played by attorneys in the administration of these services

Attorneys continue to play an important role for their client after assignment to a service provider. First, they can encourage their client to take advantage of all of the offers they are receiving from their service provider, from education and job placement to housing and counseling. These services can be exceptionally beneficial to victims of trafficking, often building the help and support system they need to begin a new life all their own, free from the confines and abuses of their traffickers.

For many victims, attending the court-mandated counseling sessions can be perceived to be more difficult than accepting a guilty plea and walking away. It can often involve reliving the traumas they have faced, and discussing them with someone new whom they may not feel they can fully trust. A victim's attorney can play a beneficial role in encouraging their client to complete the counseling sessions, and ensuring that their client is fully aware of the legal consequences of failure to attend.

It should be explained to the victims that skipping these sessions or not engaging in them can have the exact opposite effect a victim may be looking for, and could jeopardize their chances of receiving assistance and having their records cleared. Attorneys must also ensure that their clients are aware that even when they complete these sessions, they are not free of the criminal charges pending against them. They still need to go six months without any arrests before their case is officially dismissed.

2. Other legal remedies available: Immigration relief and vacatur

In addition to the services that court-assigned providers are able to provide, victims will often be in need of legal help with multiple other issues, including immigration.[53] With the signing of the Trafficking Victims Protection Act (TVPA) into law in 2000, and re-authorizations in 2003, 2005, and 2008, a new class of visas—known as "T visas"—was created specifically for victims of human trafficking, with a total of 5,000 per year being available to victims.[54]

Interestingly, the cap of 5,000 T visas is never reached within one fiscal year due to extreme underutilization.[55] With these visas, victims are allowed to remain legally within the United States, to continue to aid law enforcement in the building of a case against their traffickers, and to begin to establish new lives for themselves.[56] Upon issuance of a T visa, victims are also granted an Employment Authorization Document, meaning they are legally eligible to work in a legitimate job during their stay.[57] These visas, once issued, are valid for a period of four years; however, after three years a victim may become eligible to apply for permanent residency in the United States should they choose to do so.[58]

In order to qualify a victim for a T visa under the TVPA, an attorney must first be able to establish that their client is a victim of trafficking as defined by the law, and must currently be within the United States as a result of the victimization.[59] Though a victim does not need to be able to prove that they knew they were going to be forced into labor or the sex trade upon their arrival, their journey into the United States must have been the direct result of the trafficking—whether through kidnapping, coercion, force, or some other manner.[60]

Victims must also comply with any reasonable request from law enforcement officials for information or assistance, with the only exceptions being if the victim is under the age of 18, or is unable to cooperate as a result of serious trauma.[61] The attorney must be able to show that, should their client be sent back to the country from which they came, they would suffer from some form of extreme hardship or severe harm.[62] This can be done in a variety of ways, from showing the individual would be at risk of bodily harm or re-victimization, to showing that as a result of the psychological and physical trauma a victim had faced, being away from doctors and counselors could be dangerous to their health and well-being.[63]

Finally, a victim must be considered an admissible immigrant, meaning free from health-related or criminal issues, prior deportations, national security concerns, or other bars to citizenship outlined by United States Citizenship and Immigration Services.[64] However, for victims of trafficking seeking T visas, this is generally not an issue, since the admissibility challenges they could potentially face may be waived based on their victimization.[65] In order to be eligible to apply for permanent residency after the three-year waiting period, a victim must maintain this admissibility status, as well as continue to comply with law enforcement when reasonable and necessary.[66]

In addition to T visas for the victims of human trafficking, the TVPA created derivative T visas for qualifying family members of the victims.[67] These derivative visas do not factor into the cap of 5,000 visas per year allotted to trafficking victims.[68] This type of visa is available to victims under the age of 21 for their spouses, children, parents, and unmarried siblings under 18.[69] Therefore, an attorney can work with their client to determine if the victim has any family members who may qualify for such a visa, and help to bring them to the country and allow them to stay and work legally close to the victim. Those who receive these derivative visas would be on the same pathway to citizenship as the victims, being allowed to apply for a green card in three years so long as they maintain admissibility and eligibility, and the victim has also either applied or been granted their green card.[70] They are also available to the spouses or children of victims over the age of 21.[71] Often times family visas are factored into the holistic approach to these cases favored by service providers.[72]

In addition to immigration issues, attorneys may also assist their client victims in having any previous convictions they may have obtained while under the control of their traffickers vacated.[74] This is possible as a result of an amendment made by the New York State Legislature in August of 2010 to New York Criminal Procedure Law 440.10, which deals with the vacating of convictions and setting aside of sentences.[75] Under the amended law, victims of trafficking under state or federal law may move to vacate convictions for prostitution and other related offenses resulting from their being a victim of trafficking.[76]

In order for these convictions to be vacated, victims need to establish two things.[77] First, that the client is a victim of trafficking under the federal TVPA, or the New York State penal laws governing sex, labor, or aggravated labor trafficking at the time they were arrested.[78] Under the TVPA, one is considered a victim of sex trafficking if they are recruited, transported, or solicited for the purpose of commercial sex.[79] One could be further deemed a victim of a severe form of trafficking if they were forced into commercial sex through force, fraud, or coercion, or if they were forced into commercial sex prior to turning 18. In the alternative, New York State law defines sex trafficking as the situation where one intentionally advances or profits from prostitution in a variety of ways, including withholding or destroying a government identification document, or using force or coercion.[80] Establishing that an individual is a victim under these laws can be done in a variety of ways, from a narrative from the victim to official documentation from a law enforcement agency.[81]

a. Case Study: Bronx, 2011

Once an individual has been deemed a victim, it must be shown that the charges upon which they were arrested came as a direct result of the victimization.[82] One of the first cases of this nature was seen in a Bronx, NY court in late 2011. In this case, the victim, known as Doe to protect her identity after she willingly provided law enforcement valuable information regarding her traffickers, presented the Court with information that detailed her time as a victim of trafficking, beginning when she ran away from home at the age of thirteen.

At that time, Doe entered into a violent cycle of abusive relationships with several traffickers who forced her into prostitution. At one point during the time she was held by her last trafficker, she was gang-raped and assaulted, and subsequently refused medical treatment out of fear of drawing attention. When Doe told this same trafficker she wanted to return to her family, he forced her to tattoo his nickname on her arm so that she would always remember she "belonged" to him. After finally freeing herself from her final trafficker, Doe was able to begin a new life working, attending school, and building a relationship with her children.

After establishing a new life, Doe filed a motion for vacatur, along with an affidavit reflecting her assistance to law enforcement, of the three loitering-for-the-purpose-of-prostitution convictions she obtained while a victim. The People, upon reviewing the motion and documentation, presented no objections, rather asking the Court to grant Doe's motion with their well wishes. While a very straightforward case in which little interpretation or dispute was necessary, this case shows the potential that this new amendment to CPL 440.10 has to allow former victims to erase the convictions that were obtained during their time as victims, permitting them to move on with their lives free from the restraints of their criminal records.

b. Case Study: Queens, 2013

In 2013, the range of charges that could be vacated under CPL 440.10 in Queens, NY was expanded beyond prostitution and loitering charges. Here, the victim, known only to the courts as LG, lost her job after her employer discovered she had prior convictions for prostitution, criminal possession of a weapon (a pocketknife), and probation violations. LG petitioned the court in an effort to have all of these convictions vacated, as all stemmed from her activities while being held captive by her traffickers. While the people did not dispute that LG was a victim, they did argue that her conviction for possession of the pocketknife did not constitute a prostitution-related offense, and thus should not be vacated. The court here held that a trafficking victim's conviction for possession of a weapon in the fourth degree qualified for vacatur, as the reason she carried a pocketknife in her pocketbook was to protect herself from her male clients if necessary.[83] The court held that this, along with the arresting charge of criminal possession of a weapon, was undoubtedly connected to her being a victim of trafficking, and the activities she had been forced and coerced into doing.[84] With the most common charges facing defendants of HTICs being prostitution or loitering for the purposes of engaging in prostitution, the majority of these victims will have little trouble having their convictions vacated under this amended law.

c. Case study: New York County, 2014

The following year in New York County Court, another case regarding the vacatur of convictions for a former victim of trafficking was heard.[85] This case, as with many cases of this nature, was concluded with no argument or fight from the People. In fact, the People consented to the vacatur, allowing the accusatory instruments to be dismissed and the records sealed. This too expanded the range of cases New York allows victims of trafficking to have vacated from their records.

Here, the victim, known as C.C., she sought to have four convictions removed from her record. While the majority of these charges were for loitering and prostitution, C.C. also had charges stemming from the drug addiction both she and her trafficker suffered from, including a conviction for promoting contraband to prisoners. This conviction came after she attempted to smuggle marijuana into the prison during a visit to her imprisoned pimp. At the time she petitioned the court, C.C. had successfully completed drug treatment programs, secured housing, and began working towards her GED. Her goal was to study cosmetology. However, the state would not grant a cosmetology license to someone with her criminal record. It is for this reason, and after hearing her narrative of her time under the control of her trafficker, that the People and the Court agreed to vacate all convictions C.C. had obtained.

D. Potential Problems and Criticisms with the Human Trafficking Intervention Courts

Though the problem-solving approach to human trafficking was implemented with the goal of identifying and assisting victims of trafficking once they have been arrested, some aspects have been criticized. First, in order to be eligible to participate in HTIC programs, a victim must have been arrested, which necessitates treatment like any other criminal. As a recent report analyzing the HTICs stated, "No other charge, whether it be domestic violence, kidnapping, labor exploitation, or sexual assault, calls for the person being exploited to be arrested."[86] However, in order for victims to receive the services being offered through the specialized courts, they must first be arrested. Arguably, this arrest and subsequent dealings with police would re-traumatize someone who is already the victim of a crime.

Additionally, critics argue, victims will often be re-arrested while doing the same thing out of fear or necessity during or shortly after the completion of their court-mandated programs, and enter into a never-ending cycle of arrests and mandated programs. While the HTICs do grant an ACOD for six months after completion of the program, this can still act as a bar to employment until the charges have been dismissed and records sealed. Therefore, the victims may be forced to do the only thing they know how to do or are able to do to make money until such a time as they can get a legitimate job. They are then rearrested on prostitution or loitering charges, their records reopened, and they begin the same cycle all over again.

Victims may also be rearrested for loitering, another common charge in the HTICs, for simply being spotted with individuals who have been previously linked to prostitution, or for wearing clothes thought to be too revealing.[87] Additionally, should a victim fail to attend their sessions, a warrant is put out for them, and they will be arrested like any other criminal with a warrant for arrest. Though efforts have been made to train and educate law enforcement in the area of trafficking and how to properly identify and handle a victim, the large majority of trafficking victims who are arrested will not receive special consideration as a victim rather than a criminal.

Finally, those who have observed the specialized human trafficking courts' proceedings have reported that the availability of interpretation services in the courts is insufficient, and wait time for service providers may be long.[88] Reports show that the percentage of those in need of an interpreter can be as high as 67 percent of the court's cases.[89] There are not nearly enough interpreters to keep up with the growing demand in the HTICs. Such shortages mean that those who are in need of a translator can often spend two or three months longer in the system than those who speak English.[90] Furthermore, not being able to communicate with the people around them can heighten the confusion and trauma of the victims who are without translation services.[91] This has led to issues and delays not only in these individuals' legal proceedings, but also in their counseling sessions and receipt of services.[92] Additionally, due to the rapidly growing influx of victims through the court's doors, a number that tripled in only three years, many service providers are having trouble keeping up with the number of clients they are receiving.[93] This only further delays an individual's time in the court system, as well as the amount of time it takes for them to be able to get help.

1. How attorneys can help with potential solutions to current problems

Advocates and critics of these specialized courts agree that the large majority of the problems seen within the courts are not without solutions. The most difficult of these problems is that of the victims being arrested and treated as a common criminal in order to receive the help they need. As Judge Toko Serita, who presides over the Queens HTIC, said in a 2014 *New York Times* article surrounding the HTICs, "This court is not devised to solve the problems of trafficking, but to address one of the unfortunate byproducts, which is the arrest of these defendants on prostitution charges."[94] As one would not generally enter into any court system, problem-solving or otherwise, without an arrest, the fact that victims are being arrested and treated as criminals is not an easy problem to solve.

That said, it is possible to limit the secondary trauma experienced by victims as they go through the court system. This could be done through more training for the law enforcement officers and attorneys who are likely to be arresting and processing the victims before they enter the court. Though New York, along with the majority of other states, have created task forces and distributed some training materials, there is certainly more that could be done.[95]

As for the criticism that the courts are aimed at anyone arrested for prostitution or related offenses, there is, again, no simple solution. Unfortunately, separating those who commit prostitution offenses because they are forced or coerced from those who do it as a conscious decision, is not at all an easy task. Many individuals processed through these courts do not recognize or hold themselves out to be trafficking victims, and no one throughout the course of the court proceedings will ask.[96] There is an innate silence around the crime of human trafficking, and many victims will go back to their traffickers before calling themselves victims and asking for help.[97] In the large majority of cases, this is out of fear of what may happen to them should they choose to acknowledge what has happened to them. Therefore, every individual who passes through the HTICs is treated as if they are a victim at risk, and are provided with the same options and services, as these services could prove beneficial.

Should an individual not wish to receive those services, they are also given the option to plead guilty to a lesser charge to proceed to trial, just as they would were they to have been processed through regular courts. Under this current problem-solving model, services and assistance are occasionally offered to more people than need it. With that in mind, should an attorney be able to establish that their client is not in fact a victim, but rather voluntarily in the sex trade, a different approach and different outcome may be desirable.

Perhaps the simplest problem for which to craft a solution is that of the lack of translation services and the backlog among service providers. As such, it is a problem that advocates of the human trafficking courts, including Judge Kluger and Queens Councilman Rory Lancman, have made plans to address.[98] In early 2015, the City Council's Committee on Courts and Legal Services held a preliminary budget hearing, in which they were to consider increasing the amount of funding the HTICs and their service providers received.[99] Among those who testified before the council were Judge Kluger, representatives from some of the court service providers, and a young woman who fell victim to human trafficking in 2001.[100] An increase in funding for the court system and its providers is needed to address the problems of a lack of services or long wait times.

Individual attorneys can assist on this front by having their own translators available for cases in which the attorney is dealing with a victim of trafficking who does not know any English. Whether this is an attorney on staff who speaks multiple languages, or one that can be brought in on an as-needed basis, providing the necessary translation services for one's client can help them avoid many potential issues, and work to build the attorney-client relationship and trust.

The Red Umbrella Project, an advocate group for voluntary sex workers, also offers recommendations including examination of police profiling and treatment of sex workers, as well as examining service provider programs services and benefits.[101] Chief among their recommendations is that those involved in the creation and management of the HTICs open a line of communication with those involved in sex work.[102] Attorneys can play a crucial role in helping to open this line of communication and may play a unique and unparalleled role in instigating the formulation of ideas and procedures for handling some of the major issues sex workers find with the system.

E. Minor Clients who are Victims of Human Trafficking

Many victims of trafficking have no documentation verifying their names or their ages, as their traffickers seize identifying documents as a way to control their victims. Victims are also often told by their traffickers to lie about their age to authorities, making themselves either older or younger, to attract clients or to get themselves out of trouble. However, practitioners should take care to determine the true age of their clients, as there are certain legal remedies and social service programs only available to minors, and individuals under the age of seventeen are diverted away from these human trafficking courts, and into a family court environment.

A 2012 United Nations report shows that in the United States, 31 percent of human trafficking victims are children.[103] In 2015, the Department of Justice reported that half of human trafficking victims were under the age of eighteen, placing the average age of victims between twelve and fourteen years old.[104] This puts the United States on par with the rest of the world, where children make up, on average, 50 percent of victims, with an estimated 2 million children being subject to forced sex work.[105]

In addition to the HTICs, New York has put in place legislation that redirects young victims of trafficking away from the court system entirely, shielding them from any potential charges, and allowing them to obtain the help and services they need in an environment safe for children. This was done through the 2008 passing of the Safe Harbor for Exploited Children Act. Under this act, along with more recently added provisions, it becomes a mandated assumption that anyone under the age of 17 charged with a prostitution-related crime is a victim of trafficking, and thus should be treated as a Person in Need of Supervision (PINS).[106] Through this, rather than being processed through a court proceeding typical of a juvenile who had committed a crime, these youth are processed through a non-criminal proceeding in family courts, and provided with the services they need. Additionally, the young victims are placed into safe houses while they are obtaining these services, rather than going to jail. Thus, if one believes they are dealing with a young victim of human trafficking, they should be referred to family court and be designated a PIN, rather than being placed through the HTIC system.

Several prosecutors have argued that that in doing this, New York eliminated a powerful leverage tool that they could use to identify and arrest the traffickers who were responsible for placing the child into sex work.[107] They argue that the threat of being locked up as a child, a threat no longer able to be used under the new laws, was often strong enough that children would be willing to provide information about their captors when in court.[108] However, courts should arguably not be attempting to force this information out of young children, due to the high risk of further traumatization. Additionally, as with adult victims of trafficking, once children had been arrested through the old system and released, they were often simply placed back into the hands of their traffickers to be re-victimized.

Now, under the new laws, minors are being treated like the child victims they are, and are being supervised and provided assistance by the state. Additionally, they are avoiding collateral consequences that would have the potential to affect their ability to get educational and job opportunities in their future. These young victims, many of whom were forced into the sex trade after fleeing abusive or neglectful parents, have suffered lives of trauma and abuse.[109] Coming into contact with the legal system should not be an event that heightens this trauma, but rather one that helps to alleviate or repair the damage done by traffickers or parents. By having systems in place that allow young victims who have been arrested to receive help and begin to heal, New York is working to solve the problem not only of what happens to these young victims upon arrest, but also of the continued trauma they may endure for the rest of their lives if no one steps up to help.

When handling the case of a child victim, attorneys may face even more issues and trauma than when handling adult victims. However, much like when dealing with adults, attorneys for these child victims must work to build a relationship of trust with the child. As young victims of human trafficking in the United States do not often have the luxury of having a parent with them throughout the proceedings and processes, the attorney may end up being one of the people with whom the child feels most comfortable. They should make sure that the child understands what is happening as much as possible accounting for their age, and should ensure that they feel safe and are well cared for during the process. Furthermore, attorneys may reach out to any service providers, such as GEMS, and attempt to receive help from them in dealing with the child. Providers such as this will be able to assist in providing the child with a safe house to stay in, counseling services, education, and the opportunity to be around other children and to socialize.

3.3 Favorable Outcomes for Trafficking Victims

Despite the criticism and alleged flaws in the system, these problem-solving style courts may be the best option for victims of human trafficking who have been arrested, consistently leading to a much more favorable outcome than with a typical court proceeding. Defining success within the HTICs, much like the majority of other problem-solving courts, does include reducing recidivism rates for these victims.[110] However, contrary to other problem-solving courts, where reducing recidivism is the main goal and measure of success, HTICs' measures of success go much deeper.

For these specialized human trafficking courts, success is measured not only by ceasing the cycle of recidivism among individuals who proceed through its doors, but rather doing so while assisting these individuals to leave behind a life of abuse and victimization. For these courts, success comes when a victim of trafficking, brought before the court on prostitution-related charges, receives help and support from the legal system and service providers, allowing them to escape their captors and begin a new life.

The 11 HTICs across the state of New York now handle close to 95 percent of all prostitution-related crimes committed in New York, providing services and options to thousands of individuals.[111] While not all of the individuals who pass through the doors of the HTIC will accept or need their services, for many these courts are considered to be a lifesaver. One such success comes from the Queens human trafficking court where a young victim, forced into prostitution at the age of twelve, was able to escape with the help of these courts.[112] According to this young victim, now 27, the courts not only provided her with the vital services she needed to change her life, but also with the support system that allowed her to do it. She is now living and flourishing on her own, having obtained one college degree, and working towards another.[113] Another young woman from the same court fell victim to her traffickers at the age of 15 when she decided to migrate to the United States alone from Mexico.[114] For her, the HTIC was "the best thing that ever happened" to her, finally allowing her to become a legal resident, as well as helping her to find safe housing and employment.[115] It is stories like these, only two of many, that show just how large of an impact these courts can have on the lives of trafficking victims who come before them.

In only one year, from November 2013 to November 2014, 639 cases were brought before the HTIC in Queens, New York.[116] Of these cases, 398 of the defendants—roughly 62 percent—received an ACOD following a successful completion of their court-mandated program.[117] This is only one of the 11 courts now operational in the U.S., bringing the number of cases likely to be before this particular court system as a whole well into the thousands each year. The Queens branch of the HTIC, which sees 62 percent of its defendants successfully complete their programs and receive their promised ACOD, paints a promising picture of the success of the HTIC system as a whole.[118] If all of the 11 courts had a success rate even within five or ten percent of this, these courts would be a clear success in helping thousands of victims. In fact, a 62 percent success rate puts the HTICs on par with New York's highly successful drug courts, which boast a 67 percent success rate.[119]

As of October 2014, the HTICs in New York had handled over 4,200 cases, providing what Judge Kluger describes as an "unprecedented lifeline" to many victims.[120] In contrast to the old court systems, which treated victims as common criminals and quickly returned them to their traffickers, HTICs remove victims from that life, and give them the tools and support needed to start afresh, free from victimization and abuse. On the other hand, these courts will not provide an all-around solution for the issue of human trafficking, nor will it work to prevent it to happening to new victims. As Judge Kluger stated, this was not their intention when they were created.[121]

Many of the successes the HTICs have seen in recent years can be attributed to the attorneys who work within them. In order for an attorney to achieve the most favorable outcome for a victim of trafficking, it is imperative that attorneys fully understand the workings of the HTIC system, the options they provide for victims, and the potential outcome each of these options can provide. These attorneys, often trained in identifying and handling cases involving human trafficking victims, are often the first line of defense for the victims. They are frequently the first point of contact for victims entering the legal system, and are responsible for guiding and advising them through the entire legal process. They will often help them to avoid immigration issues, as well as ensure that their criminal records are clear and do not cause problems in the future. The attorneys also serve as the guiding voice for victims, encouraging them to complete their programs, and helping to link them with the services they need.

With the success of New York's HTICs, other states and localities have begun to follow suit, implementing a similar problem-solving approach in their areas. One such court in Wastenaw County, Michigan, received high marks for its effectiveness in a recent report by the University of Michigan's School of Social Work.[122] All individuals actively participating in the Court and the programs they provide were screened through a Severe Human Trafficking Assessment.[123] Of those screened, two-thirds were considered positive, meaning they were deemed to be victims.[124] This specialized Michigan court, which operates in the same manner as the New York courts, boasts high compliance rates in several different areas, including participation in bi-weekly reviews by the judge.[125] Victims who participated in the courts also demonstrated higher levels of self-sufficiency after the court process.[126] Therefore, while the report does cites some issues such as a lack of availability of some essential services, overall, the Human Trafficking Court was deemed to be a great success.[127]

3.4 Conclusion

Human trafficking is a 32-billion-dollar industry, affecting millions of people worldwide, and touching nearly every nation.[128] New York State was the first to announce a problem-solving approach to handling this issue through their successful HTIC system which, if properly implemented across the nation, could provide thousands of trafficking victims nationwide with the services and support they need. Attorneys play a vital role in a victim's journey through the HTIC, guiding them through the system to achieve the best outcome possible. They may often take on several roles, from attorney and advocate to supporter and listener. In this way, attorneys can aid the legal system in putting an end to the cycle of arrests and re-victimization that human trafficking victims often face in the traditional court system, and provide their clients with the help and support necessary to escape their captors and begin a new life for themselves.

However, these courts alone cannot solve the overall global issue of human trafficking. The fight against trafficking worldwide requires the collaboration of many different agencies, systems, and organizations across the globe, from anti-trafficking groups and coalitions to governments. Groups like the Polaris Project, in conjunction with the National Human Trafficking Resource Center, have made great strides in the fight against trafficking, identifying and assisting with nearly 20,000 cases of human trafficking in just seven years.[129] In the

U.S., federal government, law enforcement, and military have established task forces and training programs aimed at identifying and rescuing victims, as well as prosecuting alleged traffickers within borders. Looking internationally, the United Nations and many countries across the globe have also begun to implement laws and programs aimed at some of the causes of trafficking, such as lack of education and economic opportunities for women, as well as the prevention and prosecution of trafficking.[130] The media, both in the United States and worldwide, has also begun to enter into in the fight against human trafficking, taking to films, news articles, posters, billboards, and other forms to bring the issue of human trafficking further into the spotlight. It is through this type of highly collaborative approach that victims emerge out of the shadows and their traffickers are brought to justice.

Endnotes

1. International Labour Organization, "New ILO Global Estimate of Forced Labour: 20.9 million victims," 1 June 2012 (http://www.ilo.org/global/about-the-ilo/newsroom/news/WCMS_182109/lang--en/index.htm).

2. "Who are the victims?" Blog post published on September 1, 2015 (http://www.allwewantislove.org/blog/r4fnw8lth959o869il4wdiggnp75tj).

3. Rafael Romo, "Human trafficking survivor: I was raped 43,200 times," *CNN*, November 10, 2015 (http://www.cnn.com/2015/11/10/americas/freedom-project-mexico-trafficking-survivor/).

4. Jessica Lipscomb, "Story of victims illustrate horrors of human trafficking," *Naples Daily News*, March 13, 2015 (http://www.naplesnews.com/news/crime/story-of-victims-illustrate-horrors-of-human-trafficking-ep-980682616-340608821.html).

5. *Id.*

6. Sarah Pierce, "Top 4 States for Human Trafficking," November 4, 2014 (http://humantraffickingsearch.net/wp/top-4-states-for-human-trafficking/).

7. Polaris Project, "2014 State Rankings on Human Trafficking Law," September 2014 (http://www.polarisproject.org/resources/2014-state-ratings-human-trafficking-laws).

8. Sarah Pierce, "Top 4 States for Human Trafficking," November 4, 2014 (http://humantraffickingsearch.net/wp/top-4-states-for-human-trafficking/).

9.   Malika Saada Saar, "US Should Stop Criminalizing Sex Trafficking Victims," *CNN*, February 7, 2011 (http://www.cnn.com/2011/OPINION/02/05/saar.ending.girl.slavery/).

10. Elanor Goldberg, "Sex Trafficking Victims Usually Can't Escape Prostitution Charges. This Lawyer's Working to Change That," *The Huffington Post*, May 18, 2015 (http://www.huffingtonpost.com/2015/05/18/sex-trafficking-prostitution-charges_n_7119474.html).

11. *Id.*

12. *Id.*

13. *Id.*

14. Bruce J. Winick, *Therapeutic Jurisprudence and Problem-solving Courts*, 30 Fordham Urb. L.J. 1055 (2003).

15. *Id.*

16. *Id.*

17. *Id.*

18. Ryan J. Winter, PhD & Jonathan P. Vallano, PhD, "Can specialty courts turn lives around?" *Monitor on Psychology*, Volume 42 No. 3, March 2011 (http://www.apa.org/monitor/2011/03/jn.aspx).

19. *Id.*

20. *Id.*

21. *Id.*

22. *Id.*

23. Greg Berman & John Feinblatt, *Problem-Solving Courts: A Brief Primer*, 23 LAW & POL'Y 125, 125–26 (2001).

24. New York State Problem-solving Courts (https://www.nycourts.gov/courts/problem_solving/PSC-FLYER4Fold.pdf).

25. The Honorable Peggy Fulton Hora et. al., *Therapeutic Jurisprudence and the Drug Treatment Court Movement: Revolutionizing the Criminal Justice System's Response to Drug Abuse and Crime in America*, 74 Notre Dame L. Rev. 439 (1999).

26. "Problem-solving Courts Overview" (https://www.nycourts.gov/courts/problem_solving/index.shtm.

27. "Drug Treatment Courts" (https://www.nycourts.gov/courts/problem_solving/drugcourts/overview.shtml.

28. Hon. Barry Kamins, Justin Barry, & Lisa Lindsay, "Drug Court Initiative Annual Report 2012" (https://www.nycourts.gov/COURTS/nyc/criminal/drug_annual_report_2012.pdf).

29. "Problem-solving Courts Overview" (https://www.nycourts.gov/courts/problem_solving/index.shtml).

30. *Id.*

31. "Drug Treatment Courts" (https://www.nycourts.gov/courts/problem_solving/drugcourts/overview.shtml.

32. *Id.*

33. Ryan J. Winter, PhD, MLS and Jonathan P. Vallano, PhD, "Can Specialty Courts Turn Lives Around?" American Psychological Association website, 2011 (http://www.apa.org/monitor/2011/03/jn.aspx).

34. "Problem-solving Courts Overview" (https://www.nycourts.gov/courts/problem_solving/index.shtm).

35. Gregory M. Maney et al., *Meeting the Service Needs of Human Trafficking Survivors in the New York Metropolitan Area: Assessment and Recommendations* (2011).

36. Chief Judge Jonathan Lippman, "Announcement of New York's Human Trafficking Intervention Initiative" (http://www.courtinnovation.org/research/announcement-new-yorks-human-trafficking-intervention-initiative).

37. Holly Smith, "Interviewing victims of human trafficking: Survivors offer advice," March 2, 2014 (http://www.commdiginews.com/life/interview-

ing-victims-of-human-trafficking-survivors-offer-advice-11238/#sepLWB-7chAxZhx9W.99).

38. *Id.*

39. Red Umbrella Project, "Criminal, Victim, or Sex Worker?" October 2014 (http://redumbrellaproject.org/wp-content/uploads/2014/09/RedUP-NYHTIC-FINALweb.pdf).

40. *Id.*

41. *Id.*

42. *Id.*

43. *Id.*

44. *Id.*

45. *Id.*

46. *Id.*

47. *Id.*

48. *Id.*

49. Sanctuary for Families, "Anti-Trafficking Initiative" (https://www.sanctuaryforfamilies.org/our-approach/client-services/anti-trafficking-initiative/#Counseling).

50. Lindsey Getz, "Trauma-Focused Cognitive-Behavioral Therapy—Hope for Abused Children," *Social Work Today*, Vol. 12 No. 3 at 22, May/June 2012 (http://www.socialworktoday.com/archive/051412p22.shtml).

51. Sanctuary for Families, "Anti-Trafficking Initiative" (https://www.sanctuaryforfamilies.org/our-approach/client-services/anti-trafficking-initiative/#Counseling).

52. Sanctuary for Families, "Shelter Services" (https://www.sanctuaryforfamilies.org/our-approach/client-services/shelter-services/).

53. Sanctuary for Families, "Economic Empowerment Services" (https://www.sanctuaryforfamilies.org/our-approach/client-services/economic-empowerment-services/).

54. Sanctuary for Families, "Anti-Trafficking Initiative" (https://www.sanctuaryforfamilies.org/our-approach/client-services/anti-trafficking-initiative/).

55. USCIS, "Victims of Human Trafficking: T Non Immigrant Status" (http://www.uscis.gov/humanitarian/victims-human-trafficking-other-crimes/victims-human-trafficking-t-nonimmigrant-status).

56. Katya Botwinick, "Labor Trafficking: Unidentified Victims, Underutilized Fixes," *The Legal Intelligencer*, 22 February, 2016 (http://www.thelegalintelligencer.com/id=1202750203790/Labor-Trafficking-Unidentified-Victims-Underutilized-Fixes?slreturn=20160324140518).

57. USCIS, "Victims of Human Trafficking: T Non Immigrant Status" (http://www.uscis.gov/humanitarian/victims-human-trafficking-other-crimes/victims-human-trafficking-t-nonimmigrant-status).

58. USCIS, "Questions and Answers: Victims of Human Trafficking, T Nonimmigrant Status" (http://www.uscis.gov/humanitarian/victims-human-trafficking-other-crimes/victims-human-trafficking-t-nonimmigrant-status/questions-and-answers-victims-human-trafficking-t-nonimmigrant-status-0).

59. *Id.*

60. 22 USCA § 7102.

61. Kristina Gasson, "Differences Between T and U Visas for victims of human trafficking, two different visa options are available" (http://www.nolo.com/legal-encyclopedia/differences-between-t-u-visas.html).

62. *Id.*

63. USCIS, "Victims of Human Trafficking: T Non Immigrant Status" (http://www.uscis.gov/humanitarian/victims-human-trafficking-other-crimes/victims-human-trafficking-t-).

64. Kristina Gasson, "Differences Between T and U Visas for victims of human trafficking, two different visa options are available" (http://www.nolo.com/legal-encyclopedia/differences-between-t-u-visas.html).

65. USCIS Policy Manual Volume 8, November 10, 2015 (http://www.uscis.gov/policymanual/HTML/PolicyManual-Volume8.html).

66. USCIS I-192, "Application for Advance Permission to Enter as Nonimmigrant" (http://www.uscis.gov/i-192).

67. USCIS, "Questions and Answers: Victims of Human Trafficking, T Nonimmigrant Status" (http://www.uscis.gov/humanitarian/victims-human-trafficking-other-crimes/victims-human-trafficking-t-nonimmigrant-status/questions-and-answers-victims-human-trafficking-t-nonimmigrant-status-0).

68. USCIS, "Victims of Human Trafficking: T Non Immigrant Status" (http://www.uscis.gov/humanitarian/victims-human-trafficking-other-crimes/victims-human-trafficking-t-).

69. USCIS, "Questions and Answers: Victims of Human Trafficking, T Nonimmigrant Status" (http://www.uscis.gov/humanitarian/victims-human-trafficking-other-crimes/victims-human-trafficking-t-nonimmigrant-status/questions-and-answers-victims-human-trafficking-t-nonimmigrant-status-0).

70. *Id.*

71. USCIS, "Victims of Human Trafficking: T Non Immigrant Status" (http://www.uscis.gov/humanitarian/victims-human-trafficking-other-crimes/victims-human-trafficking-t-).

72. *Id.*

73. Sanctuary for Families, "Anti Trafficking Initiative" (https://www.sanctuaryforfamilies.org/our-approach/client-services/anti-trafficking-initiative).

74. *Id.*

75. *People v G.M.*, 32 Misc 3d 274, 279 (Crim Ct 2011).

76. Criminal Procedure Law § 440.10.

77. *People v L.G.*, 41 Misc 3d 428, 435 (Crim Ct 2013).

78. *People v L.G.*, 41 Misc 3d 428, 435 (Crim Ct 2013).

79. 22 USCA § 7102.

80. Penal Law § 230.34.

81. *People v G.M.* at 280.

82. *People v L.G.*, 41 Misc 3d 428, 437 (Crim Ct 2013).

83. *Id.*

84. *Id.*

85. *People v. CC*, NY County 2014.

86. Mary Emily O'Hara, "Not Everyone Is Happy with the NY Courts Treating Sex Workers as Trafficking Victims," October 4, 2014 https://news.vice.com/article/not-everyone-is-happy-with-the-ny-courts-treating-sex-workers-as-trafficking-victims).

87. Mike Ludwig, "Want the Truth About New York's Human Trafficking Courts? Ask a Sex Worker," October 26, 2014 (http://www.truth-out.org/news/item/27036-want-the-truth-about-new-york-s-human-trafficking-courts-ask-a-sex-worker).

88. Red Umbrella Project, "Criminal, Victim, or Sex Worker"? October 2014 (http://redumbrellaproject.org/wp-content/uploads/2014/09/RedUP-NYHTIC-FINALweb.pdf).

89. *Id.*

90. Melissa Etehad, "Do New York's Human Trafficking Intervention Courts Hurt the Women They're Meant to Help?" October 27, 2015 (http://theink.nyc/do-new-yorks-human-trafficking-intervention-courts-hurt-the-women-theyre-meant-to-help/).

91. *Id.*

92. *Id.*

93. *Id.*

94. Liz Robbins, "In a Queens Court, Women in Prostitution Cases Are Seen as Victims," *New York Times*, November 21, 2014 (http://www.nytimes.

com/2014/11/23/nyregion/in-a-queens-court-women-arrested-for-prostitu-tion-are-seen-as-victims.html?_r=0).

95. New York State Interagency Task Force on Human Trafficking, August 2008 (http://www.criminaljustice.ny.gov/pio/humantrafficking/human_trafficking_rpt_aug08.pdf).

96. Liz Robbins, "In a Queens Court, Women in Prostitution Cases Are Seen as Victims," *New York Times*, November 21, 2014 (http://www.nytimes. com/2014/11/23/nyregion/in-a-queens-court-women-arrested-for-prostitu-tion-are-seen-as-victims.html?_r=0).

97. *Id.*

98. Gloria Pazmino, "Advocates seek more city funds for human trafficking victims," March 27, 2015 (http://www.capitalnewyork.com/article/city-hall/2015/03/8564950/advocates-seek-more-city-funds-human-trafficking-victims).

99. *Id.*

100. *Id.*

101. Red Umbrella Project, "Criminal, Victim, or Sex Worker"? October 2014 (http://redumbrellaproject.org/wp-content/uploads/2014/09/RedUP-NYHTIC-FINALweb.pdf).

102 *Id.*

103. Human Trafficking (http://www.unis.unvienna.org/unis/en/events/2015/crime_congress_human_trafficking.html).

104. Theresa Fisher, "Humans Not For Sale: Federal and State Trafficking Leg-islation," January 23, 2014 (http://jjie.org/humans-not-for-sale-federal-and-state-trafficking-legislation/).

105. Human Trafficking (http://www.unis.unvienna.org/unis/en/events/2015/crime_congress_human_trafficking.html).

106. Jill L. Goodman & Dorchen A. Leidholt, *Lawyers Manual for Human Trafficking*, (https://www.nycourts.gov/ip/womeninthecourts/pdfs/MUL-LEN%20_HUMAN%20TRAFFICKING_1_d.pdf).

107. "A Victory for Exploited Children," *New York Times*, September 26, 2008, (http://www.nytimes.com/2008/09/27/opinion/27sat3.html).

108. *Id.*

109. *Id.*

110. Rachel Porter, Michael Rempel, & Adam Mansky, "What Makes a Court Problem Solving," Center for Court Innovation, February 2010 (http://www.courtinnovation.org/sites/default/files/What_Makes_A_Court_P_S.pdf).

111. Chief Judge Jonathan Lippman, "Announcement of New York's Human Trafficking Intervention Initiative" (http://www.courtinnovation.org/research/announcement-new-yorks-human-trafficking-intervention-initiative).

112. Erik Badia & Corky Siemaszko, "NYC soon to launch courts aimed at helping prostitutes out of sex work," *New York Daily News*, September 26, 2013 (http://www.nydailynews.com/new-york/nyc-launch-courts-aimed-helping-prostitutes-sex-work-article-1.1467102).

113. *Id.*

114. Sadhaba Walsh, "New court helps New York's human trafficking victims," October 21, 2013 (http://america.aljazeera.com/articles/2013/10/31/new-court-systemhelpsvictimsofhumantraffickinginnewyork.html).

115. *Id.*

116. Liz Robbins, "In a Queens Court, Women in Prostitution Cases Are Seen as Victims," *New York Times*, November 21, 2014 (http://www.nytimes.com/2014/11/23/nyregion/in-a-queens-court-women-arrested-for-prostitution-are-seen-as-victims.html?_r=0).

117. *Id.*

118. Red Umbrella Project, "Criminal, Victim, or Sex Worker?" October 2014 (http://redumbrellaproject.org/wp-content/uploads/2014/09/RedUP-NYHTIC-FINALweb.pdf).

119. Hon. Barry Kamins, Justin Barry, & Lisa Lindsay, "Drug Court Initiative Annual Report 2012" (https://www.nycourts.gov/COURTS/nyc/criminal/drug_annual_report_2012.pdf).

120. The Hon. Judy Kluger, "New York's trafficking courts save lives," *New York Daily News*, October 12, 2014 (http://www.nydailynews.com/opinion/judy-harris-kluger-new-york-trafficking-courts-save-lives-article-1.1970657).

121. Liz Robbins, "In a Queens Court, Women in Prostitution Cases Are Seen as Victims," *New York Times*, November 21, 2014 (http://www.nytimes.com/2014/11/23/nyregion/in-a-queens-court-women-arrested-for-prostitution-are-seen-as-victims.html?_r=0).

122. Katie Vloet, "Human Trafficking Court Earns High Marks in First Year," April 1, 2015 (https://www.law.umich.edu/newsandinfo/features/Pages/humantraffickingcourt04115.aspx).

123. *Id.*

124. *Id.*

125. *Id.*

126. *Id.*

127. *Id.*

128. *A Global Alliance Against Forced Labour*, International Labour Conference, 93rd Session, 2005 (http://www.ilo.org/wcmsp5/groups/public/@ed_norm/@declaration/documents/publication/wcms_081882.pdf).

129. Polaris Project, "2014 Statistics" (https://polarisproject.org/sites/default/files/2014Statistics.pdf).

130. "Prevention" (http://www.humantrafficking.org/combat_trafficking/prevention).

Chapter 4

Human Trafficking and Exploitation in Australia

By Fiona McLeod, SC

The trafficking and exploitation of human beings is one of the most confronting challenges facing humanity today. Globally, millions of people live in conditions of exploitation and abuse facing coercion, deception, fraud, and violence in conditions akin to slavery.

This is a multi-dimensional problem driven by complex social and economic factors; flourishing in conditions of conflict, poverty, poor governance and cruel indifference; driven by the constant ingenuity of exploiters; and often involving the desire of the victims and their families to escape desperate circumstances. The problem is exacerbated by highly sophisticated criminal networks, unethical commercial enterprise, environmental degradation and the social denigration of women and girls in developing countries.[2]

4.1 What is Trafficking?

Trafficking is defined in Article 3 of the UN Protocol to Prevent, Suppress, and Punish Trafficking in Persons, especially Women and Children ("Trafficking Protocol")[3] as:

> [T]he recruitment, transportation, transfer, harbouring or receipt of persons, by means of the threat or use of force or other forms of coercion, of abduction, of fraud, of deception, of the abuse of power or of a position of vulnerability or of the giving or receiving of payments or benefits to achieve the consent of a person having control over another person, for the purpose of exploitation. Exploitation shall include, at a minimum, the exploitation of the prostitution of others or other forms of sexual exploitation, forced labour or services, slavery or practices similar to slavery, servitude or the removal of organs.

The Trafficking Protocol is the first global legally binding instrument to contain an agreed definition of trafficking in persons. The intention behind this definition is to "facilitate convergence in national approaches with regards to the establishment of domestic criminal offences that support efficient international cooperation in investigating and prosecuting trafficking cases."[4] An additional objective of the Trafficking Protocol is to protect and assist the victims of trafficking with full respect for their human rights.[5]

Contrary to common misconception, trafficking does not require movement across national borders. The key requirements are movement, the absence of consent, and the purpose of exploitation.

State parties to the Trafficking Protocol are required to adopt legislative definitions that are dynamic and flexible so as to empower the legislative framework to respond effectively to trafficking that: occurs both across borders and within a country; is for a range of exploitative purposes; victimises children, women, and men; and takes place with or without the involvement of organised crime groups.[6]

Human trafficking is a serious problem in the Asia Pacific region, with many of the countries in this region being widely recognised as origin and destination countries for trafficking.[7] Of the 600,000 to 800,000 people trafficked annually in the region, about 250,000 are estimated to be from South-East Asia.[8] The majority of Asian victims are identified as having been trafficked for the purpose of sexual exploitation.

The ILO has noted an increase in persons being identified as trafficked for the purpose of labour exploitation. Poorly regulated industries, as well as an increase in the numbers of "labour recruiters, agents, immigration officials, document forgers, [and] travel providers" willing to facilitate labour migration, are just some of the factors that have been attributed to such an increase.[9] The introduction of the Trafficking Protocol itself may have spurred a growing international awareness and reporting of labour exploitation as a human rights violation.

The 2015 U.S. State Department Trafficking in Persons Report estimates that approximately 800,000 people are trafficked across borders each year.[10] UN Women and the UN High Commissioner for Refugees estimate that figure to be closer to 2 to 2.5 million people per year.[11] It is estimated that 32 percent of trafficking victims are used for forced economic exploitation, with 56 percent of these victims being women and girls.[12] Whilst the majority of trafficking victims are between 18 and 24 years of age, it is estimated that 1.2 million children are trafficked every year.[13] The Global Slavery Index estimates that 35.8 million people are living in conditions of modern day slavery.[14]

The social, economic, and moral impact of those numbers are staggering when we consider that it is predominantly the world's women and children who are being exploited on such a massive scale. These numbers mean tens of millions of displaced and vulnerable individuals are subject to abuse, entrenched poverty, and ongoing violation of their human rights. The ILO estimates that the profits from labour exploitation exceed $150 billion annually.

The nature of human trafficking varies from region to region. Most commonly, it involves trafficking in women and children for sexual exploitation. The International Labour Organisation (ILO) estimates that 43 percent of trafficking victims are used for forced commercial sexual exploitation, with 98 percent of those victims being women and girls.[15] Men, women, and children can also be trafficked for a diverse range of other purposes, including: forced labour in industries such as hospitality, construction, forestry, mining or agriculture; domestic and sweatshop labour; illicit adoption; street begging and scrounging; forced recruitment into militia or armed forces; and the harvesting of body organs.[16]

4.2 What is Slavery?

It is also useful to understand what is meant by "slavery" in the modern age. Slavery is defined in Article 1 of the UN International Convention to Suppress the Slavery Trade and Slavery 1926 ("Slavery Convention") as "the status or condition of a person over whom any or all of the powers attaching to the right of ownership are exercised."[17] Forced labour is defined in Article 2 of the ILO's

Forced Labour Convention 1930 as "work or service extracted from any person under the menace of any penalty and for which the person has not offered himself or herself voluntarily." In addition to these international instruments, the International Covenant on Civil and Political Rights (ICCPR) provides that no one shall be required to perform compulsory or forced labour, or shall be held in slavery or servitude,[18] and the International Covenant on Economic, Social and Cultural Rights protects the right to freely choose one's work, and to just and favourable conditions of work.[19] According to the ILO, some 12 million people are enslaved worldwide for the purpose of forced labour. Of these 12 million people, 55 percent are in South East Asia, and 40 to 50 percent are children.[20]

The United Nation's Recommended Principles and Guidelines on Human Rights and Human Trafficking (UN Guidelines) emphasise the need to separately criminalise forced labour as part of a broader legal framework which addresses trafficking.[21] The United Nations Office on Drugs and Crime's (UNODC) Model Law against Trafficking in Persons also criminalises the use of forced labour and services.[22]

4.3 The Position in Australia

The extent to which slavery and human trafficking exists in Australia is unclear. Estimates and other reported figures of trafficked persons vary significantly depending on the source of the information, and obtaining reliable and detailed statistics from relevant agencies is challenging. Reports of trafficking remain relatively low, with growing awareness amongst immigration and law enforcement officers and, increasingly, industrial regulators and unions.

Australia is primarily a destination country for women and girls subjected to sex trafficking and adults subjected to forced labour. There is a growing awareness of the prevalence of forced marriage occurring within some communities in Australia.

On average, around 25 allegations of trafficking in persons are reported to Australian authorities each year, although only very few of those will lead to prosecutions. Almost all victims that have been reported and identified by official sources are adult females of Asian background who were trafficked from Thailand, South Korea, Malaysia, and the Philippines to Australia for the purpose of commercial sexual exploitation. Other forms of trafficking involving men or children are rare, or not otherwise known to Australian authorities.[23] Between January 2004 and June 2012, the Australian Federal Police (AFP) undertook 346 investigations and assessments of slavery and people trafficking-related offences.[24] As at May 2016, there had been less than 20 prosecutions for people-trafficking-related offences,[25] and only 14 of these cases have resulted in a criminal conviction.[26]

4.4 Case Studies

A. *R v Wei Tang*

The case of *R v Wei Tang*[27] involved the owner of a brothel in Victoria who employed five women bought into Australia from Thailand under a "purchase" arrangement with recruiters. She was the first person to be convicted under anti-slavery laws introduced in Australia in 1999.

Each woman came to Australia voluntarily, on visas obtained illegally, expecting to perform paid sex work. Tang told each of the women that they had to work six days a week to pay off a debt of $45,000, approximating 900 clients each, before they were free of debt. Clients paid $110 for their services. Of that fee, $43 went to Tang as the brothel owner, $50 was used to pay off the debt to the recruiters, and the balance was shared by the "owners". On every seventh day, the women could keep $50 per client, although sundry expenses were sometimes deducted from this sum.

Tang exercised almost complete control over the women's lives. They had little money, limited English, and their passports were retained. Their visas were obtained illegally, and they feared detection by immigration authorities working long hours. The convictions were overturned in the Victorian Court of Appeal but upheld by the High Court. Tang was convicted of slavery offences under s 270.3(1)(a) of the Commonwealth *Criminal Code* and ultimately sentenced to ten years imprisonment with a non-parole period of six years.

In a personal message to the Justices of the High Court following the decision, the women described the conditions under which they had worked:

> Sometimes we worked until we couldn't walk. We had to work until we were very sick and the customers refused to take us. Only then were we allowed to rest, for one day![28]

The *Tang* case established the constitutional validity of the slavery provisions of the *Criminal Code,* and that a broad interpretation of the definition of slavery was appropriate, consistent with Article 1 of the Slavery Convention. The essence of slavery is the exercise of rights of ownership over another person. The inequality of their relative bargaining position and inability to assert control over their working environment amounted to slavery-type conditions and thus the offences had been made out, regardless of what Tang knew or believed about her rights of ownership.[29]

B. Ning's Case

The first claim for victims of crime compensation in Australia was made on behalf of a young woman known as "Ning" who, in 1995, was trafficked to Australia at the age of 13 from Thailand. She was put to work in a Sydney brothel. Before she arrived, she was physically and emotionally abused by her traffickers in Malaysia. This involved repeated rapes and imprisonment, deprivation of basics and her passport. Upon arrival in Australia, Ning was told that she owed a "debt" to her traffickers of $35,000, which she would pay off by having sex with 650 clients. She could then earn money for herself. She was not permitted to leave the brothel, had little money of her own, spoke no English, and had no contacts in Australia. She was told to lie about her age and circumstances if questioned, and was threatened with violence if she did not comply.

Ten days after her arrival, Ning was discovered at the brothel following a customer tip-off during a joint AFP and Immigration raid. In those ten days, she had been required to have sex with more than 100 men. A complaint was made to police, and subsequent information provided to them positively identified the brothel owner, but no action was ever taken to prosecute him.

Following the raid, Ning was promptly deported back to Thailand and found her way to a women's shelter. She eventually found her way home and gave evidence against two Thai individuals involved in trafficking her. They were subsequently convicted and imprisoned.

The AFP officer involved in the raid, Chris Payne, formerly head of the AFP Trafficking Unit, was disturbed by Ning's story and collaborated with documentary film-makers Luigi Acquisto and Stella Zammataro to find her, and the family of another young woman, Phuongtong Simaplee, who had died in immigration detention.[30] They approached the author to act pro bono for Ning in a compensation claim in NSW and for Phuongtong's family in a wrongful death claim against the Commonwealth Government.

Ning was ultimately awarded the maximum compensation available under the NSW Victims of Crime Compensation scheme for the abuse she suffered—including multiple statutory rapes of a child—and she became the first person in Australia to be compensated as a victim of trafficking and slavery.[31] Since that time, a number of claims in Victoria and New South Wales have proceeded to an award of compensation, and there are other claims underway in Victoria and in NSW.

As a post-script, Ning returned to Australia to visit and spoke to anti-trafficking organisations about her ordeal. She invested her compensation award in a small business in Thailand. Tragically, she was sexually assaulted in an act of revenge and contracted HIV before she passed away.

The author also negotiated an ex-gratia payment from the Australian government for the family of Phuongtong Simaplee, for the neglect of detention centre operators — in particular, the failure to provide adequate medical treatment.

C. *R v Kovacs*

In *R v Kovacs*,[32] a married couple, Mr. and Mrs. Kovacs, were charged with offences relating to a sham marriage under the *Migration Act 1958* (Cth) and slavery under the *Criminal Code*. They arranged and paid for a male friend to travel to the Philippines to marry and return with a Filipino woman with the intention that she would work in their take-away shop and home as a domestic servant. Once the woman was in Australia, she was effectively enslaved by the Kovaks. She was sexually assaulted, threatened, and abused. She worked up to 18 hours a day, seven days a week for a pittance. Her ability to escape was constrained by coercion, manipulation, lack of funds and the confiscation of her passport. Mr. Kovacs was convicted of slavery and sentenced to eight years imprisonment and Mrs. Kovacs to four years.

The Kovacs appealed, challenging the findings of slavery, arguing the victim in this case had a "degree of personal freedom" inconsistent with the existence of slavery as defined in the Code.[33] They argued that she was not prevented from leaving the shop or house, she was not locked in her room, she was able to send and receive letters, and she was able to use the telephone.[34] The Queensland Court of Appeal rejected the appeal, finding that the victim's freedom was "illusory or non-existent."[35] However, it set aside a number of the verdicts, and retrials were ordered, resulting in Mr. Kovacs being sentenced to nine years and Mrs. Kovacs to four years imprisonment.[36]

The case is important because it highlighted the issue of trafficking for domestic servitude and sham marriages in Australia, as well as the need to expand the legislative and policy framework to respond to cases that did not feature sexual exploitation.[37]

Reports continue in recent times of the trafficking and prostitution of children by family members and forced marriage of young girls in Australia.[38]

D. *DPP v Ho*

In *DPP v Ho*, four individuals were accused of playing a part in a scheme to bring Thai women to Australia and to profit from their willingness to work for minimal reward in the sex industry in Australia. The women were variously traded, possessed, and used as items of property, reducing them to the condition of slavery as prohibited by s 270.3(1)(a) of the *Criminal Code* (1995) (Cth).

Each of the women entered Australia on a three-month tourist or business visa issued in Bangkok, arranged by persons overseas who created false cover stories for their travel to Australia, including their attendance for "team building" exercises. Each of the women were chaperoned into Australia ,and handed over to the controllers with a view to keeping them in Australia for as long as possible and able to work without breaching their visas. Protection visas were applied for when the short stay visas were due to expire; each case using migration agents to make false claims of persecution.

All of the women came to Australia from Thailand with the knowledge they were going to work in the sex industry, and all but one had previously worked in that capacity. They understood that the price of their trip to Australia and the opportunity to earn money to assist their families was a contract to incur a debt that involved servicing between 650 or 750 clients. The debt owed by the women in each case and the gross value of their work during the period was in the order of $80,000 to $95,000 each. Each of the women usually took three to four months to repay their debt, working six days a week. On each of the days the subjects were paid $5 for each $125 service they performed, and $50 was deducted from the debt. The seventh day of each week was titled their free day when they could work and keep $50 of each $150 service.

In order to support the extended stay in Australia of one of the women, the accused assisted her with obtaining a protection visa under cover of a false story concerning her fear of persecution in Thailand as a Mormon. She continued to work in a brothel, and her clients were charged $125 for half an hour of sexual services. That money was placed in a locked box by employees, and for each client, $50 of the "debt" was deducted. After she had paid off her debt, she was entitled to earn $50 of the $125 herself from each customer; however, at this point, she asked whether she could stop working and was told she could not because there were no girls at the shop. She worked from 11 A.M.–2 A.M., and would see as many as 16 customers each day. When she was working, the premises were locked and she could not leave. Her request to work lesser hours was refused, although she was permitted to send money back to Thailand and to purchase gifts.

In sentencing the accused in this case, the Trial Judge Justice Lasry noted:

> There could be no doubt that this arrangement under which KW performed the services that she did was highly exploitative. KW was in Melbourne and unable to speak English. She had no money and was entirely dependent. The so-called "debt" seemed particularly exploitative. There was strict control of significant aspects of KW's daily life and particularly onerous for her in a foreign country, unable to speak the language and that she was not permitted to keep possession of her passport... Such offences have been recently described as offences against humanity.

For his role of architect of the scheme, Kam Tin Ho was sentenced to six years imprisonment and, having been sentenced to other offences by Cummins J on 29 September, 2009, a total effective sentence of 14 years. Sarissa Leech was sentenced to a total effective sentence of six years on the count of intentionally possessing a slave and intentionally using a slave. Ho Kam Ho was sentenced to a total effective sentence of ten years for his role as an active organiser of the scheme.

The Trial Judge noted that all of the subjects were mature adults, educated and aware, acting voluntarily as sex workers, and entering Australia knowingly on false documentation. Each came to Australia to help their families, who were in difficult and impoverished situations at home. Each found themselves in a situation of personal, social, and cultural isolation under work conditions that were strictly controlled. They were denied freedom and were effectively prisoners in the residences provided to them. As the trial Judge noted:

> The confluence of control over work and residents' situation constituted slavery. This was in part physical–the inability to leave–but essentially mental. You controlled the subjects by their vulnerability–you knew that they feared apprehension and deportation; by the removal of their passports–critical to their self-image as persons with an identity, in a foreign country with little language skills and no personal support; and by the ever present shadow of a minder under the veneer of a helper. In the context of the personal isolation of the subjects–no family, no friends, no language or personal help here to help them–all this achieved your intention: to disempower these subjects. A consequence was that this was modern slavery: not with physical chains but with mental chains. The modern world unfortunately is replete with the effectiveness, and at times illegibility of mental techniques of control.

E. *R v Rasalingham*

R v Rasalingham was the first labour exploitation trafficking matter prosecuted in Australia.[39] Mr. Rasalingham was an Australian citizen who owned and operated four Indian restaurants; the victim was introduced to him in India. During this meeting, Mr. Rasalingham offered the victim employment in his restaurants in Australia. The arrangement involved the victim working 365 days a year, without payment for the first year, but during this time Mr. Rasalingham would provide money to his family each time he returned to India. When the victim arrived in Australia, Mr. Rasalingham took possession of his passport, ticket, and other documents. The victim was required to work long hours at the restaurants and received no payment for his work; no payments were made to his family in India. By the time the victim was located, he had been working for the defendant for approximately one month.

Mr. Rasalingham was charged with one offence of organising or facilitating the entry or receipt of a person into Australia, being reckless as to whether that person would be exploited after entry into Australia contrary to the *Criminal Code*, and one offence of dishonestly influencing a Commonwealth public official by the submission of false documents. He was found guilty of dishonestly influencing a Commonwealth public official and received a suspended sentence of four months' imprisonment. Proceedings were also taken under workplace laws for failure to meet minimum award standards of pay and entitlement. The defendant was fined for eight breaches of the applicable award and required to pay the victim $11,500 in wages.[40]

F. *Ram v D + D Indian Fine Food Pty Ltd*[41]

The case of *Ram v D + D Indian Fine Food Pty Ltd* proceeded in the Federal Circuit Court of Australia. Mr. Ram was a 45-year-old Indian national who was functionally illiterate with poor English-speaking skills. He was approached through a mutual acquaintance to work in Australia as a cook. In India he lived in very modest circumstances, providing for his wife and two children. He accepted an offer of employment in Australia and came to work in an Indian restaurant in New South Wales. The employer company arranged for Mr. Ram's move to Australia on a temporary business visa (457 visa) as a skilled worker, namely, a cook.

Mr. Ram was exploited during the course of his employment. His possessions were retained by the employer, and he was told he could not leave Australia unless he repaid $7,000—the cost of bringing him to Australia. During a period of four months he worked seven days a week, 12 hours a day as a cook, and was paid total wages of just under $7,000. He lived in a small storeroom next to the kitchen at the restaurant. He had very few contacts in Australia, poor English and literacy skills, no direct wages from the employers, and he could not organise alternative accommodation for himself. There was no bathroom with a shower at the restaurant, and he had to bathe in the kitchen using buckets of hot water. The only alternative permanent accommodation offered to him by the employer was the use of his garage at his house; however, the conditions were worse than the storeroom. Mr. Ram was subjected to threats of physical and emotional abuse, and threats of such abuse led him to believe that if he did not do as he was told his employer would take his house and property in India and sell them, harm his family, and have him arrested when he returned to India.

Mr. Ram had also given evidence to the Australian Federal Police and the Commonwealth Director of Prosecutions. This evidence was relied upon to obtain a conviction of the employer for trafficking in persons.

Mr. Ram sought relief under the *Workplace Relations Act 1996* (Cth) and the general law in relation to underpayment of salary and failure to pay annual leave entitlements in breach of contract. The applicant was represented by Anti-Slavery Australia and pro bono solicitors. The Respondent's company cross-claimed against Mr. Ram for allegedly abandoning his employment and breaching his contract of employment, alleging a conspiracy to injure the company and characterise the Respondent's defences as one based on lies and fabrications.

The securing of the 457 visa involved a criminal enterprise, resulting in convictions of the employer under section 271.2(1)(B)of the *Criminal Code 1995* (Cth) of organising Mr. Ram's entry into Australia where he was reckless as to whether Mr. Ram would be exploited.

In January 2011, Mr. Ram was granted a Witness Protection (Trafficking) Visa, which granted him and his family permanent residence in Australia. Mr. Ram sought relief against the employer for underpayment of wages and entitlements under the relevant industrial award and the *Workplace Relation Acts,* and he also sought the imposition of penalties against the employer in respect of those contraventions. Alternatively, he claimed damages for breach of his employment with the company. Mr. Ram also claimed that the conditions in which he was required to live and work were degrading and exploitative.

Judge Driver accepted the claims of Mr. Ram entirely. He found that the respondents built a façade based upon sham documents to deceive the Department of Immigration and the Australian Taxation Office, and attempted to deceive the Court in an effort to create the illusion that there was employment arrangements in accordance with Australian law. The Federal Circuit Court found that Mr. Ram had been underpaid more than $100,000 and was entitled to superannuation, leave, and other entitlements. Both the employer and the individual director were ordered to pay the total sum of more than $125,000 in respect of the underpayment of his wages over time, leave entitlement, and superannuation with interest.

4.5 Australia's Responses to Human Trafficking

In 2008, the Vienna Forum to Fight Human Trafficking considered the drivers of human trafficking in detail. These drivers include the vulnerabilities of the exploited, the demand for labour and sexual exploitation, communities in crisis, corruption, and the failure of local and international law enforcement responses.[42]

The Vienna Forum[43] discussed and considered appropriate action and agreed that legislation alone was inadequate to address the scope of the problem. A suite of responses—ranging from the protection and empowerment of potential victims, policing and prosecution, national and regional responses, and the repatriation and reintegration of victims—were all recommended.[44] The cost, in terms of human misery and lost economic and social contribution, has not been estimated, but must measure many billions.

A number of challenges impact on the Asia Pacific region's capacity to effectively respond to trafficking and slavery, including a lack of awareness of people trafficking and related offences, differences in approach and trafficking legislation between countries, and differing capacities to address the problem.[45]

Very few Asian countries are a party to the Trafficking Protocol. The absence of legislation in many Asian countries which specifically targets people trafficking further limits the effectiveness of these countries' efforts to combat trafficking practices, individually and regionally. Even in countries where such legislation does exist, there is often insufficient law enforcement capacity to effectively enforce these laws.[46]

Australia ratified the Trafficking Protocol on 14 September 2005 and under successive governments, we have seen more than a decade of attention to policy and legislation, resourcing of research, domestic and foreign programs, and the work of committed NGOs dedicated to assisting victims.[47]

The Australian government has taken a number of steps to address slavery and human trafficking, both in Australia and as a leader in the Asia-Pacific region, in accordance with its obligations under Article 9 of the Trafficking Protocol.

In 2014, the government introduced the *National Action Plan to Combat Human Trafficking and Slavery 2015-2019*, setting strategic aims and measures to monitor its impact and efficacy. The Action Plan sets Australia's strategy to combat human trafficking and slavery, is founded on four central pillars: prevention and deterrence, detection and investigation, prosecution and compliance, and victim support and protection.

While Australia has been largely effective at establishing policies, programs and other measures to prevent a combat human trafficking and has provided support for research and information campaigns, it has failed to adequately address the fourth pillar of the Action Plan, namely, victim support and protection.

In order to address the momentous transnational problem, an integrated approach is critical. The four features of this approach might be described under four headings:

A. **Removal**—Identify and remove to safety those trafficked or trapped in exploitative conditions
B. **Justice**—Pass legislation criminalising trafficking and exploitation, bring criminals to justice, seize profits, strengthen law enforcement and public awareness, build the capacity of courts and prosecutors

    C. **Restoration**—Restore the physical, emotional and financial wellbeing of victims, compensating them for harm, empowering them to rebuild new lives and reunite with family and community

    D. **Resilience**—Build the capacity of communities to lift the socio-economic standing of women and girls, develop ethical corporate supply chain practices through co-operative action and educate consumer demand.

A. Removal

A number of government agencies and NGOs, including law enforcement agencies, working in and with victims of trafficking, are well-placed to assist with identifying and removing people from exploitative conditions, providing, of course, that they are made aware of individuals needing assistance.

The Support for Victims of People Trafficking Program, managed by the Australian Red Cross in conjunction with the Office for Women, is a most significant initiative. It provides bridging visas as well as access to accommodation, financial assistance, and access to health care and legal advice for victims of trafficking.[48] It provides additional ongoing support to those victims who are willing and able to assist in criminal investigations of trafficking cases. As at 30 June 2012, a total of 193 clients had been referred to the Support Program since its inception.[49]

In order to assist victims of trafficking and exploitation with transition it is necessary to coordinate and collaborate with welfare services to ensure victims receive comprehensive support services, including mental health care, if requested. They should be offered placement in shelters that provide care appropriate to their age, gender, and special needs and assistance to find secure, safe, long-term accommodation. It may be necessary to also conduct safety planning and extend protection to victims' relatives.

After 45 days on the Support Program, those who choose to aid the prosecution are eligible for additional support, including long-term accommodation, income and employment assistance, and skills training. Victims who are willing but unable to assist the prosecution may be eligible for extended support.

By comparison, parties to the Council of Europe's Convention on Action Against Trafficking in Human Beings must provide victims with a reflection period of at least 30 days to stabilize and carefully consider whether to participate in the prosecution of their traffickers. During this period, governments cannot make a decision to remove the victim from the country, nor can a previous removal decision be brought into effect.

One well-founded criticism of the Support Program[50] is that it links ongoing support for trafficked people to their assistance to the criminal justice process, thus "incentivising" cooperation by victims with law enforcement agencies. This approach appears to be an instinctive policy response to drive cooperation with law enforcement agencies rather than an evidence-based approach, and is contrary to the human rights approach encouraged by the Trafficking Protocol.[51] It may reflect the frustration of prosecutors when victims are threatened and refuse to testify, resulting in the collapse of prosecutions,[52] but it may in fact discourage reporting by victims.

Further, the Support Program operates in accordance with a number of arbitrary or discretionary factors, such as the requirement of the physical presence of traffickers in Australia, or an ad hoc assessment of the usefulness of the victim's support, thus involving an unscrutinised exercise of discretion of police and prosecutors. Eligibility criteria should be founded instead upon respect for the victim's human rights without the requirement of "willing and able to assist," and with permanent visas being granted on compassionate grounds, rather than the present potentially counterproductive attempt to drive criminal justice outcomes.[53]

A number of "rescue" programs operate in Asia and elsewhere seeking to physically capture and liberate victims of trafficking from conditions of exploitation and provide them with welfare supports. Some are unauthorised; some are condoned or assisted by law enforcement agencies. The long-term success of these programs is unknown and is somewhat controversial.

B. Justice

The Trafficking Protocol is primarily a criminalisation instrument,[54] and, as such, Australia's response to trafficking and exploitation has been to address the problem as an issue of criminal justice, rather than as an issue of labour, migration or human rights violations. This approach has been criticised by those arguing that sex work is, like any other form of work, a matter of choice or agency by the participants, and that human rights violations of the participants is best addressed absent moralising about prostitution, through regulation, labour rights and freedom of movement generally.[55] The competing claim is that trafficking, and especially trafficking for prostitution, is inherently exploitative, a form of gender-based violence condoned by international law,[56] and depriving participants of genuine choice.[57]

This ideological tension and the resulting disagreement about appropriate responses continues to challenge the policy debate.[58] Even the language used to describe participants (as "victims," "sex workers," "the prostituted," for example) inevitably impacts upon the policy response. In part, the tension continues because the serious focus by governments on these issues in Australia commenced with an awareness of trafficking for sexual exploitation and has thus encountered countervailing views about the role or degree of agency of the women involved. While the tension remains, the assumption of the Trafficking Protocol is that trafficking contemplates an abuse of vulnerability and absence of genuine choice, leaving State parties to interpret their own appropriate responses.[59]

In Northern Europe and in New York State, human trafficking laws seek to address the demand for prostitution driving sex trafficking by criminalising the conduct of patrons, increasing the seriousness of existing offences, and the conduct of those profiting from or promoting prostitution. These laws address the demand for sex work rather than the actions of the prostituted. In order to encourage reporting, convictions may be obtained from uncorroborated witness testimony. A range of health, migration, housing, interpreter and employment services are offered as part of a comprehensive package of human trafficking and labour exploitation laws.

At a domestic level, the Australian Government has implemented a number of programs and legislative reforms to assist victims of slavery, slavery-like conditions, and people trafficking. In 1999, the Commonwealth Government introduced offences relating to slavery, sexual servitude, and deceptive recruiting for sexual services into the Criminal Code.

In 2003, the Australian Government announced a whole-of-government package to address crimes committed against humanity—specifically human trafficking—including AFP funding to strengthen its capacity to detect, investigate, and provide specialist training in relation to slavery, trafficking, and related offences.

Australia is also a co-chair and founder of the Bali Process on People Smuggling, Trafficking in Persons and Related Transnational Crime ("Bali Process").[60] The Bali Process involves 46 member countries from the Asia-Pacific region and a number of international organisations. As part of the Bali Process, the AFP provides training to law enforcement agencies in the Asia-Pacific region to combat people trafficking and related offences. In recent times, the Bali Process has contemplated the inclusion of corporate organisations keen to assist in addressing issues of supply chain ethics and exploitation. While no formal structure has been established to support this work, the initiative is a positive step that should be encouraged.

In addition to these initiatives, the Australian Government has taken steps to strengthen Australia's legislative response to slavery and people trafficking. On 7 March 2013, the *Crimes Legislation Amendment (Slavery, Slavery-like conditions and People Trafficking) Act 2013* (Cth) came into force. This Act is designed to improve the criminal justice response to slavery, people trafficking, and related activities. The 2013 Act introduces a number of new offences relating to forced labour, organ trafficking, forced marriage,[61] and harbouring a victim of slavery or trafficking into Australian criminal law. A new, aggravated offence provision applies to offences involving a child, inhuman or degrading treatment, or a risk of death or serious harm.[62]

The new Act introduces a new definition of servitude and related offences that are designed to capture slavery-like and exploitative conduct offences.[63] These amendments recognise that a victim may be in a condition of servitude whether or not escaping from that condition is possible and whether or not an attempt at escape has been made. These provisions clarify the effect of recent case law,[64] and recognise the reality of the situation for many victims who, due to the threats, deception, and coercion in place, do not have the wherewithal to escape or to attempt to do so.

The Act also clarifies existing offences relating to exploitative behaviour and enhances the operational effectiveness of the offences. For example, a new definition of "coercion" was introduced in relation to slavery, trafficking, and related offences to reflect the fact that these offences can be committed where offenders use force, duress, detention, psychological oppression, or abuse of power, or where they take advantage of a person's vulnerability.[65] The inclusion of "coercion" in the relevant definitions acknowledges the fact that, whilst some people may initially enter a situation of their own accord, this is usually due to forms of coercive behaviour on the part of the perpetrator.[66]

As a Commonwealth enactment, the Act does not attempt to weigh into the criminalisation of prostitution by the State and Territories, preferring to leave this to each individual jurisdiction and the current state of discordant regulation. Federal jurisdiction to do so is enlivened by s 51(xxix) of the Constitution, but there appears to be no desire to intervene, no doubt reflecting the ongoing debate discussed earlier. The time will soon come, however, when a national approach must be considered in order to combat exploitation with a robust examination of the success of other international models in reducing criminality around prostitution.[67]

There are also offences under the *Migration Act* where an employer, labour hire company, employment agency or other person knowingly or recklessly allows an unlawful non-citizen or a non-citizen without work rights to work, or refers them for work.[68] Circumstances of aggravation for such offences include the prospective worker being exploited, which is currently defined as being in a condition of forced labour, sexual servitude, or slavery. The *Migration Amendment (Reform of Employer Sanctions) Act 2013* (Cth) came into force on 14 March 2013 and contains a number of amendments to the employer sanction provisions of the *Migration Act*, including amendments to the current criminal offences and the introduction of new civil penalty provisions. These provisions mean that employers who engage in exploitative behaviour involving migrant workers will face criminal or civil sanctions.

Key workplace relations and migration reforms such as the *Fair Work Act 2009* (Cth)[69] and visa changes also improve protections for vulnerable workers, including migrant workers.[70] These provisions may be used to assist workers who are subject to slavery, slavery-like conditions, or trafficking. There is also a provision in the *Fair Work Act* for orders to be made for monetary payment to be paid directly to the victim.[71] The Act requires an "employment" relationship, which may inadvertently give legitimacy to an exploitative relationship, and expose those victims working illegally to deportation or penalty.

The cooperation of victims is essential to intelligence-gathering and the investigation and prosecution of human trafficking. A major impediment to prosecuting trafficking-related offences appears, anecdotally, to be the reluctance of victims to give evidence of the offence, particularly as they (or their families) may have been the subject of violence or threats of violence and death either in Australia or their country of origin.[72] Other possible impairments are the lack of awareness of criminality of the offending conduct and availability of protection for victims, despite their participation, potentially, in migration offences.[73] Because the evidence of individual victims is critical to people trafficking prosecutions, corroborating testimony is sought in order to meet the criminal standard of proof required in criminal proceedings. This can often be challenging. However, there have been some very poignant cases where successful legal outcomes have been obtained.

Recounting exploitation and directly confronting traffickers can also be traumatising, especially when traffickers threaten retaliation or psychologically manipulate victims to distrust authorities and avoid seeking assistance. In addition to protecting victim-witnesses from their traffickers, governments should ensure victims have access to comprehensive services, including medical and mental health care, legal services, and, if desired by the victim, case management support throughout the criminal justice process. Such protections are key to minimizing the likelihood victims will be traumatized again during the investigation and prosecution of their accused traffickers.

Governments that embrace a victim-centred approach have adopted the following promising best practice guidelines in witness protection:

- Provide an opportunity for victims to consider their options and make an informed decision about participating in criminal proceedings
- Provide access to legal counsel for victims who wish to participate in the investigation and prosecution of their traffickers

- Permit a professional, such as a social worker, legal advocate, or counsellor, to accompany and support victims throughout investigations and prosecutions
- To the extent permissible by law, protect victims' identities and privacy, and allow victims to provide testimony in a manner that is less threatening, such as testimonies that are written or recorded, delivered via videoconference, or produced with audio or visual distortion
- Provide a separate waiting area for victims, for example in court, to minimize interaction with the accused traffickers or their associates
- Explain to victims how their testimony will be delivered and to what extent their identity will be revealed, if at all, to the defendant and the public
- Establish a point person to communicate in a language the victim understands and provide updates on the status of the case and information about available services
- Inform and prepare victims on what to expect before testimony and court examinations, including realistic expectations in the sentencing phase.

C. Restoration

Article 6, paragraph 6 of the Trafficking in Persons Protocol states:

> Each State Party shall ensure that its domestic legal system contains measures that offer victims of trafficking in persons the possibility of obtaining compensation for damaged suffered.

The corresponding provision of the Organised Crime Convention, found in article 25, paragraph 2, requires that at least some "appropriate procedures" are established to provide access to compensation or restitution.

The Protocol does not specify any potential source of compensation. Consequently, any or all of the following general options would probably meet the requirements of the Protocol:

- Provisions allowing victims to sue offenders or others under statutory or common law torts for civil damages
- Provisions allowing criminal courts to award criminal damages (i.e., to order that compensation be paid by offenders to victims) or to impose orders for compensation or restitution against persons convicted of offences

- Provisions establishing dedicated funds or schemes whereby victims can claim compensation from the State for injuries or damages suffered as the result of a criminal offence.

The UN Basic Principles and Guidelines on the Right to Remedy and Reparation for Victims state that:[74]

Restitution should, whenever possible, restore the **victim** to the original situation before the gross violations of international human rights law or serious violations of international humanitarian law occurred. Restitution includes, as appropriate: restoration of liberty, enjoyment of human rights, identity, family life and citizenship, return to one's place of residence, restoration of employment and return of property.

Compensation should be provided for any economically assessable damage, as appropriate and proportional to the gravity of the violation and circumstances of each case, resulting from gross violations of international human rights law and serious violations of international humanitarian law, such as:

(a) Physical or mental harm;

(b) Lost opportunities, including employment, education and social benefits;

(c) Material damages and loss of earnings, including loss of earning potential;

(d) Moral damage;

(e) Costs required for legal or expert assistance, medicine and medical services, and psychological and social services.

The International Convention on the Protection of Rights of All Migrant Workers and Members of Their Families[75] stresses the right of migrant workers to receive compensation even in the case of their expulsion. Expulsion shall not prejudice any rights of a migrant worker acquired in accordance with the law of the State of employment, including the right to receive wages and other entitlements due to her or him. Before or after departure, the person concerned shall have a reasonable opportunity to settle any claims for wages and other entitlements due to him or her and any pending liabilities. Measures to eliminate the employment of undocumented migrant workers shall not impair such workers' rights with respect to the ability to bring civil claims against their employers.

Receiving compensation is important for victims of trafficking not only because of the financial component, but also because it has symbolic meaning. Awarding compensation acknowledges that trafficking is a crime: The victim's pain and suffering are acknowledged and they are assisted in taking a step towards overcoming trauma inflicted and abuses suffered. At a practical level, compensation can assist victims rebuilding their lives and empower them; at a retributive level, compensation paid by traffickers can constitute a form of punishment and deter other traffickers.

In accordance with principles 8 to 13 of the UN Declaration of Basic Principles of Justice for Victims of Crime and Abuse of Power, compensation should include the return of property or payment for harm or loss suffered, reimbursement of expenses incurred as a result of victimisation, provision of services and restoration of rights. States should encourage the establishment, strengthening, and expansion of national funds for compensation to victims of crime.

Offenders or third parties responsible for their behaviour should, where appropriate, make fair restitution to victims, their families, or dependants. Such restitution should include the return of property or payment for the harm or loss suffered, reimbursement of expenses incurred as a result of victimisation, the provision of services, and the restoration of rights.

When compensation is not fully available from the offender or other sources, States should endeavour to provide financial compensation to:

(a) Victims who have sustained significant bodily injury or impairment of physical or mental health as a result of serious crimes
(b) The family, in particular dependants, of persons who have died or become physically or mentally incapacitated as a result of such victimisation.

The domestic legislative framework establishing mechanisms to make compensation claims is an important starting point for providing trafficked persons with access to compensation for harm suffered and wages lost.

1. State compensation schemes

While compensation is generally regarded as payment or reparation for injury or harm, restitution, on the other hand, is a form of payment or action taken to restore the victim to the position he or she would have been in but for the victimisation.

Compensation can also be paid by or through the State. Some countries such as Australia have established state-administered schemes for victims of violent crime. State-funded or state-subsidized compensation schemes have the great advantage of providing a guaranteed payment of compensation to the victim without requiring a specific perpetrator to be located or identified. A police report, together with a willingness on the part of the victim to assist the police with the investigation, is usually sufficient. State schemes may also be relatively streamlined and quicker than civil proceedings, and they develop administrative expertie and awareness of trafficking.

In order to qualify for payment, victims in many cases have to show they have reported the matter to the police and have been willing to cooperate with investigations. Investigations must have also disclosed a case of trafficking in persons. In some jurisdictions, state-funded compensation is only available if a person has been legally declared to be a victim within the meaning of the existing law.

Within Australia, State and Territory victim of crime compensation schemes provide some assistance and redress to trafficked persons, but are not ideal due to a lack of uniformity. Different thresholds for different awards under the various State and Territory schemes suggest that a uniform federal scheme for victims of federal crimes is needed,[76] tailored to meet the particular vulnerabilities of this group of victims. Applications are often characterised, for example, by a delay or failure to report to police due to fear of retribution by traffickers or fear of adverse outcomes in interactions with police and immigration authorities.

A national scheme could be administered by arrangement with existing State and Territory tribunals or through federal courts such as the Federal Circuit Court with the advantages of uniformity of approach. This could obviate the need for victims to establish a prerequisite act of violence—sometimes difficult to prove in exploitation cases—and with the benefit of special procedures to avoid the risk of re-traumatisation through confrontation with the offender.[77]

In one recent claim involving the rape of a trafficking victim, a Victorian Magistrate decided to invite the offender to attend the hearing of the application, over the AFP's and the victim's objections. The victim was required to make an election to withdraw her claim or face the probability of having to confront her abuser in court, despite the fact that her claim of trafficking had been accepted as well-founded by the AFP and Victoria Police.[78]

Any cumbersome procedure that frustrates and discourages victims from making claims will defeat the purpose of compensation. In Australia, for example, a successful claim for compensation is wrongly considered to impact upon payments due under the Support for Victims of Trafficking Program. These factors act as a disincentive, and are likely to result in victims having little confidence in the justice system.

2. Confiscation and reparation orders
Some countries connect civil actions for compensation with criminal proceedings against the perpetrator. This means that a single trial both punishes the perpetrator and compensates the victim, thus reducing the stress on victims.

This is also achieved in countries where payment of compensation is part of the sentence imposed by the perpetrator.

Where civil proceedings are appended to a criminal case, there is the dual advantage of having two procedures rolled into one, and the prosecutor is responsible for gathering and presenting evidence on the liability of the perpetrator to pay compensation.

In some countries, a court order for compensation to be paid by the perpetrator can be made at the sentencing. Criminal compensation calculations may be made on the same basis as in national civil law or on a completely different basis. These types of claims require a victim to have been identified by the authorities and for a perpetrator to have been prosecuted and found guilty in criminal proceedings. Prosecuting trafficking offences is difficult, however, if the offender is unknown or has fled the jurisdiction, or there is insufficient evidence of the involuntary nature of the work performed by the victim, or the victim is unwilling or unable to cooperate with law enforcement.

Where assets can be traced, frozen or seized, states may be empowered to confiscate them. If those assets can be used for compensation, the procedures in a civil case and in a criminal case differ. In a civil case, the confiscation is usually limited to the value of the damages awarded, but in a criminal case, all assets arising from the crime or general criminal activity may be confiscated, depending on the regulations in that jurisdiction.

There must be an explicit legal linkage of the confiscated assets to the payment of compensation orders. Where this does not exist, it can inhibit or delay the compensation payment. Alternatively, all or some of the confiscated assets could be used to establish or contribute to a fund to make compensation payments to victims of crime, including trafficking in persons.

Reparation orders following criminal trials are also available under the legislation but rarely used. A defendant must have been identified by the prosecuting authorities, been found guilty at a criminal trial, and have sufficient available assets before compensation can be considered through the offender.

Outside Australia, in some jurisdictions, a victim can file a claim for civil damages to be heard at the same time as the criminal case. This has the advantage of combining two potentially lengthy procedures into one, to be managed by one person—the prosecutor.

In other jurisdictions, there may be a specific procedure that allows compensation to be paid as part of a sentence. Calculating what may be appropriate in the circumstances may be based on the civil court procedure of assessment, or it may be a completely separate procedure.

3. Torts

In many countries, victims can pursue a civil claim for compensation on the basis of a wrongdoing that has caused them loss in tort law (or delict) or under contractual rights. Victims of trafficking may have rights in labour law, regardless of the existence of any form of employment contract.

Although civil law proceedings may seem more accessible to a trafficking victim than criminal proceedings since the police are not involved, they still require a perpetrator to have been identified and, if the victim is to receive compensation, the perpetrator must be within the jurisdiction and solvent. Damages will be calculated on the basis of national civil law.

Some jurisdictions may use payment of compensation by the defendant to the victim as a mitigating factor for reducing the sentence that may be imposed. There may be a formal opportunity to "plea bargain" where compensation is an element under discussion.

Aggravated, exemplary, or punitive damages may be available to trafficking victims in some jurisdictions. They usually serve to punish a wrongdoer for particularly outrageous conduct, therefore having a deterrent element, and can be related to the wealth of the wrongdoer. These concepts will be novel to other jurisdictions, but there is nothing to prevent states from introducing such concepts where the types of action for which compensation is being claimed warrant a particularly punitive response as a matter of public policy.

4. Labour laws

A victim may have rights under domestic labour law even if they have no employment contract. Rights and contractual breaches can be enforced against a wrongdoer (e.g., trafficker or exploitative employer) in labour courts or tribunals, and compensation can be claimed.

Claims may be based on unpaid wages and entitlements, leave not taken, work-related injuries, and under discrimination law. The standard of proof in these actions will generally be lower than in a criminal case.

As with civil court claims, a wrongdoer must be identifiable, locatable and solvent. Potential advantages of using labour courts include the fact that regulators may initiate proceedings, and employers may be insured for claims against them that may improve the chances of success of a compensation claim.

With regard to calculating the lost wages that may be part of a claim for compensation in labour law, several different possibilities exist. For example, the claimed amount could be based on the local prevailing wage, a legislated minimum wage, or on the basis of the promised contractual wage.

5. The current framework in Australia

The Australian government has not acted to ensure adequate effective compensation for victims, as required by the Trafficking Protocol.[79] While civil remedies and criminal reparations are, in theory, possible, and would meet the highly desirable goal of requiring those responsible for and profiting from the offending to pay, there is no effective mechanism to ensure that victims are compensated in practice.

Currently in Australia, statutory victim's compensation schemes are provided by each of the eight States and Territories, and trafficked people may, in limited circumstances, have access to these schemes. However, these schemes are not designed to accommodate victims of federal offences against the person, are technically complicated, and vary considerably in their application.

For example, State and Territory schemes differ in respect of categories of harm covered by the scheme, time limits, and levels of award. Under the existing schemes, the amount of compensation available to trafficked people in Australia varies,[80] depending on the State or Territory in which the offence takes place and the type of offences. Conceivably, a trafficking victim facing violent abuse and coercion could be awarded $10,000 in NSW or $75,000 in Queensland or Western Australia for the same abuse.

Trafficked people who have been moved between States and Territories can only apply for compensation relating to the harm that they suffered whilst in a specific State or Territory, which may result in a victim having to make multiple applications.[81]

State or Territory schemes also fail to expressly recognise the offences of forced labour, forced marriage and debt bondage,[82] leaving victims of these crimes without access to government compensation.

These inconsistencies between the State and Territory compensation frameworks, and the lack of coordinated federal approach to compensation, is an impediment to trafficked people obtaining fair, effective and timely access to justice, and departs from international best practice.

An over-arching federal victims compensation scheme is needed to fairly and equitably compensate victims of federal offences. There is constitutional power to create a national compensation scheme. In *R v Wei Tang*, the High Court considered that the criminalisation of "slavery" in the Criminal Code was supported by the external affairs power of the Constitution to give effect to Australia's obligations under the Slavery Convention. The Commonwealth, therefore, has at least one clear head of power to enact a national compensation scheme.

Access to compensation is closely linked to other issues, including access to information. Trafficked persons are often prevented from gaining access to compensation because they do not know about their right to receive compensation and the necessary steps to take. Therefore, information provided by law enforcement officers, private lawyers, or NGOs is an important prerequisite for such access.

Under section 21B of the *Crimes Act 1914* (Cth), there exists a mechanism for the court to issue reparation orders requiring a convicted offender to make direct reparations, by way of monetary payment or otherwise, to the victim of the offence.[83] The difficulty with this mechanism is that it requires a successful prosecution of a trafficking offence, leading to a conviction. In the area of human trafficking, there have been a low number of cases that have proceeded to prosecution and resulted in a criminal conviction. The author is not aware of any case in which section 21B has been used in relation to human trafficking.[84] This demonstrates that reparation orders are an unlikely remedy for trafficked people under the current framework. Furthermore, there is no guarantee that any orders will be made: Reparation orders are discretionary and dependant on the financial capacity of the offender to make reparations.[85]

There have been no successful torts claims litigated in Australia on behalf of victims of trafficking. A potential claim by Ms Ning (see case study above) was confounded initially by a lack of information about the identity of the Australian brothel owners, and ultimately by her death.

Civil claims may have no utility because of an inability of victims to access proceeds of crime. Traffickers often hide their money or move it abroad, which prevents trafficked persons from enforcing their compensation claims. In order to overcome this obstacle, states should confiscate any property and money resulting from trafficking and use it to compensate victims. States should also strengthen international law enforcement cooperation to secure access to the traffickers' assets moved abroad.

A claim can potentially be made up of several bases on which compensation is requested, including but not limited to:

- Pain and suffering due to physical or psychological violence
- Medical expenses
- Unpaid and underpaid wages
- Reimbursement of illegal "fees" paid to a recruitment or employment agency, or for smuggling or transportation
- "Fines" imposed by traffickers for bad behaviour
- Excessive, fraudulent or illegal "deductions" from wages for rent, subsistence, transport, tax or social security "payments."

Enforcement is far easier where assets have been traced, seized, or frozen and confiscated in the course of civil or criminal proceedings.

4.6 Resilience

In order to address the scale of the problem globally, international efforts to address poverty and the socio-economic standing of women and girls are critical.

The Australian government facilitates several programs relating to trafficking in persons in the Asia Pacific region. One of these is the Asia Regional Trafficking in Persons (ARTIP) Project, which supports the criminal justice systems of participating governments in the region by strengthening national law enforcement and judicial and prosecutorial functions,[86] bilateral and regional cooperation, and regional and national legal, policy, and research capacity. Project Childhood is another program, established in 2010 to prevent and respond to child sex tourism in the Mekong subregion.[87] Other programs include funding of the Tripartite Action to Protect Migrants in the Greater Mekong Sub-Region from Labour Exploitation project to promote safe labour migration and prevent labour exploitation, and partnering with USAID to support the End Exploitation and Trafficking campaign to raise awareness of human trafficking in South East Asian countries.[88] With the recent deep cuts to Australia's foreign aid program, these programs and those supporting the education, training, and economic empowerment of women in the region in general are continually at risk of missing out on support and ongoing funding.[89]

The Attorney-General's Department and the Department of Immigration work together with other Australian agencies to facilitate capacity-building activities and provide a number of countries with technical assistance to support their efforts to address irregular migration, with a strong focus on trafficking.[90] Bilateral agreements made directly with source countries regarding the identification and repatriation of victims and perpetrators are also instrumental in providing a strong framework to deal with both victims of trafficking (for return and repatriation) and perpetrators (for prosecution and extradition) across borders.[91]

On 8 March 2013, the Australian Government also announced a new whole-of-government strategy to reinforce ethical behaviour in procurement, so that no firm providing goods or services to the Australian Government is tainted by slavery or people-trafficking anywhere in the supply chain.[92] This work and the National Action Plan to Combat Human Trafficking and Slavery are significant developments. The critical role of the supply chain has been recognised, for example, by the creation of the Global Freedom Network, an organisation led by religious leaders, which aims to abolish slavery.[93]

Federally, governments on both sides of politics in Australia have taken significant steps in the past to address these important human rights issues both domestically and in the Asia-Pacific region, especially over the last decade. Those programs that aim to reduce entrenched poverty and improve the education and social standing of women and children abroad are critical, and support for these programs must continue if we are to have any hope of making inroads into this pandemic of human misery.

As consumers of cheap goods and services, we contribute to the perpetuation of exploitation and should be mindful of the impact of our decisions as consumers.

Australia's response in the last decade or so has been to improve law enforcement and immigration responses to victims, and provide funding for research and front-line programs. The policy response to date has been relatively encouraging, but is not yet centrally focused on the needs of victims, and recent gains will be squandered if deep cuts to foreign aid eventuate.

In time, Australia will need to review the success of its programs and grapple with the unresolved tensions and competing narratives about the causes of exploitative practices and the best way to respond to them. The momentum is moving towards hybrid approaches that maintain the criminality of trafficking and slavery-like conduct but also criminalise the purchasing of services that exploit others, especially sex. These moves have been boosted by recent developments overseas to implement the "Nordic" model.[94] However these competing views are to be resolved, the protection of human rights of victims of trafficking and slavery-like offences must remain at the forefront of our response.

4.7 The Private Sector: An Opportunity to Lead

Beyond the efforts of governments, companies can also take action to reduce the likelihood of trafficking in their supply chains and respect the rights of those who work to make their businesses successful.

There are many measures that businesses can take to mitigate the risks of human trafficking throughout their operations. For example, business leaders can create anti-trafficking policies that address the common risks in their operations and supply chains, ensure workers have the right to fair compensation and redress, train staff to understand the indicators of human trafficking, and adopt pre-emptive remediation plans to allow for appropriate corrective action. Businesses should also work with government officials, NGOs, and recruiters in source countries to gain a better understanding of workers' vulnerabilities and commit to making improvements.

The Australian Attorney-General's Supply Chains Working Group has identified a number of high-risk goods and services based on import data, complaints by visa holders, and international data.

A company can demonstrate its commitment to responsibly source goods and services by creating a clear and comprehensive anti-trafficking policy, which includes an enforcement mechanism that is applied throughout the company's supply chain. High-level executives should approve and promote such a policy and build it into company operations, so supplier consideration goes beyond price and reliability, to include an assessment of labour practices.

Among other things, an effective policy prohibits human trafficking and those activities that facilitate it—including recruitment fees charged to workers, contract fraud, and document retention. Effective policy also responds to industry- or region-specific risks; requires freedom of movement for workers; pays all employees at least the minimum wage in all countries of operation (preferably a living wage); includes a grievance mechanism and whistle-blower protections; and applies to direct employees, as well as subcontractors, labour recruiters, and other business partners.

4.8 Conclusions

In Australia, we see examples of trafficking, slavery-like exploitation, forced marriages, forced labour, and debt bondage. The driving forces behind this phenomenon are the significant economic gains that are to be derived though trafficking and exploiting the poor, coupled with a cruel indifference to human suffering.

This is a multi-dimensional problem driven by complex social and economic factors—flourishing in conditions of conflict, poverty, and poor governance; driven by the constant ingenuity of exploiters; and often involving the desire of the victims and their families to escape desperate circumstances.

The problem is exacerbated by highly sophisticated criminal networks, unethical commercial enterprise, environmental degradation, and the social denigration of women and girls in developing countries.

The legal framework in Australia is robust, and our contribution to regional initiatives is important, but our enforcement mechanisms are not working effectively. On average, around 25 allegations of trafficking in persons are reported to Australian authorities each year, although very few of those will lead to prosecutions.

Recounting exploitation and directly confronting traffickers can be traumatizing, especially when traffickers threaten retaliation or psychologically manipulate victims to distrust authorities and avoid seeking assistance.

Australia has been very effective domestically and internationally in leading the ongoing criminal justice response to human trafficking and exploitation. Despite the low numbers of prosecutions, prosecutors and investigating police would appear to be aware of the legislation and to be actively seeking an opportunity to bring test cases.

There is, however, a persistent lack of communication about individual cases between non-government organisations and authorities. Non-government organisations are aware of thousands of potential cases; however, the risk of negative immigration outcomes for potential witnesses continues to outweigh the support available to those who might potentially give evidence to federal authorities. The failure to provide certainty by way of an immigration amnesty is almost certainly preventing those subject to exploitation and abuse from complaining, and is a severe impediment to the effective implementation of the criminal justice response.

There is a clear need to conduct and prosecute a test case under the forced labour provisions of the Australian Criminal Code. Anecdotal evidence suggests there are potentially tens of thousands of cases of exploited workers within Australia. A fear of immigration outcomes is preventing these workers from reporting physical and emotional abuse and coercion by employers, effectively locking survivors in their situation—particularly in the agricultural industries.

On the international stage, Australia has led the Bali Process very successfully. There is a clear need to expand the Bali Process to include a specific focus on the human rights of victims and a survivor-centred approach to redress and compensation. The early stages of the Bali Process Human Rights Forum, involving business leaders, are at this stage promising, but they need to expand to include and take account of the views of civil society, particularly those working closely with survivors.

The Australian government is lagging in terms of the protection of victims of trafficking and exploitation. Despite the fourth pillar of the Australian National Action Plan committing government to protect the rights of victims and provide appropriate redress, the political will to design and implement a national compensation scheme is lacking. This amounts to a significant failure to protect victims of trafficking and exploitation. The harsh reality is that there is no recourse for victims of trafficking beyond pro bono lawyers and not-for-profit agencies working to secure victims of crime compensation under State and Territory schemes. Even those practices have now been inhibited by a concern that accessing victims of crime compensation will disentitle claimants to support payments under the Trafficking in Persons scheme, as has been the experience in recent times.

On a recent mission to Australia, the Human Rights Council's Special Rapporteur, Joy Ngozi Ezeilo, noted the lack of a comprehensive national framework for victims' compensation in Australia. She recommended that the Government establish a Commonwealth compensation scheme for victims of people trafficking.

This is something the author has raised with successive Attorneys General over the last decade. The Trafficking in Persons Protocol, to which we are a party, compels it. We have recognised that victims of terrorism require a national compensation framework, yet there is no such harmonised program for human trafficking.

Existing State and Territory schemes are not designed to accommodate victims of federal offences against the person. They are also technically complicated, and they vary considerably in their application.

The current system can lead to unjust results. As mentioned above, a Magistrate recently decided to invite the offender to attend the hearing of the application. The victim was required to make an election to withdraw her claim or face the probability of having to confront her abuser in court, despite the fact that her claim of trafficking had been accepted as well-founded by the AFP and Victoria police.

Victims' entitlements to financial support are also negatively impacted by the current system: A successful claim for compensation is wrongly considered to impact upon payments due under the Centrelink-administered Support for Victims of Trafficking Program.

These factors act as a disincentive and are likely to result in victims having little confidence in the justice system. It is high time that a harmonised national scheme be put into place by the Australian government to assist in expanding the scope of remedies available to human trafficking victims.

Endnotes

1. *Ram v D + D Indian Fine Food Pty Ltd* [2015] FCCA 389 (27 March 2015).

2. See OSCE Office for Democratic Institutions and Human Rights "Conference Report" (Paper presented at Ensuring Human Rights Protection in Countries of Destination: Breaking the Cycle of Trafficking, Helsinki, 23-24 September 2004).

3. "Protocol to Prevent, Suppress and Punish Trafficking in Persons, especially Women and Children, Supplementing the UN Convention against Transnational Organized Crime," opened for signature 15 November 2000, 2237 UNTS 319 (entered into force 25 December 2003).

4. See UN Office on Drugs and Crime, "United Nations Convention against Transnational Organized Crime and the Protocols Thereto" (2014).

5   Art 2.

6. See UN Office on Drugs and Crime, "Human Trafficking," (2014) (http://www.unodc.org/unodc/en/human-trafficking/what-is-human-trafficking.html).

7. Joudo Larsen J., "Migration and People Trafficking in South East Asia" (Research Paper No 401, Australian Institute of Criminology, November 2010) 3.

8. See World Vision Australia, "Policy Brief — Human Trafficking in Asia" (November 2007).

9. *Id.*, although the estimates of overall numbers of children in forced labour has dropped. See, "Making Progress against child labour, global estimates and trends 2000-2012," ILO 2012 (available at http://www.ilo.org/ipec/Informationresources/WCMS_221513/lang--en/index.htm).

10. U.S. State Department Trafficking in Persons Report (2015).

11. See, e.g., Joint UN Commentary on the EU Directive — A Human Rights-Based Approach, Prevent, Combat, Protect: Human Trafficking, 2011, 16.

12. OSCE 'Conference Report', above note 2.

13. *Id.*

14. www.globalslaveryindex.org. Fourteen million of these are in India, followed by China (3 million) and Pakistan (2 million). These countries and Nigeria, Ethiopia, Russia, Thailand, Democratic Republic of Congo, Burma and Bangladesh together make up 76% of the total number. It is estimated 4% of the total population of Mauritania and Uzbekistan are in conditions of slavery. Current estimates of 3,000-3,300 are given for Australia.

15. See UN Global Initiative to Fight Human Trafficking, "Human Trafficking: The Facts" (Fact Sheet, UN Global Compact, 2008).

16. Commonwealth Attorney-General's Department, "Discussion Paper: The Criminal Justice Response to Slavery and People Trafficking; Reparation; and Vulnerable Witness Protections," 2010.

17. International Convention to Suppress the Slavery Trade and Slavery 1926, opened for signature 25 September 1926, 60 UNTS 254 (entered into force 9 March 1927) art 1.

18. International Covenant on Civil and Political Rights, opened for signature 16 December 1966, 999 UNTS 171 (entered into force generally 23 March 1976 and for Australia 13 November 1980) arts 8(1)–8(3).

19. International Covenant on Economic, Social and Cultural Rights, opened for signature 16 December 1966, 993 UNTS 3 (entered into force generally 3 January 1976 and for Australia 10 March 1976) arts 6(1) and 7.

20. See International Labour Office, "ILO Action Against Trafficking in Human Beings" (Discussion Paper, International Labour Office).

21. United Nations Recommended Principles and Guidelines on Human Rights and Human Trafficking, E/2002/68/Add.1 (2002), Office of the High Commissioner for Human Rights.

22. UNODC, Model Law against Trafficking in Persons (United Nations, 2009), 32-34.

23. Anti-People Trafficking Interdepartmental Committee, "Interdepartmental Committee on Human Trafficking and Slavery" (Annual Report, Attorney General's Department, January 2004 – June 2012) 20; TC Beirne School of Law Human Trafficking Working Group, "Statistics and Other Data" (1 January 2013) The University of Queensland (http://www.law.uq.edu.au/human-trafficking-statistics).

24. Anti-People Trafficking Interdepartmental Committee, "Interdepartmental Committee on Human Trafficking and Slavery" (Annual Report, Attorney General's Department, January 2004 – June 2012) 20.

25. See Commonwealth, "Joint Standing Committee on Foreign Affairs, Defence and Trade: Slavery, Slavery-like conditions and People Trafficking," (2012), 6.

26. UN Office of Drugs and Crime, Human Trafficking Case Law Database (as of 4 November 2015).

27. See *R v Wei Tang* [2008] HCA 39; (2008) 237 CLR 1.

28. Open message of thanks to the Justices of the High Court of Australia, 14 November 2008, reproduced at http://projectrespect.org.au/system/files/PR-Womens-statement-2008_0.pdf.

29. *Id.* at [28]. See also, for example, *R v McIvor & Tanuchit* [2010] NSWDC 310 and *R v Sieders & Yotchomchin* [2006] NSWDC 184; (2008) 72 NSWLR 417. In the first, the defendants were convicted of offences of intentionally possessing a slave and five offences of using a slave in relation to the debt bondage and prostitution of five Thai women. In the second, the offences were of exploiting women in conditions of sexual servitude.

30. Chris Payne with the assistance of documentary film makers Luigi Acquisto and Stella Zammataro.

31. The author represented Ning. Her claim was supported by the work of Luigi Acquisto and Stella Zammataro (film makers), former AFP officer Chris Payne and local interpreter Sumalee Milne. Her claim and outcomes are featured in the films *Trafficked*, and *Trafficked, the Reckoning* by Abracadabra films and Film Australia Ltd.

32. [2009] 2 Qd R 51; (2009) 192 A Crim R 345. See also Human Trafficking Working Group, *Case Report (Criminal)*, (2011), The University of Queensland   (http://www.law.uq.edu.au/documents/humantraffic/case-reports/kovacs.pdf).

33. [2008] QCA 407 [46].

34. [2008] QCA 407, [44].

35. [2008] QCA 407, [46].

36. See also *R v Trivedi* (2011) NSWDC unreported, involving labour trafficking outside the sex industry. The victim was coerced into exploitative working conditions by a restaurant owner who sponsored him to travel to Australia on a temporary work visa (457 Visa).

37. See Schloenhardt A. and Jolly J., *Honeymoon from hell: human trafficking and domestic servitude in Australia,* 2010 Sydney LR 32 671.

38. "Brisbane Mother jailed for Child Trafficking of Daughter, Nine" 16 April, 2013; Elks, S., "The Australian; Focus on child marriage in Australia," 11 February 2014, Koc, E. SBS.

39. (Unreported, NSWDC, 2007).

40. [2008] FMCA 208.

41. *Ram v D + D Indian Fine Food Pty Ltd* [2015] FCCA 389 (27 March 2015).

42. Report of the Vienna Forum: *A way forward to combat Human Trafficking* 13 to 15 February, 2008 available at http://www.un.org/ga/president/62/ThematicDebates/humantrafficking/ebook.pdf. The failure of states to treat traf-

ficking and exploitation as human rights violations, rather than an immigration problem driven by the demand for unskilled labour, was raised by the OHCHR delegate at the time: p 43.

43. See above, note 19.

44. *Id.*

45. David P., David F., & Gallagher A., *ASEAN Handbook on International Legal Cooperation in Trafficking in Persons Cases* (Handbook, Association of Southeast Asian Nations, August 2010) iii.

46. World Vision Australia, above note 8.

47. Anti-People Trafficking Interdepartmental Committee, "Interdepartmental Committee on Human Trafficking and Slavery" (Annual Report, Attorney General's Department, January 2004 – June 2012) 20. Also informed by personal communications, National Roundtable on Human Trafficking and Slavery discussion with participants; See also Simmons F., O'Brien B., David F. and Beacroft L., "Human trafficking and slavery offenders in Australia," Australian Institute of Criminology, November 2013.

48. *See* Anti-Slavery Australia, "Fact Sheet #15: Where Can Trafficked and Exploited People Get Help" (2014) Anti-Slavery Australia (http://www.antislavery.org.au/resources/fact-sheets/209-fact-sheet-15-where-can-trafficked-and-exploited-people-get-help.html); Report of Special Rapporteur p14.

49. Anti-People Trafficking Interdepartmental Committee, above note 23.

50. The author, Anti-Slavery Australia and others have consistently argued for the delinking of a requirement of co-operation by the victim with the criminal justice system for admission to the Support Program.

51. Articles 2, see also arts 6(3) and 7.

52. As in the 2004 case of JEON and OH, 50 victims were deported following joint AFP and DIMIA raids on three brothels. Charges were dropped after victims' families received death threats and they refused to testify: AFP personal communications.

53. For example, Anti-Slavery Australia paper Senior Officials Meeting 22 November, 2013; personal communications at National Roundtables and Law

Council of Australia submissions available at http://www.lawcouncil.asn. au/lawcouncil/index.php/10-divisions/141-people-trafficking.

54. Embedded within the UN Convention against Transnational Organized Crime rather than the Slavery Convention.

55. See for example David F., "Trafficking of Women for Sexual Purposes" (Australian Institute of Criminology: Research and Public Policy Series, 2008), 5; Cullen M. and McSherry B., cited in Schloenhardt A. and Jolly J., *Trafficking in Persons in Australia: Myths and Realities* (LexisNexis Butterworths Australia, 2013), 45; Jeffreys E. "Anti-trafficking Measures and Migrant Sex Workers in Australia Intersections: Gender and Sexuality in Asia and the Pacific" Issue 19, February 2009; Hathaway J., *The Human Rights Quagmire of "Human Trafficking"*, 49 Virginia Journal of International Law 1 (2008), 35; Sanghera J., "Unpacking the Trafficking Discourse" in Kempadoo K. (ed.), *Trafficking and Prostitution Reconsidered: New perspectives on Migration, Sex Work and Human Rights* (2005, Paradigm Publishers), 4.

56. Convention of All Forms of Discrimination Against Women, article 6; General Recommendation 19. United Nations Convention on the Elimination of All Forms of Discrimination Against Women, General Recommendation 19.

57. Gallagher A., *Human Rights and Human Trafficking: Quagmire or Firm Ground? A Response to James Hathaway,* 49 Virginia Journal of International Law 789 (2009), 792; Farley M., *Prostitution, Trafficking, and Cultural Amnesia: What We Must Not Know in Order To Keep the Business of Sexual Exploitation Running Smoothly* (2006), 18 Yale Journal of Law & Feminism, 109; Farley M., Cotton A., Lynne J., Zumbeck S., Spiwak F., Reyes M., Alvarez, D. & Sezgin U., 2003, *Prostitution & Trafficking in Nine Countries: An Update on Violence and Posttraumatic Stress Disorder,* Journal of Trauma Practice 33, 37; Cho S., Dreher A., Neumayer E., "Does Legalised Prostitution Increase Human Trafficking? Courant Research Centre: Poverty, Equity and Growth in Developing and Transition Countries, Statistical Methods of Empirical Analysis" (Georg-August-Universitat Gottingen, Discussion Paper No. 96, 2011 updated January 2012), 1.

58. Parliament of Victoria, Drugs and Crime Prevention Committee "Inquiry into People Trafficking for Sex Work: Final Report" (Parliament of Victoria, Government Printer for State of Victoria, 2010), 28.

59. United Nations (2000), "Interpretative notes for the official records (travaux préparatoires) of the negotiation of the United Nations Convention against Transnational Organized Crime," 347.

60. See The Bali Process, "About the Bali Process" (2014), The Bali Process on People Smuggling, Trafficking in Persons and Related Transnational Crimes (http://www.baliprocess.net/).

61. *Crimes Legislation Amendment (Slavery, Slavery-like conditions and People Trafficking) Act 2013* (Cth) s 270.6A, 270.7B.

62. Convention on the Rights of the Child, opened for signature 20 November 1989, 1577 UNTS 3 (entered into force 2 September 1990), art 4 (http://www.2.ohchr.org/english/law/crc.htm).

63. *Crimes Legislation Amendment (Slavery, Slavery-like conditions and People Trafficking) Act 2013* (Cth) s 270.5.

64. See *R v Wei Tang* [2008] HCA 39; see also *R v. Kovacs* [2008] QCA 407.

65. *Crimes Legislation Amendment (Slavery, Slavery-like conditions and People Trafficking) Act 2013* (Cth) s 270.1A.

66. International Labour Organisation Director General, "A Global Alliance Against Forced Labour: Global Report under the Follow-up to the ILO Declaration on Fundamental Principles and Rights at Work 2005" (Paper presented at International Labour Conference, Geneva, May–June 2005), 5-6 <http://www.ilo.org/public/english/standards/relm/ilc/ilc93/pdf/rep-i-b.pdf>.

67. For example, recent consideration by Canada and the European parliament of the merits of the "Nordic" model, implemented in Sweden, Norway and Iceland, which criminalises the purchase of sex rather than the conduct of the seller: Taylor D., "If Europe votes for the 'Swedish model' on prostitution, women will be at risk," Taylor D., 24 February 2014; and Smith J., "The Tipping Point: Tackling the Demand for Prostituted/Trafficked Women and Youth," 13 February 2014.

68. *Migration Act 1958* (Cth), ss 245AA–245AK.

69. The *Fair Work Act 2009* (Cth) contains 10 National Employment standards that apply to all Federal employees. These standards guarantee the rights of all employees to certain employment conditions including leave, public holidays, termination notice and maximum weekly hours of work. In addition, the general protections scheme in Parts 3-1 of the Act enhances the range of options available to exploited workers and job applicants.

70. The *Migration Legislation Amendment (Worker Protection) Act 2008* introduced a greater level of protection for migrant workers who hold subclass 457 visas.

71. *Fair Work Act 2009* (Cth) s 546(3) with penalties up to $33,000 for each individual contravention of the Act.

72. Personal communications with victims of trafficking.

73. *Id.*

74. UN Basic Principles and Guidelines on the Right to a Remedy and Reparation for Victims of Gross Violations of International Human Rights Law and Serious Violations of International Humanitarian Law (General Assembly resolution 60/147 annex).

75. International Convention of the Protection of All Migrant Workers and Members of their Families, Arts 22 and 68 (General Assembly resolution 45/158 annex) (Art. 22, paras. 6 and 9; art. 68, para 2).

76. See, e.g., McLeod F., "Compensation for Trafficked and Enslaved Persons" (Speech delivered at the Anti-Slavery Project Seminar on Remedies for Trafficked and Enslaved People, Sydney, 8 October 2011); Law Council of Australia various submissions available at http://www.lawcouncil.asn.au/lawcouncil/index.php/10-divisions/141-people-trafficking. "Report of Special Rapporteur on trafficking in persons, especially women and children Mission to Australia," 18 May 2012, A/HRC/20/18/Add.1 (Report of Special Rapporteur) available at http://www.ohchr.org/Documents/HRBodies/HRCouncil/RegularSession/Session20/A.HRC.20.18.Add.1_En.PDF p21.

77. Report of Special Rapporteur.

78. *Application of RG*: Victims of Crime Assistance Tribunal 2010/1373 decision 22 August, 2012; Contrary to *Frost v VOCAT* (2002) VCAT 1390 per Bowman J.

79. Article 6(6).

80. *Victims of Crime Assistance Act 2009* (QLD) s38(1); *Criminal Injuries Compensation Act* (WA) s31(1).

81. Frances Simmons, *Making Possibilities Realities: Compensation for Trafficked People* [2012], 34 Sydney Law Review 511, 529.

82. *Id.*, 533.

83. *Crimes Act 1914* (Cth).

84. Law Council of Australia, [108].

85. Law Council of Australia, [107]-[109].

86. See generally, ASIA Regional Trafficking in Persons Project, "Securing Justice for Victims and Ending Impunity for Traffickers" (2014) ASIA Regional Trafficking in Persons Project (http://www.artipproject.org/).

87. Australian Government, "East ASIA Regional Project Childhood" (1 November 2013), Australian Government Department of Foreign Affairs and Trade (http://aid.dfat.gov.au/countries/eastasia/regional/Pages/initiative-project-childhood.aspx).

88. Australian Government, *East ASIA Regional MTV EXIT (End Exploitation and Trafficking) Phase III* (1 November 2013), Australian Government Department of Foreign Affairs and Trade (http://aid.dfat.gov.au/countries/east-asia/regional/Pages/initiative-mtv-exit-phase-3.aspx).

89. See note 87 above.

90. See Attorney-General's Department, "Human Trafficking" (2013), Australian Government Attorney-General's Department (http://www.ag.gov.au/Peopletrafficking/Pages/default.aspx).

91. See "Report of the Special Rapporteur on trafficking in persons, especially women and children," Mission to Australia, 18 May 2012, A/HRC/20/18/Add.1, 15 <http://www.ohchr.org/Documents/HRBodies/HRCouncil/RegularSession/Session20/A.HRC.20.18.Add.1_En.PDF>.

92. Former Prime Minister Julia Gillard, "International Women's Day Speech," (Speech delivered at the UN Women National Committee Australia, Australia, 8 March 2013) (http://www.pm.gov.au/press-office/international-women%E2%80%99s-day-breakfast).

93. Miller, N., "Andrew Forrest's dream to stop all slavery," *The Age,* 18 March 2014 (http://www.theage.com.au/national/andrew-forrests-dream-to-stop-all-slavery-20140317-34y2g.html).

94   See note 67 above. For example, recent consideration by Canada and the European parliament of the merits of the "Swedish" model, implemented in Sweden, Norway and Iceland, which criminalises the purchase of sex rather than the conduct of the seller.

Part II

Digital Aspects in Identifying and Investigating the Human Trafficking Case

Chapter 5

Using Digital Technologies to Combat Human Trafficking: Privacy Implications

By Felicity Gerry QC, Julia Muraszkiewicz, LL.M., and Niovi Vavoula, LL.M.

There is a moment in the film *Working Girl* when Melanie Griffith is in an elevator with the boss of "Trask Enterprises" and she has to prove that a radio deal was her idea before reaching the top floor, where Sigourney Weaver plans to usurp the whole show. Melanie's character, Tess McGill, produces a women's magazine and demonstrates how two separate chapters led to the creation of *her* great idea.[1] It's a great moment in cinema and led to a huge (albeit fictional) financial deal. It also neatly encapsulates the current discourse around technology as a solution to human rights abuses. As Tess McGill might say, if human rights attorneys and technology experts ever turned up to the same party, they might think they were in the right place at the right time and start looking for the guy with the money in the elevator. While this might be a fun metaphor to demonstrate that using data to combat human rights abuses can be a logical conclusion, this chapter is a reminder that such an approach must be handled in a careful way in order to recognise, adapt to, and protect privacy so that victims are not doubly abused.

5.1 Human Rights and Human Trafficking

Human rights abuses occur, as with all human behavior, in three main contexts: Past abuse, ongoing abuse, and abuse to come. Human history is understood through security, economy, health, education and culture. These are terms that scientists understand as well, and some big thinking is being done on big data. However, surveillance and manipulation by algorithm is one of the potentially greatest human rights abuses, and human society can only truly progress with understanding and knowledge that harnessing data requires ethical and careful handling to enhance rights and not further restrict freedoms.

By its intrinsic nature, human trafficking is a hidden crime, where criminal individuals or organisations quickly adapt and advance their *modus operandi* in order to respond to law enforcement strategies—often acting under the guise of legitimate operations. In addition, trying to estimate the number of people it affects or the profit criminals make is a troublesome task, given that exploitation can occur in multiple ways. While it is true that stakeholders, including government authorities, do not need 100% accurate statistics to take immediate action against human trafficking, it is widely recognised that improving our knowledge will enhance the prospects of tackling this crime effectively while ensuring full protection of the victims.

5.2 Human Rights and Technology

Over the past few years, policy makers, academics, and activists have increasingly turned their attention to the multiple role of technology in the human trafficking framework. On the one hand, scholarship has improved the understanding regarding the way perpetrators utilise technological forms as means of recruiting and controlling their victims. It has been correctly pointed out that many aspects of human trafficking have been transformed by the evolution of technology because the latter has changed not only the ways in which links are made between exploiters, purchasers, and victims, but also the circulation of information regarding how to engage in criminal activity.[2]

On the other hand, there is growing interest in finding ways to "exploit technology" with a view to disrupting human trafficking networks. For example, law enforcement authorities are using technological traces to identify traffickers, and companies perform data mining to identify suspicious transactions.[3] Furthermore, technology has facilitated the recording, storage, and exchange of victims' information after being identified as such. Reporting mechanisms for witnesses and victims via telephone or the Internet have been established.

In cases involving images, metadata may assist in proving the dates when the crimes were committed. The location of an offence may be proved by the content of images and geo-tagging. "Xif" data from devices used to take images may match those devices in the possession of a particular suspect. In cases where only circumstantial evidence exists, inferences may be drawn from evidence that the suspect used fake caller ID or spyware to rebut suggestions of innocent association and to prove criminal intent. Flight bookings and bank records of cash withdrawals abroad might assist in proving transnational trafficking. The transnational, multi-dimensional and highly adaptive character of human trafficking renders the possibilities for using technology endless.

5.3 Technology and Human Trafficking

The application of technology in the human trafficking framework inevitably raises significant concerns as to how this can be effectively done without undermining the fundamental rights of both the victims and other individuals who may collaterally be affected. In particular, privacy and, in turn, data privacy considerations lie at the heart of the analysis. Privacy concerns in human trafficking legislation tend to relate to the way criminal proceedings must take place to ensure anonymity of a victim, rather than specific guidelines that take into account the impact of the use of different technological tools on individual privacy. Some progress has been made on these issues in the "datACT" project, which is committed to ensuring that victims of trafficking are "perceived in their autonomy and not as powerless victims whose personal data must be collected and stored."[4] The project recognises that trafficked persons enjoy an equal level of protection of their right to privacy as any other citizen. It is a foundational approach that needs to be recognised globally.

Following an outline of the relationship between human trafficking and privacy, this chapter explores four ways in which technological development may be used for combating trafficking in human beings: location tracking, data collection, unmanned aircraft vehicles (UAVs, commonly referred to as "drones"), and biometrics. It concludes that, in the rush to combat human trafficking, governments must not lose sight of the balance that needs to be achieved by maintaining privacy so that technology remains useful rather than abusive.

5.4 Defining the Issues

A. Technology

Despite the fundamental changes it has brought about in human interaction, technology is relatively easy to define:

By "technology," we refer to information and communication technologies, particularly those constituting digital and networked environments. Technologies that allow users to exchange digital information over networks include the Internet, online social networks, and mobile phones. Digital and networked technologies alter the flow of information between people and thus impact social interactions, practices, and behavior.[5]

The exploitation of human beings through trafficking is a critical humanitarian issue, but the reaction of technology giants has been from a law enforcement perspective:

Microsoft believes that the technologies of today's "mobile-first, cloud-first" world can be used to help disrupt the global problem of human trafficking. Technology can not only make law enforcement more efficient, it can be used to educate those at risk and their families, and can disrupt criminal operations by increasing the risk and reducing the rewards of their activities.

We are also committed to investing in research and in government and industry partnerships to help understand the role of technology in combatting human trafficking. We have recently sponsored six different research teams in order to create a better understanding of the role of technology in the advertising, sale, and purchase of child trafficking victims.[6]

B. Human Trafficking

Human trafficking amounts to ownership, control, and exploitation of people for profit. Traffickers erode a series of human rights: the right to freedom, the right not to be tortured or treated inhumanely, and the right to dignity, to name a few. It can be committed by organised transnational criminal gangs or by a single person, and it can target women, men, and children of all ages. It is also an intrinsic part of commerce: Although communities traditionally think of human trafficking in the form of female sexual exploitation, according to the United Nations Office on Drugs and Crime (UNODC) the sectors most frequently associated with human trafficking are agriculture or horticulture, construction, garments and textiles under sweatshop conditions, catering and restaurants, domestic work, entertainment and the sex industry.[7] In other words, human trafficking targets sectors that exploit individuals for forced labour surrounded by secrecy, making it difficult to tackle.

C. Privacy and Data Privacy

Describing privacy and data privacy is not as straightforward a process as in relation to the previous notions and surely cannot be effectively done within a few paragraphs. Privacy is "large and unwieldy"[8] and "a notoriously vague, ambiguous, and controversial term that embraces a confusing knot of problems, tensions, rights and duties."[9] It has been described as "an unusually slippery concept,"[10] and as "a concept in disarray. Nobody can articulate what it means."[11]

In relation to the right to private life at an international level privacy, is recognised as a human right in Chapter 17 of the International Covenant of Civil and Political Rights (ICCPR), which mirrors the wording of Chapter 12 of the non-binding United Nations Declaration of Human Rights. Despite this lack of conceptual clarity, it is widely agreed that privacy comprises multiple dimensions that are not possible to reduce to one single notion,[12] but are divided into privacy of the person, privacy of personal data, privacy of personal behaviour and privacy of personal communication.[13] Seven types of privacy have been suggested to include privacy of thoughts and feelings, of location and of association.[14]

Data privacy is often discussed in the context of data protection, but the two overlap. Rules have been developed in most jurisdictions around the collection and storage of data with rules on remedies for the data subject. However, a definite set of data protection principles does not exist and different lists have emerged both in literature and in various data protection instruments.[15] As regards these instruments, the most important ones are the OECD Guidelines Governing the Protection of Privacy and Transborder Flows of Personal Data (1980), the Council of Europe's Convention for the Protection of Individuals with regard to Automatic Processing of Personal Data 108 (1981), and the United Nations (UN) Guidelines Concerning Computerized Personal Data Files (1990).

It seems sensible to conclude that privacy and data privacy are closely related but not identical notions, because privacy protects other dimensions of a person apart from their personal data, while data privacy is restricted to the protection of data that is personal but not necessarily part of a person's private life. In cases of processing of personal data, if viewed together as the CJEU does, individuals can be shielded more effectively at all stages of information processing—from the collection to their further use and exchange.

5.5 Relationship Between Human Trafficking and Privacy

The relationship between human trafficking and privacy arises in a law enforcement and corporate context. At the outset, it needs to be stressed that the primary focus is placed on the trafficked victims, and that privacy and data privacy are considered in relation to criminal proceedings. A first indication is Chapter 6 of the UN Trafficking Protocol, which states that: "In appropriate cases and to the extent possible under its domestic law, each State Party shall protect the privacy and identity of victims of trafficking in persons, including, inter alia, by making legal proceedings relating to such trafficking confidential."[16]

Examples of technologies now being applied to combat trafficking include Digital Crimes Units—where private companies assist government entities, biometric identification, tracking systems, and computer forensic investigation. Trafficked persons' privacy does not always appear to be a priority, and it must be remembered that in any trafficking scenario other actors are also involved. This can include those under investigation, but also others such as support services, employers, and bankers receiving proceeds of crime and subject to reporting requirements. Furthermore, personal data could be useful as an evidentiary tool, but concerns may also be raised as to the extent to which the processing of such data may have harmful repercussions: "What happens when the weapon (technology) used for the elimination of crime is the same weapon used against people's safety?"[17]

Chapter 6 of the UN Trafficking Protocol is of qualified nature: In the UN framework, privacy and data privacy play second fiddle to other duties, and therefore there is a wide margin of maneuver in relation to the protection of privacy of trafficked individuals. At present victim protection largely focuses on anonymity, often limited to naming an individual in the media. As we shall see below, the potentially invasive nature of technological advances makes such an approach far too limited. What is needed is a recognition of the privacy issues that can and do arise, in advance, throughout an enquiry, in the presentation of issues in court. There is also a need for monitoring, such as through reporting committees like the Convention on the Elimination of All Forms of Discrimination Against Women (CEDAW).

The current ad hoc approach does not address specific fundamental rights challenges related to the use of technology in combatting the crime or at corporate level. There are guides and toolkits that promote ethical research and data collection. Such examples include the UNODC toolkit on "Use of standardized data collection instruments"[18] or the "United Nations Inter-Agency Project on Human Trafficking, Guide to Ethics and Human Rights in Counter Trafficking."[19] However, in practice, this means that the increasing reliance on surveillance tools not only during criminal investigations and proceedings, but also in the context of trafficking prevention, can only be examined against the general legislation on privacy and data privacy and overarching tools against a background of competing interests. One simple example is the creation of sex offender websites where the IP addresses of those who use the website are inevitably collected by the server. One short sentence highlights the dangers for innocent individuals in a technological process ostensibly designed to protect people. Without specifically addressing the privacy issues in combatting human trafficking, the focus on human protection from exploitation and human protection from invasion of privacy risks being lost in the clamour for technological solutions.

Report: *Understanding and Improving Law Enforcement Responses to Human Trafficking*

Law Enforcement responses to human trafficking in the U.S. were set out as long ago as 2008 in a report, "Understanding and Improving Law Enforcement Responses to Human Trafficking," which was submitted to the U.S. Department of Justice by the Institute on Race and Justice at Northeastern University.

The report found that "while agencies generally think human trafficking is a rare or nonexistent problem in their community, and relatively few agencies have taken proactive steps such as developing training or protocols or assigning specialized personnel to investigate cases of human trafficking, a surprisingly larger proportion of local law enforcement agencies have investigated one or more cases of human trafficking since 2000."

The report sets out the importance of awareness, strategies and challenges for investigators, the advantages of multiagency task forces, policy implications and recommendations.

5.6 Technological Advances

The ways in which technology can facilitate and assist in the fight against human trafficking, while protecting the fundamental rights and the safety of the victims, cannot be exhaustively analysed in the limited space of a chapter. In order to highlight the debate on privacy and data protection in human trafficking issues, four key examples will be examined: location tracking, data collection, deployment of drones in border areas as well in crime scenes, and the emerging concerns around biometrics.

A. Location Tracking

As with almost all forms of digital technologies, location tracking fits in the human trafficking framework in a twofold manner: It can be used to both facilitate and disrupt human trafficking offenses.

Perpetrators may exploit location tracking to facilitate the exploitation of their victims. Indeed, one of the primary functions of a trafficker is to impose and retain control over their victims. To this end, victims' phones may be manually examined, phone records may be accessed online, and increasingly sophisticated spyware has become routinely available. Even after a victim has freed themselves from the trafficker's "grasp," they can still be tracked as abusers discover their whereabouts by using location trackers on their mobile phones.[20]

The traffickers' practices to track and monitor the activities of their victims prove that victims can be fairly easily located by direct or remote interrogation of their phone. In essence, the victim becomes a walking database of evidence. At the same time, the safety of a trafficked person, even after being liberated from the trafficking circle, should be prioritised, along with the tackling of the phenomenon.

In this context, it becomes necessary for advocates in the civil society sector to raise their awareness and become proficient at understanding technology and how it can be used. In light of the uncertainty surrounding the power and role of technology in the human trafficking context, many advocates "simply want the technology to go away," as this would "restore a comprehension of trafficking within their frame of reference."[21]

It goes without saying that the solution is not to remove technology from a victim, as this can be incredibly disempowering. It would severely increase their isolation, while giving the abuser more power. Instead, it seems a far more logical step for victims to have safe access to technology, both phones and Internet. In this context, apart from human rights advocates, it is imperative that trafficked persons learn the extent to which these technologies can be used to their benefit or against them.[22] If victims are further facilitated to use technological advances so that they obtain concrete evidence of their victimhood and are assisted to safely identify the perpetrators, their position would be empowered.

Location tracking is also used by law enforcement authorities to detect the position of suspected traffickers or other individuals participating in the trafficking network. It has already been put into place in similar contexts; for example, mobile phones have already been used to track poachers of animals.[23] Furthermore, every migrant worker entering Bahrain receives a SIM card from the Labour Market Regulatory Authority (LMRA), to enable workers to contact the LRMA immediately by text message if there are problems with their employers.[24]

This policy enables the Ministry of Labour to indirectly track migrants (by having their phone numbers on a centralised database), and officially send them information related to the risk of human trafficking, including hotline numbers. With the necessary amendments and caveats, a similar policy could be adopted to monitor the state of affairs as millions are confined to camps on the borders of Syria, travelling across Europe seeking asylum and prey to traffickers, or as individuals are trafficked and abused within countries and from one country to another.

While tracking technology can certainly offer new opportunities to intervene in human trafficking, it must be pointed out that, being a form of surveillance, it can be highly invasive on a persons' privacy. In relation to the effects of location tracking, Michael and Michael have pointed out that such practices have pushed us to live in a state of "überveillance," in which surveillance has become constant and embedded, and individuals and objects can be located and identified.[25] Indeed, location data—combined with the time and possibly the content of a specific activity—can reveal a plethora of information regarding an individual's personal life, including their affiliation with a particular religion, the development of personal relationships and associations with other individuals, as well as their everyday habits. What is more, location tracking enables telecommunication or Internet providers to record these activities and possibly transfer the relevant data to other companies without eliminating the risk of subsequent profiling.[26]

Despite the serious risks attached to tracking technology, it cannot be fully dismissed as a tool against human trafficking. As noted in the context of using tracking devices for patients with dementia: "For the sake of safety a slight loss of liberty is a price worth paying and, that concern about privacy has force only if we imagine that the person involved is trying to hide."[27] In addition, if in the question of "why is tracking being used," the answer is "for the benefit of the individual," then perhaps the concerns over power balance can be reduced.

However, a number of safeguards should be put into place in compliance with the principle of proportionality and reliance on data protection principles. First of all, it could be limited to exceptional circumstances only, for example, when there is substantiated suspicion that the safety of a victim is jeopardised. Blanket monitoring of all migrants—like the example in Bahrain—could have serious repercussions as regards the privacy of the individuals, especially since they are not suspected of committing any crime.

In any case, strong emphasis must be placed on obtaining fully informed consent from persons who will be subjected to tracking technology. Potential or former victims should be informed about the consequences of location tracking in their private lives, the temporal character of the monitoring and the way the information from their electronic devices will be used, what type of information would that be, by which authorities it will be processed, and in which context.

Further, if location tracking involves a former victim and is used for collecting evidence against their perpetrators, consent could be withdrawn at any moment, irrespective of whether the criminal investigation is finalised, without any repercussions for the individual who collaborated with the authorities. The participation in such operations should not be in any way forced upon them, as this would undermine their consent and the individuals concerned should be able to freely choose whether they wish to obtain tracking devices.

Attention also needs to be paid to the power implications of surveillance.[28] In a context where the State or a civil society body gives a victim or a potential victim a device with tracking technologies, the former is at a power advantage. Given that trafficking victims are, to a large extent, nationals of developing countries, it is vital to ensure that their location data will not increase the appetite of domestic authorities to (ab)use the information for purposes unrelated to human trafficking.

It would be unacceptable to use victims' location data for criminal law purposes in cases when national bodies suspect this group of individuals of having committed a crime or for migration control objectives, even after a criminal investigation or criminal proceedings have terminated. In light of the continuing efforts at a global level to tackle irregular migration through the constant monitoring of aliens' movement, this is a serious obstacle that needs to be thought through carefully. Otherwise, tracking devices would act as a "Trojan horse," and persons subjected to tracking technology would be trapped and further victimised at the national level.

One way to bypass this issue could be to develop a monitoring and evaluation system that would ascertain that tracking technology is not used excessively or abused. In addition, opting for a system that would not involve the centralised storage of personal data of victims or potential victims would be an important safeguard. Another method is to ensure that rules around the collection and admissibility of evidence take into account the privacy issues so that, in the same way as police might seek a warrant for searching persons or premises, there are strict procedures around monitoring systems that engage location tracking technology, breach of which could render the evidence obtained inadmissible in the event of litigation. The potential that this has to undermine victim protection has a necessary effect of focusing procedures on the appropriateness of the decision-making around technology as a force for combatting a human rights abuse.

Exploring the nexus of technology and human trafficking in this way demonstrates that the real concern should not be about whether technology can be used to combat human trafficking, but how it can be done in a manner complying with human rights. At the moment, it seems that location technology could be useful in proving the forced movement of exploited people; however, further proof would be necessary, as well as clear and strict limitations of the powers of national authorities.

Privacy in web browsing for victims

In July 2014, George LeVines reported for *The Boston Globe* on a pioneering arrangement between Cambridge domestic violence prevention organization Transition House and the Tor Project—a nonprofit that builds anonymous Web browsing and communication tools. "The Tor Browser Bundle is free software that works like most ordinary browsers but comes configured to make it harder for individuals to be tracked, obscuring or deleting things like a browser's history, location, and IP address from both the website the user is browsing as well as erasing traces from the computer the browser is hosted on."

B. Data Collection

Despite the growing efforts to eliminate human trafficking, in reality, reliable and holistic information on the magnitude of the problem is limited. "The need for better data" on both the perpetrators and the trafficked persons has been repeatedly highlighted[29] under a preventive logic that "it takes a network to defeat a network."[30] Although data collection involves information on all actors tangled in a human trafficking framework, recent efforts have largely concentrated on the collection of personal data—specifically, from trafficked victims. Interestingly, it has been suggested that the underlying rationale behind the collection is not related specifically to a criminal investigation and prosecution or the organisation of national and transnational assistance, but rather for "all other kinds of reasons," and is conducted by national governments, intergovernmental organisations, NGOs and private parties."[31]

For example, in the UK, the National Referral Mechanism (NRM) is a framework for identifying trafficked persons, but equally functions as a tool through which the State collects data about victims. According to the National Crime Agency, "this information contributes to building a clearer picture about the scope of human trafficking in the UK."[32] If one starts to consider how data collection could occur in a corporate environment, even when an effort is being made to ensure corporate responsibility, one can start to see how the right to privacy, even on a qualified basis, is lost to the government and to commercial employers.

The need for protecting the privacy of trafficked persons, including their personal data, is vital, since victims of trafficking form a particularly vulnerable group of individuals who are in need of enhanced protection. Further, having suffered at the hands of their traffickers, they face great risks related to their physical safety. First, the risk of being re-captured and abused is evident. Second, they risk carrying the stigma of being implicated in trafficking proceedings that may prevent them from integrating into a societal environment, accessing the labour market, and eventually regaining their autonomy.

The aim of protection includes the ability of human trafficking victims to recover from their experiences, irrespective of whether this takes place in the sending country or in the receiving one.[33] This is important, considering that if victims return to their country of origin, in certain populations public exposure of certain events that trafficked persons may have experienced may be deemed shameful and may result in being ostracised. As correctly summarised, "(p)rotection from further harm is inextricably linked to protection of the trafficked person's privacy. Failure to protect privacy can increase the danger of intimidation and retaliation. It can cause humiliation and hurt to victims and compromise their recovery."[34]

The danger of profiling that may lead to discriminatory treatment of trafficked persons must also be taken into serious consideration. While combatting human trafficking is a global imperative, it would be pointless if, in doing so, greater harm were caused. It is here that there needs to be real thought around depersonalisation and anonymity, given technological advances in algorithmic analysis, data processing and centralised storage in large-scale databanks, where the risk of unauthorised access and abuse is significantly higher. Currently, the voiced criticism that data collection bodies lack awareness and sufficient knowledge of what data protection laws signify and require means that there is a long way to go before data collection can be a safe resource in the context of tackling human trafficking.[35]

Handbook on Anti-Trafficking Data Collection in South-Eastern Europe

The International Centre for Migration Policy Development has produced a *Handbook on Anti-Trafficking Data Collection in South-Eastern Europe*, and is a useful reference point for Developing Regional Criteria. The handbook:

> ... provides the practical tools needed to work with two databases—the victim-centred database and the trafficker-centred, criminal justice database—including the range of information to be collected in each context and standardised methodologies and terminologies for collecting this information from a wide range of data sources.
>
> This handbook also aims to equip national data repositories with some basic skills in the inputting, maintenance and analysis of this data in accordance with legal and ethical parameters at a national and regional level. The handbook is intended for the specific

government institutions responsible for the collection, maintenance and analysis of the victim-centred database and the trafficker-centred, criminal justice database in each of the SEE countries/territories.

This format is a useful template for any jurisdiction.

C. Drones

The third example of a technological advance that can assist in the fight against human trafficking relates to the employability of drones. Drones can generally be defined as aircraft devices—although land and sea-based vehicles are under development—that are used, or intended to be used, without a human pilot on board.[36] Technically, they are also known as unmanned aerial vehicles (UAVs), remotely piloted vehicles (RPVs), or, in conjunction with their ground-based control stations, unmanned aerial systems (UAS) or remotely piloted aerial systems (RPAS).[37] In their latest forms, they can be "as small as an insect or as large as charter flight."[38]

Since drones are merely aircraft devices, they do not process personal data as such; however, in most cases they carry video camera devices with specialised software that processes the video feed. They can be equipped with Wi-fi sensors, microphones, biometric sensors processing biometric data, GPS systems processing the location of the person filmed, or systems reading IP addresses of all devices located in a building over which the RPAS will fly.[39] Apart from the ability to be attached to numerous payloads that can modify their functionalities, drones carry a number of operational benefits: They can be almost undetectable from the persons under surveillance, they decrease personnel costs, they are more expandable as they can stay airborne much longer than a human crew, they are flexible in tasking, and they can cover remote areas.[40]

Although drones have been primarily deployed in war zones for around a century,[41] in light of their attributes their application has been recently expanded from the military framework to other fields such as environmental monitoring, observation of large-scale human constructions, energy infrastructure, border management, and law enforcement.[42] In relation to human trafficking in particular, drones are relevant in two forums: First, they are used in domestic police operations for the surveillance of criminal activities, including human trafficking. For example, they can be used to track illegal cannabis farms, which are often staffed by victims of human trafficking. This involves the prescription of strict conditions such as the acquisition of a warrant. The second, and far more common, application of drones involves the patrol of external frontiers and combines border control with law enforcement purposes. Under this logic, which has been criticized as being part of the growing trend towards the militarisation of border surveillance,[43] drones are used to monitor the external borders of a specific State as a tool to prevent irregular migration and cross-border crime while rescuing—when needed—the lives of developing-country nationals when in danger in their attempt to cross the border. As a matter of fact, the humanitarian element of these operations has been presented as their flagship in an attempt to justify the necessity of such border-management mechanisms.[44]

As for the function of drones in this context, considering that in numerous cases migrants are also victims of smuggling or trafficking, drones can gather evidence of their victimhood and information on the trafficking networks, such as images of the perpetrators or those connected to them, the chosen routes and the timings of the border crossing. At the same time, information collected by drones can be processed for the purposes of risk analysis and thus improve the understanding on human trafficking. Both operations will depend on whether drones carry devices that can record images and are subject to the mind-set that is based on migration prevention rather than victim protection. The latter may well necessitate increased immigration to combat human trafficking, whereas the former is dedicated to keeping borders closed.

The transfer of drones from the military domain to the non-military one is currently high. In the U.S., where the deployment of drones for enhancing border control is established, it is confirmed that "drones have been used by the U.S. Customs and Border Protection Agency (part of the Department of Homeland Security) on the U.S.-Mexican border to monitor illegal immigration, human trafficking and drug smuggling."[45] Further, through the use of drones, U.S. intelligence was able to establish that the Mexican army is involved in human trafficking and other crimes.[46] Ironically, as reported by the *Independent*, criminals may be one step ahead of the law enforcement bodies as they have "reportedly started using unmanned drones fitted with heat-seeking cameras to steal from and extort illegal cannabis farms."[47]

Here we can quickly see how surveillance is maximised and not targeted to suspects, thus raising serious privacy concerns regarding the individuals monitored. U.S. case law on aerial surveillance has developed but does not go far in addressing some of these concerns. The police can validly fly over a garden and spot elements constituting part of a criminal offence. The U.S. Supreme Court has held that such activities would not signify an intrusion into the person's privacy as "any member of the public flying in this airspace who glanced down could have seen everything that these officers observed."[48]

So, drones can be used without a specific target, but they are surveying an area more generally looking for the "unnamed," thus potentially encroaching on innocent individuals pursuing legitimate activities. When used at borders, they may capture images of fishermen and tourists, or when used to dismantle trafficking networks in urban areas they may also survey individuals living in neighbouring regions, or, in cases of sex trafficking, people who have chosen the company of a victim (especially in cases when they do not know about their trafficked status).

The privacy of trafficked individuals is put at high risk and low regard in such circumstances, with a "chilling effect" on personal freedom.[49] The Article 29 Data Protection Working Party was set up under the Directive 95/46/EC of the European Parliament and of the Council of 24 October 1995 on the protection of individuals with regard to the processing of personal data and on the free movement of such data. It has pointed out that what matters is not the use of drones as such, but the other technologies they can be equipped with, and the subsequent use and processing of personal data that takes place.[50]

As mentioned above, the use of video cameras will allow for the identification of persons whose images have been captured; thus, the relevance of data protection law cannot be underestimated. In this context, the risk of function creep and the use of recorded material for purposes incompatible with the ones for which drones are originally employed must be carefully scrutinised. The danger of using recorded material to further victimise and criminalise trafficked persons is particularly evident.

While trafficked individuals may be in need of international protection, the safety and fundamental rights of victims should remain central.[51] The rhetoric converging around border control, irregular migration, and fighting human trafficking demonstrates that the position of trafficked persons in particular may be precarious if the use of drones is regularised. Otherwise, the effect would be to target "the usual suspects" and "undesirables."[52]

One solution would be to employ drones only in specific investigations as a targeted response or for a longer period of evidentiary collection under strict criteria, and only when there are no other less-intrusive means to achieve the same purpose. Prior authorisation for an independent judicial authority could also be necessary in order to ensure that police authorities do not over-rely on drones.

The underlying aim should not be to allow for government authorities to invest in new toys of surveillance, but rather to "exploit" already existing means in cases where other mechanisms have failed to provide for a solution. As regards specific guidelines, sensors could be turned on and off in flight in order to avoid continuous recording, and private areas could be automatically masked. Other individuals who are accidentally captured in images and videos should be automatically detected and pixelated.[53] Similarly, the depersonalisation of trafficked victims' images should also be foreseen in order to guarantee both their safety and privacy. In this regard, a proper regulatory framework concerning the use of drones for civilian purposes, including law enforcement, would be a significant development.

Drones in Rio

In July 2015, Rachel Browne reported for Vice News that:

> The Brazilian government will start deploying a small army of drones as part of its latest effort to eradicate human trafficking in remote parts of the country. Starting next month in the state of Rio de Janeiro, six drones mounted with video cameras will be sent to fly around and record businesses in rural areas suspected of forcing workers to toil away in slave-like conditions. Exactly what will be done with the footage is still unclear.

"Drones are no substitute for the inspector's physical presence, but they will be useful out in the country, in the case of farms that are hard to reach by road, for example," Bruno Barcia Lopes, coordinator of Rural Supervision for Rio de Janeiro's Labor Secretariat, told the Thomson Reuters Foundation.

There are no reliable statistics about slave labor in Brazil, but estimates range between 25,000 and 40,000 people.[54]

D. Biometrics

Biometrics is the scientific study of biological data through measurement. It can provide material in relation to face, eyes, fingerprints and voice. Such material is used both to verify (one-to-one searches) and to identify (one-to-many searches) individuals, and is widely deployed in the criminal investigative context. Oliver Munday reported the following in January 2014:

> Since 2011, police departments across the U.S. have been scanning biometric data in the field using devices such as the Mobile Offender Recognition and Information System (MORIS), an iPhone attachment that checks fingerprints and iris scans. The FBI is currently building its Next Generation Identification database, which will contain fingerprints, palm prints, iris scans, voice data and photographs of faces. Before long, even your cell phone will be secured by information that resides in a distant biometric database.[55]

More worryingly, over the past few decades, biometrics have also been widely deployed in the framework of immigration control and human trafficking. Apart from the use of biometric identifiers at the borders where part of the official rhetoric in favor of their use involves the fight against human trafficking, national governments are currently exercising their creativity in exploiting biometrics. A key example in this context originates from the UK, where a lack of process for consistently capturing biometric data of human trafficking victims (photographs or fingerprints) has been noted. It has been further pointed out that "collection of such data will help the location and later identification of victims." However, consent of the victim must be ensured so that there is no risk of re-traumatization in such a process.[56]

This progressive expansion and implicit overreliance on the use of biometrics, which stems from the over-optimistic view that this type of data is infallible, has significant implications.[57] As Munday observed, "Unfortunately, this shift to biometric-enabled security creates profound threats to commonly accepted notions of privacy and security. It makes possible privacy violations that would make the National Security Agency's data sweeps seem superficial by comparison."

The concerns do not just relate to the collection and storage of data through surveillance devices, but also to the manipulation of that information. For example, the science of biometrics has also developed in tandem with enhancement techniques through algorithm technology in order to improve quality. Biometric data can be collected and stored without individual consent. It already occurs through street CCTV. Technological developments enable the collection of iris scans of every person in a crowd from a distance of 10 meters.[58] New technologies, including voice identification, are attractive to law enforcement and are potentially being used without proper evaluation of scientific reliability.[59]

The potential for misuse, theft, and misidentification is a huge concern that, combined with the issues around drones, data collection, and location tracking, means that globalized rules protecting individual liberty around technology must be a priority. Since human trafficking has the criminal-corporate crossover outlined above, it is the perfect context for internationally accepted legislative codes of practice to be identified and implemented.

Oliver Munday wrote in *Scientific American* that biometrics had the potential to turn existing surveillance systems into something more powerful, and much more invasive. He cited the Domain Awareness System, which is a network of 3,000 surveillance cameras in New York City: "Currently if someone commits a crime, cops can go back and review sections of video. Equip the system with facial-recognition technology, however, and the people behind the controls can actively track you throughout your daily life." Munday wrote that while "face-in-a-crowd detection is a formidable technical problem," researchers working on projects like the Department of Homeland Security's Biometric Optical Surveillance System (BOSS) are making rapid progress.

Source: "Biometric Security Poses Huge Privacy Risks", *Scientific American*, 2014. Read the full article at http://www.scientificamerican.com/article/biometric-security-poses-huge-privacy-risks/.

5.7 Conclusion

Combating human trafficking has become an important priority from both a political and human rights perspective. Reliance on technological developments is a trend that is growing faster than the corresponding procedural considerations. The consequence is that individual privacy for victims is endangered, with the consequential effect on human safety and security. Ignoring the potential effect of using technology to combat human trafficking fails to respect fundamental human rights discourse. Evidence collected through technological forms must interact with balanced justice systems and balance needs to be achieved in the context of surveillance in order to ensure we are combating and not exacerbating human trafficking. If the lift was still running for Tess McGill in *Working Girl*, she would tell Mr. Trask that the issues are complex, but not insurmountable with an approach that protects society's freedoms rather than characterising society as problematised.[60] Attorneys putting the ink on such a deal should have regard to the wider issues, because technology is not the automatic solution to human exploitation.[61]

Endnotes

1.   Taken in part from F. Gerry, "Data Uses to Combat Human Rights Abuses," *IEEE Technology & Society Magazine Refereed Viewpoint.*

2.   M. Latonero, G. Berhane, A. Hernandez, T. Mohebi, L. Movius, "Human Trafficking Online: The Role of Social Networking Sites and Online Classifieds" (*Technology and Human Trafficking*, 2011); M. Latonero, J. Musto, Z. Boyd, E. Boyle, A. Bissel, K. Gibson, and J. Kim, "The rise of mobile and the diffusion of technology-facilitated trafficking" (USC Annenberg Center on Communication Leadership and Policy, 2012); J. Musto, "The post-human anti-trafficking turn: Technology, domestic minor sex trafficking, and augmented human–machine alliances" in K. K. Hoang and R. Salazar Parreñas (eds), *Human Trafficking Reconsidered: Rethinking the Problem, Envisioning New Solutions* (International Debate Education Association, 2014).

3.   Mitali Thakor and D. Boyd, *Networked trafficking: Reflections on technology and the anti-trafficking movement*, Dialectical Anthropology (2013) Vol. 37, 277–90.

4. The aim of datACT is to promote the rights of trafficked persons to privacy and autonomy and to protect their personal data: "DATACT - Data Protection In Anti-Trafficking Action," DatAct.

5. Latonero, Mark, Jennifer Musto, Zhaleh Boyd, and Ev Boyle, *op. cit.*, pp. 9-10.

6. "Fighting human trafficking with technology" (https://news.microsoft.com/apac/2015/06/22/fighting-human-trafficking-with-technology/).

7. United Nations Office on Drugs and Crime, "Human Trafficking frequently asked questions."

8. Raymond Wacks, *Law, Morality, and the Private Domain* (Hong Kong University Press, 2000) p. 222.

9. C.J. Bennett, *Regulating Privacy Data Protection and Public Policy in Europe and the United States* (Cornell University Press, 1992) p. 13.

10. James Q. Whitman, *The Two Western Cultures of Privacy: Dignity versus Liberty*, Yale L.J. (2004) Vol. 113, pp. 1153-4.

11. Daniel Solove, *Understanding Privacy* (Harvard University Press, 2008) p.12.

12. Solove, *op. cit.*

13. C. Roger, "What's 'privacy?'" (Australian Law Reform Commission workshop, 28 July 2006) (http://www.rogerclarke.com/DV/Privacy.html > accessed 15 October 2015).

14. Rachel L. Finn, David Wright and Michael Friedewald, "Seven Types of Privacy," in Serge Gutwirth et al. (eds.), *European Data Protection: Coming of Age* (Springer, 2013) pp. 4-5.

15. The OECD Guidelines of 1979 are often used as a starting point. See also the six "core fair information principles" of Bennett: principles of openness, individual access and correction, collection limitation, use limitation, disclosure limitation and security, Bennett, *op. cit.*, p.101.

16. Trafficking Protocol, Art. 6.

17. Athanasia Zagorianou Technology and Human Trafficking (http://www.uhrsn.org/2015/07/technology-and-human-trafficking/).

18. United Nations Office on Drugs and Crime, "Toolkit to Combat Trafficking in Persons" (United Nations Office on Drugs and Crime).

19. United Nations, "Guide to ethics and human rights in counter trafficking" (United Nations Inter-Agency Project on Human Trafficking, 2008).

20. WESNET in Australia has identified these issues and provides training on the misuse of technology to target, track, stalk, harass and commit other acts of violence against women (http://wesnet.org.au/2015/10/safetynet-training-canberra-3/).

21. Thakor and Boyd, *op. cit.*, p. 287.

22. See, for example, WESNET, "Internet Safety" (http://wesnet.org.au/safetynet/Internet-safety/).

23. R. A. Butler, "Discarded cell phones help fight rainforest poachers" (Mongbay, 24 June 2014).

24. United States Department of State, "2014 Trafficking in Persons Report - Bahrain" (20 June 2014).

25. M.G. M. and K. Michael, *Toward a State of Überveillance*, IEEE Technology and Society Magazine (2010) Vol. 29(2), 9.

26. For an overview of the effects of location tracking see among others: K. Michael and M. G. M., *The Social and Behavioural Implications of Location-Based Services*, Journal of Location Based Services (2011) Vol. 5, 121; A. S.Y. Cheung, *Location privacy: The challenges of mobile service devices*, Computer Law & Security Review (2014) Vol. 30, 41-54.

27. J. Hughes and S. Louw, *Electronic tagging of people with dementia who wander*, British Medical Journal (2002) Vol. 325, 847-848.

28. Raab and Wright, *op. cit.*

29. F. Laczko, *Data and Research on Human Trafficking*, International Migration (2005) Vol. 43, 5-16.

30. United Nations Office on Drugs and Crime, "Transnational Organised Crime in East Asia and the Pacific: A Threat Assessment" (UNODC, 2013).

31. Marjan Wijers, "Where do all the data go? European data protection law and the protection of personal data of trafficked persons" (chapter presented at the datACT – Conference on data protection and trafficking, Berlin, 25-27 September 2013).

32. National Crime Agency, "National Referral Mechanism."

33. Council of Europe, Explanatory Report on the Convention on Action Against Trafficking in Human Beings, ETS 197,16.V.2005, para. 138.

34. Ann Gallagher, *The International Law of Human Trafficking* (New York: Cambridge University Press, 2010), p.303.

35. Wijers, *op. cit.*

36. This definition combines those submitted by B. Hayes, C. Jones and E. Töpfer, "Eurodrones Inc." (Statewatch, 2014) 7, and P. McBride, *Beyond Orwell: the application of unmanned aircraft systems in domestic surveillance operations*, Journal of Air Law and Commerce (2009) Vol. 74(3), 628. Roger Clarke has identified four characteristics of drones: The device must be heavier than air (i.e., balloons are excluded), the device must have the capability of sustained and reliable flight, there must be no human on board the device (i.e., it is "unmanned"), and there must be a sufficient degree of control to enable performance of useful functions. See R. Clarke, *Understanding the Drone Epidemic*, Computer Law & Security Review (2014) Vol. 30(3), 230-246.

37. B. Hayes, C. Jones and E. Töpfer, *op. cit.*, p. 7.

38. E. Bone and C. Bolkcom, "Unmanned Aerial Vehicles: Background and Issues for Congress" (Washington D.C., 2003) 1.

39. EPDS, Opinion of the European Data Protection Supervisor on the Communication from the Commission to the European Parliament and the Council on "A new era for aviation—Opening the aviation market to the civil use of remotely piloted aircraft systems in a safe and sustainable manner."

40. A. Brecher et. al., "Roadmap to near-term deployment of unmanned aerial vehicles (UAV) for transportation applications charge to participants" (UAV 2003: A Roadmap for Deploying UAVs in Transportation Specialist Work-

shop, Santa Barbara, 2003); P. C. Nolin, "Unmanned Aerial Vehicles: Opportunities and Challenges for the Alliance Special Report" (NATO Parliamentary Assembly, Canada, 2012).

41. For an overview of the history behind the deployment of drones in the military framework, see R. L. Finn and D. Wright, *Unmanned aircraft systems: Surveillance, ethics and privacy in civil applications*, Computer Law & Security Review (2012) Vol. 28, 185.

42. For an overview of the different uses of drones, see European Parliament, Directorate General for Internal Policies, "Privacy and Data Protection Implications of the Civil Use of Drones" (PE 519.221, June 2015), 11.

43. D. Bigo, "Migration and Security" in Virginie Guiraudon and Christian Joppke (eds.), *Controlling a New Migration World* (Routledge, 2001) 121-149.

44. Jørgen Carling and María Hernández-Carretero, *Protecting Europe and Protecting Migrants? Strategies for Managing Unauthorised Migration from Africa*, The British Journal of Politics and International Relations (2011) Vol. 13, 42-58; Ben Hays and Mathias Vermeulen, *Borderline. EU Border Surveillance Initiatives. An Assessment of the Costs and Its Impact on Fundamental Rights* (Heinrich-Böll-Stiftung, 2012).

45. J. I. Ross, "Drones Are Different" (Baltimore Sun, 19 June 2012).

46. M. Webster, "U.S. ABP & U.S. Drones Flying Over Mexico Detecting Military Drug/Human Trafficking Camps" (Renew America, 1 April 2011).

47. A. Withnall, "Criminals 'Using Unmanned Drones And Infrared Cameras To Find Illegal Cannabis Farms' – And Then Steal From The Growers" (*The Independent*, 17 April 2014).

48. U.S. Supreme Court, *California v. Ciraolo* (1986).

49. R. L. Finn, D. Wright and A. Donovan (Trilateral Research & Consulting, LLP), L. Jacques and P. De Hert (Vrije Universiteit Brussel), "Privacy, data protection and ethical risks in civil RPAS operations" (7 November 2014), 28; Roger Clarke, *The Regulation of Civilian Drones' Impacts on Behavioural Privacy*, Computer Law & Security Review (2014) Vol. 30(3) 286-305.

50. Chapter 29 Working Party, Opinion 01/2015 on Privacy and Data protection Issues Relating to the Utilisation of Drones, 16 June 2015.

51. For instance, Chapter 20(5) of the EUROSUR Regulation prohibits the transmission of personal data of persons needing international protection and of asylum applicants.

52. Finn and Wright, *op. cit.*, p. 188.

53. EDPS, *op. cit.*, p. 15.

54. Source: The Thomson Reuters Foundation, the charitable arm of Thomson Reuters, that covers humanitarian news, women's rights, trafficking, corruption and climate change. Visit www.trust.org. http://news.trust.org// item/20150728135023-q1ldw/?source=jtOtherNews1.

55. Oliver Munday, "Biometric Security Poses Huge Privacy Risks" Scientific American.

56. UK Home Office, "Review of the National Referral Mechanism for Victims of Human Trafficking," November 2014.

57. For a general overview on the privacy concerns, see Patricio Campisi (ed.), *Security and Privacy in Biometrics* (2013, London/Heidelberg/New York/ Dordrecht, Springer).

58. Munday, *op. cit.*

59. Singh. C., *Quis custodiet ipsos custodes? Should Justice Beware: A Review of Voice Identification Evidence in Light of Advances in Biometric Voice Identification Technology,* Int. Comment. Evid. 2013; 11(1): 1-28.

60. *Id.*, and see Lyon, D. (2001), *Surveillance Society: Monitoring Everyday Life*, (Philadelphia, PA: Open University Press).

61. This chapter is taken in part from F. Gerry, J. Muraszkiewicz, and N. Vavoula, *The role of technology in the fight against human trafficking: Reflections on privacy and data protection concerns*, 32 Computer Law & Security Review 2, April 2016, pp. 205–217.

Chapter 6

Human Trafficking in the Dark: Sex Trafficking on the Dark Web

By Bryanne Perlanski

In addition to traditional forms of recruitment and trafficking of victims, new technologies, specifically the Internet, have changed the game of trafficking. As investigations and prosecutions begin to pinpoint traffickers and purchasers of victims visiting everyday websites, it should be anticipated that the trafficking of persons, like other illegal transactions, will move to a more anonymous cyber location—the Dark Web. This discussion focuses mainly on sex trafficking because labor trafficking does not appear to be as prevalent online. The regional attorney for the Equal Employment Opportunity Commission in the Los Angeles District Office stated that the use of technology to facilitate labor trafficking in the cases she saw was very unlikely.[1] To have successful prosecutions and convictions of traffickers using the Dark Web, the tools used to investigate these cases must be more sophisticated than the technological tools traffickers will be using to remain hidden.

6.1 How the Internet Facilitates Human Trafficking

Recognizing that sex trafficking is taking place can be one of the biggest challenges faced by law enforcement and service providers, especially when the trafficking is being done online. "The Internet has made access to commercial sex essentially effortless."[2] The Internet allows for traffickers to remove sex trafficking from where it was being recognized by those who came across it and making it more public in some aspects.[3] The Internet creates a new way for traffickers to locate and lure in their victims.[4] Social networking sites, specifically, have increased the access to potential victims—both adults and children.

Traffickers using the Internet to recruit sex trafficking victims are not bound by geography, allowing them to reach a greater number of victims, located anywhere.[5] Children are more vulnerable to predators because their lives are much more exposed through social networking sites, they live their lives online, and they are readily accessible through mobile devices.[6] Traffickers can also exploit children they meet online through "sextortion"—"sexual exploitation that uses non-physical forms of coercion by threatening to release sexual images or information to extort sexual favors from the victim."[7]

Over 10 years, there were 715 federal cases of sex trafficking in the U.S.
78% of those cases involved the use of technology, totaling 557 cases.

Source: Mary Graw Leary, *Fighting Fire with Fire: Technology in Child Sex Trafficking,* 21 Duke J. Gender L. & Pol'y 289, 290 (2014).

Traffickers can also connect to people wishing to purchase the sexual services provided by victims. A commercial sex transaction online is beneficial to both purchasers and traffickers: It creates a safer environment for the parties, buyers and victims can be connected rapidly, the traffickers are distanced from the transaction, and the purchasers are not risking being exposed publicly.[8] Women and children can also be advertised for sale with the appearance of being a legitimate business.[9]

When it comes to the selling of children for sex quickly to the broadest market, online advertising websites seem to be the traffickers' choice.[10] "Craigslist, an online site that provides classified ads and discussion forums for jobs, housing, items for sale, service, local events, and more, has been the subject of numerous anti-trafficking efforts."[11] Craigslist received a lot of attention for advertisements of commercial sex being posted in their "Adult Services" section, which Craigslist has voluntarily shut down worldwide.[12] However, these efforts did not prevent traffickers from conducting business online. Sex trafficking advertisements were being moved into other categories on Craigslist and there are a number of other competing websites that are making millions in revenue from sex advertisements.[13]

75% of child victims are advertised online

Source: Drew Olanoff, "Thorn to Set Up an Innovation Lab in Silicon Valley to Fight Child Sex Trafficking," *Tech Crunch* (Nov. 12, 2015).

In 2010, about half of online adults in the U.S. have used online classified advertising sites.

Source: Mark Latonero, "Human Trafficking Online: The Role of Social Networking Sites and Online Classifieds," Ctr. on Commc'n Leadership & Policy, 17.

After the shutdown of Craiglist's "Adult Services" category, Backpage became the number-one website for sex advertisements online.[14] Backpage is similar to Craigslist in that it is a host to online classified ads. There have been some efforts to make Backpage verify the age of those posting ads on their website; however, this does not prevent an individual from posting an ad depicting minors for escort services or a minor posting pretending to be an adult.[15] In practice, there is very little that can be done to verify age online. For example, in Washington three teens were being forced to have sex with clients 20 times per day because their pimp, who was an adult, posted ads depicting them on Backpage and legally verified that he was over the age of 18.[16] This minor formality, a user

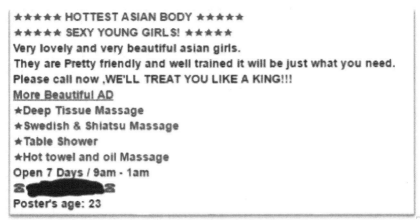

Figure 6.1 *Ad found on Backpage.com under the "escorts" category.*

verifying their age, does little to prevent child sex trafficking and nothing to prevent sex trafficking of adults. While these websites are providing a playground for sex traffickers to exploit their victims, getting rid of Craigslist and Backpage will not resolve the problem. As quoted by ABC NEWS, general counsel for Backpage stated that, "'[t]he endgame is that the same activity will continue to occur, but it will just move into the deeper part of the web – or offshore[.]'"[17]

The ad depicted above was found under the "escorts" section on Backpage, only vaguely disguising sexual services for legitimate massages. The ad also shows the age of the poster; however, as previously mentioned, there is no way to verify this. Additionally, it is very hard to recognize the difference between posts offering sex willingly (voluntary prostitutes) and those who are being forced to sell their bodies against their will (victims of sex trafficking).[18] The only sure way to determine if there is trafficking involved with online commercial sex is if the ad makes clear that the person being advertised is a minor.

Under U.S. law, all minors engaged in commercial sex acts are victims of trafficking.[19] The attorney for Backpage says that "in the adult and dating category, a team of moderators looks at every single ad."[20] However, the ad depicted below was found under the "escorts" section and may suggest a younger girl being advertised.

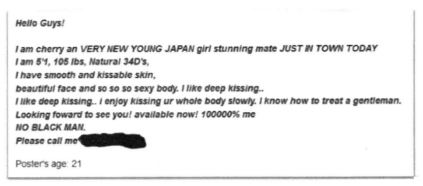

Figure 6.2 Backpage ad using keyword language that may suggest an underage girl.

Given the amount of ads found like the one above, it is unclear if this review process is actually working in practice. Despite ads not outright saying those involved are children, there are keywords within the ads that those looking to engage in sex with minors would recognize.[21] Backpage's attorney also says the website's terms of use policy "already ban[s] using 'codes' to advertise sexual favors for money, any material that exploits minors, and human trafficking."[22] With authorities narrowing in on identifying traffickers, purchasers, and victims based on transactions taking place online, the risk of these transactions moving to more anonymous corners of the Internet is increasing.

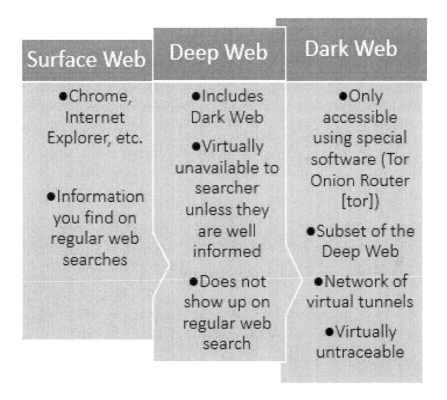

Surface Web	Deep Web	Dark Web
•Chrome, Internet Explorer, etc. •Information you find on regular web searches	•Includes Dark Web •Virtually unavailable to searcher unless they are well informed •Does not show up on regular web search	•Only accessible using special software (Tor Onion Router [tor]) •Subset of the Deep Web •Network of virtual tunnels •Virtually untraceable

Figure 6.3 Lisa M. Browniee, "The Deep Web and the Dark Web—Why Lawyers Need to be Informed," Legal Solutions Blog (Jan. 30, 2015); Larry Greenemeier, "Human Traffickers Caught on Hidden Internet," Scientific American (Feb. 8, 2015).

6.2 The Dark Web

Thus far, the discussion has focused on one part of the Internet—the Surface Web. There are actually three different layers to the Internet: the Surface Web, the Deep Web, and the Dark Web. Below is a chart that explains the essential differences between each of these layers.

The Deep Web is a portion of the Internet that includes the Dark Web, but they are not the same. Rather, the Dark Web is a subset of the Deep Web. Much of the information on the Deep Web is "unstructured data gathered from sensors and other devices that may not reside in a database that can be scanned or 'crawled' by search engines."[23] This Deep Web is "a goldmine of data not precisely unavailable to the general public, but virtually unavailable unless the searcher is well-informed."[24]

The Dark Web is even more difficult to maneuver for the average person: "Some areas of the Deep Web are accessible using only special software such as the Tor Onion Router [Tor], which allows people to secretly share information anonymously vis peer-to-peer connections rather than going through a centralized computer server."[25] "Tor is 'a network of virtual tunnels that allows people and groups to improve their privacy and security on the Internet.'"[26] The Dark Web is designed to be inaccessible to ordinary browsers and is a global network that is virtually untraceable.

It is difficult to narrow down who is using the Dark Web due to the anonymity of cyberspace. Though navigating the Dark Web takes some computer sophistication, after looking at websites describing the process of how to reach and use this portion of the Internet, with some effort any individual who uses a computer regularly could figure out how to use the Dark Web.[27] The anonymity of this portion of the Internet raises some important questions: Who created it and how have others found out about it? Interestingly enough, in 1996 the United States Naval Research Laboratory gave a presentation in England describing the process of using the Internet without divulging a person's identity to servers or routers—the United States military was the creator of the Deep Web.[28]

55% of Internet users have tried to avoid being observed online.

Source: Lev Grossman, "The Secret Web," *TIME* (Nov. 11, 2013), http://time.com/630/the-secret-web-where-drugs-porn-and-murder-live-online/.

On a website that gives instructions on how to maneuver through the Deep Web and Dark Web, there is a brief warning concerning human trafficking. It reads: "Since the authorities might want to monitor the activities of groups involved in these trafficking activities, many of the culprits have been known to conduct their communication activities on the [D]eep [W]eb, away from the prying eyes of the government."[29] The Dark Web "has offered the Internet's savvier users a chance to develop marketplaces at which people can order just about anything—controlled substances included—for delivery to their doors."[30] The United States Attorney's Office in Atlanta attributed underground and quasi-underground chat rooms as a source for sex trafficking.[31] The Defense Advanced Research Projects Agency (DARPA) says that "human trafficking has a significant Dark Web presence in the form of forums, advertisements, job postings and hidden services (anonymous sites available via Tor)."[32]

In order for sex trafficking to take place, there must be a transfer of something of value for the return of a sex act.[33] Similar to transfer of money on the Surface Web, the transfer of anything with value can happen on the Dark Web. To

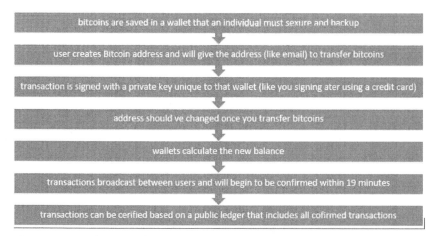

Figure 6.4 *Reuben Grinberg, Bitcoin: An Innovative Alternative Digital Currency, 4 Hastings Sci. & Tech. L.J. 159, 162 (2012); "How does Bitcoin work?" (https://bitcoin.org/en/how-it-works).*

preserve anonymity, the currency of choice on the Dark Web is bitcoin, which is digital money.[34] There is a difference between "Bitcoin" and "bitcoin": "Bitcoin with a capital B means the software and the system; bitcoin with a lowercase b means the actual money."[35] The process of transferring bitcoins is actually quite technical, and is explained in the chart below.

In order to own or trade Bitcoin, an individual can either run a program on their computer or open an account on a website that will run the Bitcoin protocol.[36] This Bitcoin protocol, called "Bitcoin client," saves bitcoins in a wallet that the individual must secure and backup.[37] A Bitcoin user then creates a Bitcoin address, and in order to transfer bitcoins to others or have them transfer their bitcoins to you, you need to give each other your Bitcoin addresses; once the transfer is made, the Bitcoin address should be changed. The wallets calculate the spendable balance and all new transactions can be verified based on a shared public ledger, or block chain, that includes all confirmed transactions. In order to sign transactions, Bitcoin wallets have a secret piece of data—a private key—to prove they came from the owner of the wallet. "All transactions are broadcast between users and usually begin to be confirmed by the network in the following 19 minutes, through a process called mining."[38] Mining confirms "waiting transactions by including them in the block chain."[39] Recently, there has been controversy in creating regulations surrounding Bitcoin because a large part of the proposed regulation is attempting to remove the anonymity involved with Bitcoin, one of the benefits to the virtual currency, by forcing merchants to collect names and addresses for transactions, exposing consumers' personal information that would not otherwise be exposed.[40]

6.3 Process of Criminal Online Sex Trafficking Cases

"The United Nations Office on Drugs and Crime estimates there are about 2.5 million human trafficking victims worldwide at any given time . . . [i]n its 2014 study on human trafficking the U.N. agency found that 40 percent of countries surveyed reported less than 10 convictions per year between 2010 and 2012."[41] The proliferation of trafficking over the Internet has only magnified the problems involved in identifying these victims and prosecuting those who profit from this crime.

A. Step 1: Identifying Sex Trafficking

One of the most challenging steps in the prosecution of a sex trafficking case is identifying if an individual is a trafficking victim. As shown in the Backpage ad earlier in this chapter, there is not a clear-cut way to identify if the individual being advertised is a victim of sex trafficking or if he or she is voluntarily partaking in prostitution. The easiest way to identify a sex trafficking victim is if he or she is a minor—because any child involved in commercial sex is considered a victim. In cases involving the Internet, whether it is Backpage or via the Dark Web, the way to identify victims is to be able to come into contact with them. This could be increasingly complicated if the Dark Web is being used for the selling of commercial sex.

B. Step 2: Investigation

The Defense Advanced Research Projects Agency (DARPA) has created a program called "Memex" to investigate sex trafficking cases taking place via the Dark Web.[42] Though developed to "provide the mechanisms for improved content discovery, information extraction, information retrieval, user collaboration and other key search functions[,]" Memex's initial focus was to assist the Department of Defense in addressing the issue of human trafficking.[43] This program allows them "to scour the Internet in search of information about human trafficking, in particular advertisements used to lure victims into servitude and to promote their sexual exploitation."[44] The program was named after converging the terms "memory" and "index."[45] This program can explore the portions of the Internet that one could not reach through a regular search on a search engine. However, it is noteworthy that if something is protected by a password, meaning it cannot be accessed by the public, Memex will not search it.[46]

When Memex was created, the idea behind it was to allow "users to quickly and flexibly search huge amounts of information and more efficiently gain insights from it."[47] In order to combat sex trafficking with Memex, the Pentagon specified three developments that need to be involved:

(1) Domain-specific indexing, referring to scalable [W]eb crawling infrastructure for link discovery and information extraction and overcoming counter-crawling measures, including bans on robot behavior, paywalls, human detection, member-only forums and non-HTML content[;] (2) Domain-specific searching, including designing query language for crawling and information extraction algorithms[; and] (3) Domain-specific applications such as Counter Human Trafficking, and, during the life of the program, may include possible indexing for found data, missing persons and counterfeit goods or the next Silk Road.[48]

The program indexes content found on the Web that would not be caught by regular search engines in the effort to identify hidden links between the content.[49] For example, Memex can take a name or phone number that shows up in a sex trafficking ad and create a diagram with dots that represent the Web pages that contain the name and number; clicking on the dots would give the location and time where the ads were posted.[50] This allows investigators to gather information to locate criminals they would not be able to locate using regular search engines.[51] The Dark Web users' identities and IP addresses are still not being revealed with Memex; however, patterns and relationships can be used to track the users.[52]

At times, a criminal investigation can begin with as little information as an e-mail address.[53] The government focuses on forums, chats, advertisements, job postings, and other tools used to lure victims of human trafficking.[54] The Memex program, in accordance with the New York County District Attorney's (NYDA) Office, has played a major role in generating active sex trafficking investigations and has been applied to open indictments with their office.[55] "In September 2014 sex trafficker Benjamin Gaston was sentenced to a minimum of 50 years in prison having been found guilty of 'Sex Trafficking, as well as Kidnapping, Criminal Sexual Act, Rape, Assault, and Sex Abuse – all in the First Degree.'"[56] Gaston was subject to prosecution by the NYDA after he reportedly held a 28-year-old female victim for 42 hours, took her phone and cash, threatened her, and then ordered her to perform sexual acts, which he profited from.[57] This victim escaped by jumping out a sixth story window, subsequently breaking her vertebrae, pelvis, arm, and leg.[58] This new program allows offices to build evidence-based prosecutions, which are crucial to combating human trafficking because victims are often too traumatized or fearful to testify, so having an option to prosecute cases without them is necessary.[59]

In addition to government efforts to investigate sex trafficking on the Dark Web, non-governmental organizations also attempt to aid in the effort to end the exploitation of individuals for commercial sex. Thorn is an organization that combines efforts of its employees, tech companies, law enforcement, and everyday users of the Internet to fight the issue of sex trafficking that occurs online, specifically child sexual exploitation.[60] Thorn built and utilizes a tool called Spotlight, which helps identify "chatter, content, and other data to help law enforcement catch perpetrators" of human sex trafficking.[61] Additionally, there are several private companies taking on the fight against human trafficking. Google is working to identify victims and coinciding traffickers with targeted search results. The company is also partnering with anti-trafficking organizations, such as Polaris Project and Palantir, to support new initiatives using technology to combat trafficking.[62] Google has attempted to connect human trafficking victims with organizations that can provide help to them: If certain keywords are searched on Google, human trafficking hotline numbers will show up.[63] Google has teams of engineers, research scientists, product managers, and issue experts that work for Jigsaw, formerly known as Google Ideas, that researches issues with technology and international security.[64] Using Google Ideas, Google partnered with Palantir and The Polaris Project to package their technology and provide it to other human trafficking support groups throughout the world.[65]

In addition to Google's efforts, JP Morgan Chase created "tools for applying anti-money-laundering protocols to human trafficking networks," because the two seem to be interconnected.[66] Both seem to "involve hidden financial transactions," and technology used to detect money laundering have been useful in discovering other unlawful activities.[67] "Homeland Security and JP Morgan officials developed a detailed M.O. for the banking habits of businesses involved in human smuggling for prostitution and other forms of forced labor," such as credit card transactions after business hours.[68] Further, LexisNexis has "been instrumental in promoting and introducing an array of technology driven tools to assist in detecting, monitoring, and researching human trafficking."[69] "In collaboration with the NHTRC, LexisNexis developed a national database of social service providers."[70] In addition to other actions to counteract human trafficking, LexisNexis created an online resource center for attorneys who work with human trafficking victims, and is working with the American Bar Association to establish a training institute on civil remedies for victims."[71]

C. Step 3: Federal Prosecution

Once victims of sex trafficking are identified and there has been an investigation, the final step in the process is to determine whether to prosecute a case or not. The criminal prosecution has been described as the "linchpin to eradicating human trafficking."[72] "[P]rosecution deters further trafficking, incapacitates current traffickers, and removes the powerful financial incentive to traffic."[73] The Department of Justice (DOJ) prosecutes cases involving human trafficking "through the 94 United States Attorney's Offices and two specialized units that serve as DOJ's nationwide subject-matter experts."[74] In addition to federal laws criminalizing sex trafficking, most states also have legislation specific to sex trafficking. State legislation allows for local law enforcement to be trained on sex trafficking provisions, so there is a greater chance that more victims would be identified in traditional venues for sex trafficking; however, the means of prosecution may not equate to those of federal agencies.[75] Some suggest that federal courts should be handling the prosecution of traffickers while states play more of a support role.[76] The interstate commerce element allows federal prosecutors to charge a greater amount of sex trafficking cases involving online activity under federal trafficking laws.[77] But, regardless of who prosecutes these cases, the challenge of identifying hidden victims must first be overcome.

In 2014, the Department of Justice charged 335 people in 208 federal human trafficking cases, and 184 traffickers were convicted.

Source: Trafficking in Persons Report, July 2015

In an effort to counteract human trafficking and identify more victims, in 2000 the federal government passed the Victim of Trafficking and Violence Protection Act (VTVPA).[78] The Trafficking Victims Protection Act (TVPA), a provision of VTVPA, was "the first comprehensive federal law in the United States that tackles the issue of human trafficking through a three-tier approach of prevention, prosecution, and protection."[79] The purpose of this Act is "to combat trafficking in persons, a contemporary manifestation of slavery whose victims are predominantly women and children, to ensure just and effective punishment of traffickers, and to protect their victims."[80] It provides an increase in penalties with sentencing enhancements while increasing the protections for victims.[81] Additionally, this Act "strengthened the federal government's ability to prosecute traffickers."[82] It "added four new criminal offenses to the U.S. Criminal Code: (1) forced labor; (2) trafficking with respect to peonage, slavery, involuntary servitude, or forced labor; (3) sex trafficking[;] and (4) the unlawful seizure of documents in furtherance of trafficking[,]" and "expanded the definition of coercion to include psychological coercion."[83] The chart below breaks down the elements that need to be proven for federal crimes that a sex trafficker could be charged with.

In cases where sex trafficking is taking place online, the advertisements are instrumental to satisfying the elements of each of these crimes. However, the cooperation of the victims is just as important in proving that coercion existed, unless the victim is under the age of 18. Using programs like Memex will pro-

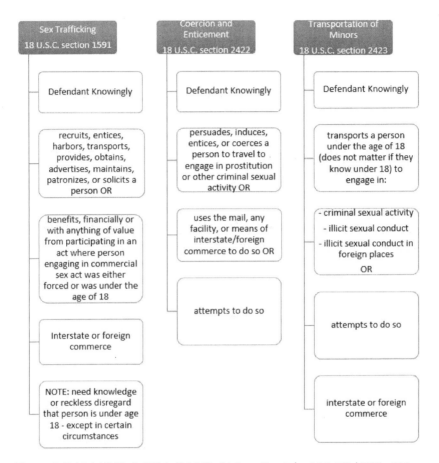

Figure 6.5 *18 U.S.C. § 1591 (2015); U.S. v. Daniels, 653 F.3d 399, 411 (6th Cir. 2011) 18 U.S.C. § 2422 (2006); 18 U.S.C. § 2423 (2015).*

vide evidence against a trafficker, rather than relying on the word of a victim against the word of the trafficker. Traffickers' use of the Internet, whether it is the Surface Web or the Dark Web, is enough to fulfill the interstate commerce requirement needed for a federal prosecution.

The Commerce Clause gives Congress power to regulate three types of activity: (1) "the use of channels of interstate commerce;" (2) "the instrumentalities of interstate commerce, or persons or things in interstate commerce, even though the threat may come only from intrastate activities;" and (3) "those activities having substantial relation to interstate commerce, … i.e., those activities that substantially affect interstate commerce."[84]

In addressing whether interstate commerce has been established, "because of the very interstate nature of the Internet, once a user submits a connection request to a website server or an image is transmitted from the website server back to user, the data has traveled in interstate commerce."[85] Though this is a case involving child pornography, the Court came to the conclusion that "the Internet is an instrumentality and channel of interstate commerce" and that it is "a system that is inexorably intertwined with interstate commerce."[86] In a case where a man was charged under 18 U.S.C. § 1591, the Court determined that the TVPA "deals with commerce within the power of Congress to regulate."[87] This case involved the use of Craigslist to advertise the sex trafficking victims, which includes advertising across state lines.[88]

There are several cases that can be found where traffickers were using the Internet to advertise their trafficking victims, enabling the federal government to establish that the Commerce Clause has been satisfied. Given the information provided from these cases, in theory if sex trafficking is taking place on the Internet, then the element involving interstate commerce can always be satisfied. Even if interstate commerce is triggered by the use of the Internet (an instrumentality of interstate commerce), which means that because a case can be prosecuted federally, this does not mean that federal law enforcement and federal prosecutors will take the case on.

6.4 What Can Practitioners Do to Aid in this Process?

If practitioners are looking to assist in criminal prosecutions of traffickers, there are a few things that they can do to aid investigations. Going through the process as described above, the first step is to identify a victim. If a practitioner comes into contact with an individual they suspect is a victim of trafficking, he or she should listen to the victim and take them at their word. Practitioners may find they are soon out of their depth with the amount of issues and trauma a victim may be experiencing. Therefore, contact with a local service provider who specializes in these types of cases should be initiated as soon as possible. If a practitioner is unaware of what resources are available in their area, they may contact local state agencies, or call the National Human Trafficking Resource Center at 1-888-373-7888 (USA).

When preparing for prosecution, evidence is always key: The more evidence the better. But, practitioners, particularly those working in a law enforcement capacity such as district attorneys or federal prosecutors, should understand that a victim may be unwilling to talk with anyone until a trust relationship can be established, due to victims' real or imagined beliefs about authority figures (which can arise as a result of their traffickers' psychological manipulation tactics). Specifically in cases involving the Internet, if a victim can provide their advertisement, such evidence should be preserved by printing or writing down any and all contact information. If a state or federal investigation commences, technical professionals may be able to assist with obtaining additional information, even if an ad or website is taken down or removed.

Endnotes

1. Mark Latonero, *Human Trafficking Online: The Role of Social Networking Sites and Online Classifieds*, Ctr. on Commc'n Leadership & Policy, 17 (2011).

2. Abby R. Perer, *Policing the Virtual Red Light District: A Legislative Solution to the Problems of Internet Prostitution and Sex Trafficking*, 77 Brook. L. Rev. 823, 828 (2012).

3. Mary Graw Leary, *Fighting Fire with Fire: Technology in Child Sex Trafficking*, 21 Duke J. Gender L. & Pol'y 289, 290 (2014); Kendall Vitale, *Barricading the Information Superhighway to Stop the Flow of Traffic: Why International Regulation of the Internet is Necessary to Prevent Sex Trafficking*, 27 Am. U. Int'l L. Rev. 91, 107 (2012).

4. Vitale, *supra* note 3, at 109.

5. Latonero, *supra* note 1, at iv; Leary, *supra* note 3, at 309 ("The 2013 TIP Report noted that '[a]s technology and globalization make the world more interconnected traffickers' ability to recruit and exploit their victims was also intensified'").

6. Leary, *supra* note 3, at 310.

7. Drew Olanoff, "Thorn to Set Up an Innovation Lab in Silicon Valley to Fight Child Sex Trafficking," *Tech Crunch* (Nov. 12, 2015); Definition of "sextortion," Collins Dictionary.

8. Latonero, *supra* note 1, at 15; Leary, *supra* note 3, at 313.

9. Vitale, *supra* note 3, at 109.

10. Leary, *supra* note 3, at 309.

11. Herbert B. Dixon, Jr., "Human Trafficking and the Internet* (*and Other Techonologies, too)," *The Judges' Journal*, ABA.

12. Marissa Louie, "Craigslist Saga: The Great Migration of Sex Trafficking Ads," *Huffington Post* (Jan. 13, 2011, 3:16 p.m.); Perer, *supra* note 2, at 830 (Craigslist was not legally required by under the Communications Decency Act of 1996 (CDA) and correlating case law to shut down its Adult Services

category. The CDA was Congress' first act trying to regulate Internet activity. Section 223 and 230 of the CDA were enacted in response to online sex sales).

13. Louie, *supra* note 12 (A list of websites competing with Craigslist and the amount of money made off of sex advertisements includes: (1) Backpage, $20 million; (2) Eros.com, $6.8 million; (3) CityVibe.com, $3 million; (4) Escots.com, $265,000; and (5) MyRedBook.com, $230,00).

14. *Id.*

15. Esme Murphy, "Talking Points: Child Sex Trafficking & Backpage.com," CBS Minn.; "Backpage.com Lawsuit: Judge Stops Age Verification in Sex-Related Ads," *Huffington Post* (July 28, 2012) [hereinafter *Lawsuit*]; Kevin Dolak, "Three Teens Sue BackPage.com over Sex Trafficking," *abcNEWS* (July 30, 2012).

16. Dolak, *supra* note 15.

17. *Id.*

18. Perer, *supra* note 2, at 828.

19. Latonero, *supra* note 1, at 18.

20. Tammie Fields, "Backpage.com: A haven for underage prostitution?" 10NEWS (May 14, 2013).

21. Latonero, *supra* note 1, at 18.

22. Fields, *supra* note 20.

23. Larry Greenemeier, "Human Traffickers Caught on Hidden Internet," *Scientific American* (Feb. 8, 2015).

24. Browniee, *supra* note 23.

25. Greenemeier, *supra* note 25.

26. Browniee, *supra* note 23.

27. Wendy Boswell, "How to Access the Dark Web," (July 24, 2014); "What is Dark Internet, How to Access Onion Domains and Configure Hosting for the Dark Web" (June 25, 2011).

28. Lev Grossman & Jay Newton Small, "The Secret Web: When Drugs, Porn, and Murder Live Online," *TIME* (Nov. 11, 2013).

29. "Human Trafficking, a Tale of Misery," Hidden Wiki, (http://www.hidden-wiki.org/human-trafficking.html) [hereinafter *Misery*].

30. Will Tucker, "Tech-Savvy Drug Traffickers Using the Deep Web," *The Bulletin* (July 21, 2013, 5:00 am).

31. Latonero, *supra* note 1, at 19.

32. Stockley, *supra* note 24.

33. Sex Trafficking, Nat'l Human Trafficking Res. Ctr.

34. Grace Caffyn, "Bitcoin on the Dark Web: The Facts," CoinDesk (Sept. 23, 2015), Kate Cox, "Bitcoin: What the Heck Is It, and How Does It Work?" *Consumerist* (Mar. 4, 2014).

35. Cox, *supra* note 38.

36. Reuben Grinberg, *Bitcoin: An Innovative Alternative Digital Currency*, 4 Hastings Sci. & Tech. L.J. 159, 162 (2012).

37. *Id.*

38. *Id.*

39. *Id.*

40. Trevor Murphy, "The Big Problem with Bitcoin Regulations," CNBC (Nov. 20, 2014).

41. Greenemeier, *supra* note 25.

42. *Id.*

43. Wade Shen, *Memex*, Def. Advanced Research Projects Agency (http://www.darpa.mil/program/memex); Stockley, *supra* note 24.

44. Greenemeier, *supra* note 25.

45. Wade Shen, *Memex*, DARPA (http://www.darpa.mil/program/memex).

46. Greenemeier, *supra* note 25.

47. Shen, *supra* note 52.

48. "DARPA Memex: How It Works and What It's Up To – Really," DARK-NETPAGES (Sept. 18, 2015).

49. Christian de Looper, "Memex Is DARPA's Latest Tool to Search Dark Web, Catch Human Traffickers," *Tech Times* (Feb. 16, 2012, 5:20 am).

50. Nicole Arce, "Meet Memex, DARPA's Dark Web Search Engine: What Can It Do That Google Cannot?" *Tech Times* (Feb. 14, 205).

51. *Id.*

52. Anthony Cuthbertson, "Death of the Dark Web? DARPA's Memex Search Engine Allows Tor Tracking," *IBTimes* (Feb. 16, 2015).

53. Greenemeier, *supra* note 25.

54. Stephanie Mlot, "DARPA Search Engine Battles the Dark Web, Human Trafficking," *PC* (Feb. 13, 2015).

55. Greenemeier, *supra* note 25.

56. Stockley, *supra* note 24.

57. "Man Sentenced to 50 Years to Life After Woman Forced Into Prostitution Jumps From Sixth-Story Window," CBS New York (Sept. 3, 2014).

58. *Id.*

59. Greenemeier, *supra* note 25.

60. Olanoff, *supra* note 7.

61. *Id.*

62. Derrick Harris, "DARPA-funded Research IDs Sex Traffickers With Machine Learning," *Gigaom* (Jan. 13, 2015); Dixon, *supra* note 11.

63. *Id.*; "UPDATE: Helping Human Trafficking and Modern Day Slavery Victims Around the World," Google Pub/ Policy Blog (Jan. 12, 2015).

64. Jigsaw (https://jigsaw.google.com/vision/).

65. Katie Fehrenbacher, "Data can help fight human trafficking, here's how," GIGAOM (Mar. 19, 2014).

66. Dixon, *supra* note 11.

67. "Private-Sector Initiatives," Tech. & Human Trafficking [hereinafter *Private*]; Michael Hudson, "JPMorgan Chase's record highlights doubts about big banks' devotion to fighting dirty money flows," The Int'l Consortium of Investigative Journalists (Apr. 30, 2013); *Private*, *supra* note 74.

69. Dixon, *supra* note 11.

70. *Private*, *supra* note 74.

71. *Id.*

72. Eileen Overbaugh, *Human Trafficking: The Need for Federal Prosecution of Accused Traffickers*, 39 Seton Hall L. Rev. 635, 642 (2009).

73. *Id.*; 18 U.S.C. § 1593 (2008) (mandatory restitution); 18 U.S.C. § 1594 (2015) (forfeiture of assets).

74. U.S. Dep't of State, Trafficking in Persons Report, 53, 353 (July 2015), http://www.state.gov/documents/organization/245365.pdf [hereinafter Report].

75. Stephanie Richard, *State Legislation and Human Trafficking: Helpful or Harmful?* 38 U.Mich.J.L. Reform 447, 459, 460 (2005).

76. Overbaugh, *supra* note 79, at 661-662 (The supportive role that this law review article suggests entails: State and local prosecutors should be active members on task forces with federal officials, high-level prosecutors should attend meeting with the local U.S. Attorney to share information on potential human trafficking cases, local agencies should continue to provide

information to other agencies, precursor crimes such as identity theft and/or promoting prostitution should be prosecuted, lower level trafficking crimes should be prosecuted as instructed by the U.S. Attorney, and there should be an agreement between local prosecutors and federal prosecutors to refer cases to one another under the right circumstances).

77. Latonero, *supra* note 1, at 20.

78. Richard, *supra* note 82, at 448.

79. *Id.* at 451.

80. 22 U.S.C.A. § 7101(a) (2000).

81. Richard, *supra* note 82, at 451.

82. Marisa Nack, The Next Step: *The Future of New York State's Human Trafficking Law*, 18 J.L. & Pol'y 817, 826 (2010).

83. *Id.* at 826-27.

84. *United States v. MacEwan*, 445 F.3d 237, 244 (3d Cir. 2006).

85. *MacEwan*, 445 F.3d at 244.

86. *Id.*at 245.

87. *United States v. Todd*, 627 F.3d 329, 333 (9th Cir. 2010).

88. *Todd*, 627 F.3d at 333.

Part III
Special Issues

Chapter 7

Using the New Social Influence Model (SIM) to Pursue Justice for Trafficking Victims

By Nora M. Cronin and Alan W. Scheflin

7.1 Introduction: Trafficking Victims Are Victimized Twice—by the Trafficker and by the Legal System

The 13th Amendment prohibits "involuntary servitude," but few other laws actually give teeth to this laudable moral principle when it involves human trafficking. The result is that girls, boys, women, and men who are trafficked are often victimized twice.

The first victimization occurs when the traffickers lure, induce, coerce, and eventually convert the innocent into the injured. Trafficked persons suffer physical, emotional, and sexual exploitation so severe and dehumanizing that it is even difficult to speak about, because the public cannot stand to learn or hear about it.

The second victimization occurs when the trafficked persons encounter the legal system.

In general, there are three situations in which victims and courts interact:

(1) The trafficked victim may be seeking legal redress against a trafficker in a civil context, such as a wage and hour claim for unpaid labor
(2) The trafficked person may appear as a witness against their trafficker in a criminal context
(3) And finally, the victim themselves may be facing criminal charges.

7.2 Force, Fraud, and Coercion in the Context of Human Trafficking

The terms "fraud" and "coercion" should be familiar to legal practitioners, as they are among the common elements in many human trafficking statutes worldwide. As Professor Kathleen Kim points out in her excellent article, "The Coercion of Trafficked Workers" (2011), these elements were created as contradictions in jurisprudence regarding whether the "force" element required in prior involuntary servitude claims needed to rise to the level of physical force.[1]

The U.S. Trafficking Victim's Protection Act (TVPA), enacted in 2000, and the first piece of federal legislation to target these criminal actions, defines "severe forms of trafficking in persons" (22 U.S.C. § 7102) as:

• Sex trafficking: The recruitment, harboring, transportation, provision, obtaining, patronizing, or soliciting of a person for the purpose of a commercial sex act which is induced by force, fraud, or coercion. Any child under the age of 18 who has been subjected to a commercial sex act is a victim of trafficking regardless of force, fraud, or coercion.

• Labor trafficking: The recruitment, harboring, transportation, provision, or obtaining of a person for labor or services, through the use of force, fraud, or coercion for the purpose of subjection to involuntary servitude, peonage, debt bondage, or slavery.

Congress has voted to reauthorize the Act in 2003, 2005, and 2008. Since then, a majority of states have created local statutes under their criminal code. For purposes of comparison, consider the states such as New York, California, Texas, and others listed in the comparative charts found in the Appendices of this book. All have written their trafficking statutes with some nod to the elements of force, fraud, or coercion used in the federal law.

Internationally, the Palermo Protocol, to which the United States is a signatory, also uses these key terms in its definition of "trafficking in persons":

> [R]ecruitment, transportation, transfer, harbouring or receipt of persons, by means of the threat or use of force or other forms of coercion, of abduction, of fraud, of deception, of the abuse of power or of a position of vulnerability or of the giving or receiving of payments or benefits to achieve the consent of a person having control over another person, for the purpose of exploitation. Exploitation shall include, at a minimum, the exploitation of the prostitution of others or other forms of sexual exploitation, forced labour or services, slavery or practices similar to slavery, servitude or the removal of organs.

But, there is little guidance as to what these terms actually mean in practice. And so legal practitioners who practice in jurisdictions where force, fraud, or coercion are elements of the crime of trafficking may find an understanding of undue influence to be helpful in showing that this undue influence is, in fact, the element of coercion that is required to be met in order to sustain a trafficking conviction.

Due to the fact that traffickers profit from the exploitation of keeping their victims in the shadows, many victims find that they themselves are the ones being arrested and prosecuted for criminal activity engaged in at the behest of their traffickers. So, rather than a depth of case law of trafficking cases, instead we have a population of low-level offenders who are actually the victims of undue influence—force, fraud, and coercion—at the hands of their traffickers.

In particular, victims of sex trafficking are arrested and prosecuted at a far greater rate than their traffickers for the low-level crimes of prostitution, loitering for the purposes of prostitution, and misdemeanor weapons or drug possession charges. Victims of labor trafficking are seen as perhaps being victims of their own choices, such as moving to a country "illegally" and facing the consequences through their inability to find paying work, or work that pays a fair wage.

Numerous jurisdictions have already begun to recognize that these individuals need special treatment under our law. Jurisdictions such as New York State have begun to innovate through the court system by creating "Human Trafficking Intervention Courts," which are discussed at length in Chapter 3 in this book.

Through the decisions of these courts,[2] vacatur has become a popular remedy for victims who have found themselves saddled with criminal convictions as a result of their human trafficking situations. However, vacatur as a necessary condition requires that a criminal conviction has already attached. Even a misdemeanor conviction or merely having an "open case" can have devastating consequences for a victim when seeking future employment, resolving custody disputes over children, and obtaining housing.

These economic and social consequences may often pale in comparison to the psychological consequences of a conviction for a person who is labeled a criminal in the eyes of the justice system, on top of a victim's often already marginalized place in society. As Judge Toko Serita, who currently sits in the Queens County Human Trafficking Intervention Court, wrote in 2013:

> On any given Friday in my courtroom, you will see rows and rows of female and, occasionally, transgender defendants who are present to answer to prostitution charges. The majority are American-born young black or Latina women, or older foreign-born Asian women. There is also a growing number of gay male and transgender female defendants... Virtually all of the cases before my court involve low-level prostitution offenses taking place on the street, or in brothels, massage parlors, and hotels targeted by law enforcement.[3]

On the other hand, traffickers themselves are rarely prosecuted because they need not be directly involved in the criminal activity, since their victims do this work for them. Even though many states have anti-trafficking laws as part of their penal code, the number of cases brought by prosecutors remains small for a variety of reasons—including resources needed to conduct the type of large-scale investigations required in trafficking cases, prosecutorial uncertainty and avoidance of risk, and general lack of familiarity with the laws due to the low number of attorneys with experience with these cases, which leads to a vicious circle of inaction in this area of prosecution.[4]

Another possible reason these cases are rarely brought may be due to the lack of available witnesses to testify against their traffickers. As described above, once a person has encountered the justice system as a defendant, there may be understandable reluctance to engage as a witness, even though they were always truly a victim of their trafficker.

7. 3 Getting to the Undue Influence Defense in Courts

There is a great history of creative thinking being used to apply existing laws to problems, seemingly without legal remedies, in the name of social justice. Today, in cities across the country, tenants living in apartments enjoy and take for granted rights bestowed to them by law despite not being landowners themselves. These protections are not an accident, nor were they created by design (although they have certainly been strengthened) through legislation. These rights are based in contract law, and if it hadn't been for a lawyer working in Washington, D.C. in the 1960s, these rights may never have been articulated for tenants.

Florence Roisman represented tenants living in squalid apartment buildings owned by wealthy slumlords. In case after case, she successfully appealed to the hearts of the judges, but not to their minds. Their message to her was that she was presenting a case of property law, and it is clear that the owners of property have all the legal rights. Her clients had none. One day, however, everything changed. Florence entered the courtroom and said in essence that, "I am not here arguing the law of *property*. I am arguing under the law of *contracts*. My clients have a right to habitable dwellings; otherwise, the rent contracts they signed are illusory." The judges similarly answered, "Oh, you are arguing contract law. That is an entirely different thing."

Notice that the facts of the squalor in which Ms. Roisman's clients were living did not change— only the legal theory that she used to argue for redress. Roisman won her case, and within a decade every state in the country required landlords to supply tenants with decent sanitary dwellings because every contract for housing carried with it a judicially created, implied warranty of habitability.

With the spirit of the story of Florence Roisman and her triumph in mind, it would be worth reconsidering the concept of undue influence as a way to:

(1) Allow victims to attain civil redress against their traffickers
(2) Explain why a victim may not be criminally liable for actions done on behalf of or for the benefit of their traffickers
(3) Or, from a prosecutorial perspective, to satisfy the elements of force, fraud, or coercion required to be shown in trafficking prosecutions, through evidence demonstrating that the trafficker exerted undue influence over their victim.

Using the concept of undue influence would help not only in philosophically understanding trafficking victims, but would position these victims for potential legal remedies as well. However, in order for undue influence to be able to be introduced as evidence in a trafficking case—either to show lack of criminal liability or as evidence of force, fraud, or coercion—it first has to be allowed as evidence in court, which will take some finessing.

A. Distinguishing Undue Influence and Brainwashing

Florence Roisman's strategy of describing an old problem in a different way found support in the world of cult victimization. Because the operative term for cult involvement had been "brainwashing," there were several problems that prevented victims from getting legal remedies. Trafficking victims may also be seen as having been "brainwashed," but using that term will frustrate getting legal relief. In tort law, a plaintiff cannot bring a case directly alleging that they have suffered a loss as a result of brainwashing—no causes of action or civil remedies exist to redress that particular wrongdoing. Additionally, using brainwashing as a defense to criminal liability is virtually without precedent.

As a federal appellate court noted when a defendant attempted to introduce such a theory in the context of a murder conviction due to a severe dietary restriction placed on members of a religious organization ("Cult-brainwashing arguments rarely succeed"),[5] judges often look at such theories at best as an argument of last resort, or at worst as an admission that no other recognized theory will help the client.

Furthermore, many experts who have attempted to testify about the extreme influence that a cult leader may have over their client inevitably fail the *Daubert* test of admissibility:

1) Whether the expert's theory or technique can be tested;
2) Whether the expert's theory or technique has been subjected to publication or peer review;
3) Whether the expert's testimony has a known error rate; and
4) Whether the expert's testimony or technique is generally accepted in the relevant scientific community.[6]

Experts must be able to support their opinions with the relevant scientific literature. To the extent that "brainwashing" fits into virtually no legal category, it is difficult for experts to qualify, even if the science exists to support their views. In that way, the juridical concept closes the courthouse doors to the relevant science that might have opened an avenue for legal relief via this defense for victims.

Brainwashing may be mistakenly understood by some practitioners to be, in fact, no different than undue influence; however, brainwashing is best understood as a colorful description for extreme social processes that have occurred at times in history, and have been invoked by attorneys to show how their client's free will has been overcome to explain often inexplicable behavior.

B. Solution: Undue Influence As a Defense

The California Supreme Court, in the 2002 case *Rice v. Clark*, has defined undue influence as "pressure brought to bear directly on the testamentary act, sufficient to overcome the testator's free will, amounting in effect to coercion destroying the testator's free agency."[7] If the influencer is determined and clever enough, and the techniques used are sophisticated and powerful enough, or well-hidden, experts believe that few people will be able to resist becoming victims of undue influence. Likewise, it is arguable that almost everyone, under certain circumstances, is potentially vulnerable to undue influence.

Therefore, the undue influence doctrine should not be limited to cases involving wills or other financial misdeeds. The shift by influencers from targeting bank accounts to targeting ideas, beliefs, identities, and, in fact, entire life cycles, makes the undue influence doctrine of even more immediate concern. Courts may now be willing to accept that this undue influence satisfies the coercion element in many human trafficking statutes, as the *Rice* case indicates how undue influence amounts in effect to coercion.

But, when undue influence escapes from the confines in which it was largely contained in trusts and estates law, a very serious issue arises: where to draw the line. There are no clear demarcations as one passes from guidance, to advice, to education, to suggestion, to seduction, to indoctrination, to thought-reform. And the concept itself of "policing" thoughts and actions that are not, in and of themselves, prohibited by law may give some pause.

The policy behind the law—rather than the law itself—may be a helpful area of focus. The law of undue influence must find what may be called *the point of unacceptable interaction*. This point occurs when one might witness someone's conduct and think, *"You just can't treat people like that. And if you do, the law will step in and you will be punished."*

In all civil cases, the person who brings the lawsuit is saying that the status quo is wrong and the court should remedy it. That person has the burden of proving that the judge should step in and not just leave the parties in their current situation. No law could ever precisely, and in advance, define when the judge should act, because each fact pattern is unique. But an informal test might be an articulation of the idea that "You just can't treat people like that," and that the evidence and science must support that claim.

There are two analogies in law that help us understand this perspective. The law of contracts recognizes the concept of *unconscionability*. When two people meet to bargain and eventually sign a contract that memorializes their final agreement, the law will enforce this contract because it was a mutually agreed-upon exchange. The fact that one party gets the better deal is not a sufficient reason to decide that the contract should not be enforced. But what if the agreement is grossly unfair, as was the case in the situations Florence Roisman argued for her tenant-clients? Unfairness generally is not judicially remedied. However, if the unfairness is a product of exploitation, to the point at which a person's vulnerability has been so compromised that the choices made cannot be considered to have been voluntary, judges will declare the contract void.

The other analogy involves the law of torts. Courts have long recognized the tort of intentional infliction of emotional distress. In these cases, one person's behavior toward another is so morally and socially outrageous that it "shocks the conscience" and demands judicial redress.

Unconscionability cases and intentional-infliction-of-emotional-distress cases have precisely the same sliding-scale problem as do the undue-influence cases. All of them are resolved with a "shock the conscience" test that basically says, "You cannot treat another person that way." Arguably, all three types of cases involve the point of unacceptable interaction. It is generally the function of triers of fact, be they judges or juries, to decide when that point has been reached.

C. The Freedom of Choice Paradox

One may argue that the only true way to protect freedom of thought is not to interfere with it at all. People make decisions; let them be bound by them. There is a very strong preference in the law for free will, individual autonomy, and holding people accountable for their choices. And this is a good thing—it protects the right to be oneself. For this reason, there is reluctance to expand the scope of justifications and excuses to override choices, no matter how unfortunate those choices might turn out for the person who made them.

This judicial hands-off policy clearly pits undue influence against freedom of choice. Thus we have a paradox: Courts are asked to protect your freedom of choice by *denying* or *altering* the choices you already made. In the context of a human trafficking case, one can say—and some advocates argue it is the right of an individual to do so—that a man or a woman made the choice of their free will to become engaged in selling sex for money. But what if that individual lacked the autonomy to make that decision because of undue influence?

Some states, including California, used to have a test for answering these questions. The test was whether the influencee had been duped by an "artful and designing person." In its Dickensian language, this test attracts our attention to the key ingredients of undue influence—a vulnerable victim outmatched by a self-interested and clever manipulator.

But whatever the test, the paradox remains. Do you protect freedom of mind by upholding the choices actually made, or by undoing the decisions on the grounds that they were the product of a sophisticated fraud?

7.4 Use of the Concept of Undue Influence in Court

A. Social Influence Model (SIM)

The Social Influence Model (SIM) was first devised by Professor Alan Scheflin in 2015 for use by experts who would be giving in-court testimony.[8] The SIM was based on the older but rarely used SODR test, named for its following four elements:

(a) **S**usceptibility to undue influence
(b) **O**pportunity to exert influence
(c) **D**isposition to exert influence
(d) **R**esult of the influence.

The Social Influence Model (SIM), on the other hand, is designed to accommodate several different goals. First, it is layperson-friendly. It succinctly conveys the relevant dimensions of an influence process, and it does so in an understandable manner. Second, it is expert-friendly. The SIM allows the presentation of the relevant science that supports mind manipulation. It provides a way to simplify complex studies and present them more easily. Third, it is judge-friendly. Judges who research or preside over undue influence cases may be familiar with the SODR test. Because the SIM is similar to the SODR test, it will more likely be accepted as an appropriate vehicle for the presentation of factual and scientific evidence. Finally, the SIM lends itself to visual learning. Lawyers can make a chart of the SIM to aid jurors (and judges) in seeing how they may assess and understand the evidence. Thus, it serves as an effective persuasive tool.

Here is the SIM:

(a) INFLUENCER (Identity and Status)
(b) INFLUENCER'S MOTIVES (Purpose)
(c) INFLUENCER'S METHODS (Techniques)
(d) CIRCUMSTANCES (Timing and Setting)
(e) INFLUENCEE'S RECEPTIVITY/VULNERABILITY (Individual Differences)
(f) CONSEQUENCES (Results)

B. Using the SIM to Present Evidence in a Trafficking Case

Some examples of how the SIM may be used to present expert scientific evidence in court include:

(a) INFLUENCER (Relationship to the Influencee) [WHO]

Authority Figure
Confidential Relationship
Advisor
Family Member

(b) INFLUENCER'S MOTIVES (Purpose) [WHY]
Financial Gain
Behavioral Acquiescence
Ideological Adherence
Ego Gratification
Political or Social Power

(c) INFLUENCER'S METHODS [WHAT/HOW]
"Foot in the Door" [Small request, then larger one]
"Door-in-the Face" [Large request, then small one]
"Help Me Help You"
"Won't You Help?"
"Don't You Want to Do the Right Thing?"
"I'm Really Depending on You"
"This May Be Your Only Chance"
"Everyone's Doing It" ["Don't Be Left Behind"]
"God Has Selected You"
"Love-Bombing"
"Grooming"/Progression of Seduction[9]
    –The Bait
    –Building Trust
    –Sweetening the Scam
    –Closing the Fraud

(d) CIRCUMSTANCES [WHERE/WHEN]
Location
Control of Physical Environment
Control of Information (Input and Output)
Access to Independent Advice
Frequency, Duration, and Nature of the Contacts

(e) INFLUENCEE'S RECEPTIVITY/VULNERABILITY [WHO][10]
Personality Type (Individual Differences)
Hypnotic Induction Profile (HIP)
Revised Stanford Profile Scales of Hypnotic Susceptibility, Forms I and II
Gudjonsson Suggestibility Scales

(f) CONSEQUENCES [WHAT]
Financial
Behavioral
Ideological

One can imagine the practical application in the defense of a client in court accused of drug sales, or any related charge done at the behest of a trafficker:

(a) **INFLUENCER** (Identity and Status): The trafficker is an individual the target has seen in the community; the trafficker is wealthy in an area that is mostly poor, and is able to have luxury items that the target themselves could not afford. In this way, the trafficker may be seen as an authority figure, or may establish a relationship as a mentor to an individual in a lower social standing.

(b) **INFLUENCER'S MOTIVES** (Purpose): Trafficker is motivated to maintain this status within the community, and to increase his or her own personal wealth.

(c) **INFLUENCER'S METHODS** (Techniques): Upon meeting the target, the trafficker immediately begins to build a trust relationship with their target. Then, when the trafficker needs something from the target, it is provided as part of an ongoing relationship of trust. The trafficker may say things to the target such as "I'm really counting on you…" or "You are the only person I can ask," adding to both the value and the sense of reliance on the part of the target, without the target knowing the true motive behind these requests.

(d) **CIRCUMSTANCES** (Timing and Setting): In many cases, the trafficker meets the target through social media and gets to know their needs and desires. Or, the target may be approached within the community in a public setting. This could be on the street, in a bar or club, or even be at an otherwise reputable institution, such as a school or church, making the encounter seem even less likely to have a nefarious purpose. The traffickers may be very likely to combine the meeting places with the target's needs and desires, such as bringing a young man who is having difficulty coming out to his family to a gay club, or taking a young woman who is unable to afford to buy clothes to a mall to go shopping.

(e) **INFLUENCEE'S RECEPTIVITY/VULNERABILITY** (Individual Differences): In this case, our influencee is the target in this case. Likely, for this model to be introduced in court, the expert who is providing this testimony would have the ability to assess the client based upon tests that are available to registered psychologists, such as the Gudjonsson Suggestibility Scale.

(f) CONSEQUENCES (Results): In the context of a trafficking case, the consequences for the trafficker are most often financial gain. Some tangible non-monetary results may also include ego gratification or enhanced community status. For the target, he or she may experience an ideological shift that may decrease his or her risk aversion, leading him or her to be more likely to engage in criminal activity. In some cases, individuals who would otherwise not be inclined to engage in sex work may do so at the behest of their traffickers. To demonstrate the extent of this influence, the sex work may not even correspond with the individual's own sexual identity.[11]

7. 5 Conclusion

While innovations do exist in trafficking cases—like New York's Human Trafficking Intervention Courts and the increasing number of vacatur motions on behalf of attorneys working with clients who have prior criminal convictions—these are solutions to problems created by the criminalization of behavior associated with trafficking, rather than the prevention of criminalizing this activity in the first place.

Some advocates may offer alternative solutions, such as eliminating the crimes that often bring trafficking victims into court in the first place. Decriminalizing prostitution is a popular suggestion, but there are serious objections that exist and have been cited elsewhere, including testimonials from women involved in sex work.[12] Additionally, legalizing prostitution says nothing for individuals who may be arrested because they were trafficking drugs on behalf of a trafficker, or carrying a weapon because they were afraid of their trafficker, or are victims of labor trafficking.

Introducing evidence that an individual was unduly influenced or coerced into engaging in behavior as a defense would allow an avenue for relief for these victims. Another potential step forward would be to craft these concepts into a portion of the penal code, so that rather than raising this as a defense at a later time, it would prevent victims of the heinous crime of trafficking from being treated like criminals in the first place.

Additionally, exploring this concept of undue influence will allow for acceptance as a defense in other types of cases not yet contemplated. There is simply no reason why an individual should be made to suffer once at the hands of their exploiters and again at the hands of the legal system.

Endnotes

1. Kim, *The Coercion of Trafficked Workers*, 96 Iowa L. Rev. 409 (2011).

2. *See, e.g., People v. G.M.*, 922 N.Y.S.2d 761 (Crim. Ct. 2011).

3. Serita, *In Our Own Backyards: The Need for a Coordinated Judicial Response to Human Trafficking*, N.Y.U. Rev. L. & Soc. Change 36 (2013), at 640.

4. *See, e.g.*, A. Farrell, et al., *The Prosecution of State-Level Human Trafficking Cases in the United States*, Anti-Trafficking Review, (2016).

5. *Robidoux v. O'Brien*, 643 F.3d 334 (2011).

6. *Daubert v. Merrell Dow Pharmaceuticals, Inc.*, 509 U.S. 579 (1993).

7. *Rice v. Clark*, 120 Cal.Rptr.2d 522 (2002).

8. Scheflin, *Supporting Human Rights by Testifying Against Human Wrongs*, International Journal of Cultic Studies 6 (2015), at 69-82. Thank you to Michael Langone and the publishers of IJCS for allowing the extensive use of the SIM in this article.

9. "Grooming" is a stage particularly relevant in trafficking cases, but there has been some movement away from the term because it suggests a positive result.

10. Brown, Scheflin, and Hammond identify six different types of compliance with suggestions:

    (a) Source Credibility
        Expertise
        Training and Experience
        Familiarity [agrees with your prior beliefs]
        Charisma

Authenticity/Sincerity
Perceived Status [Awards; Appointments]
(b) Post-Event Misinformation Effect
(c) Interrogatory Suggestibility
(d) Hypnotic Suggestibility
(e) Exposure to Systematic and Sustained Influences
(f) Brainwashing/Coercive Persuasion/Extreme Influence

From D. Brown, et al., *Memory, Trauma Treatment, and the Law* (W.W. Norton, 1998).

11. *See, e.g.*, Dank, et al., *Surviving the Streets of New York: Experiences of LGBTQ Youth, YMSM, and YWSW Engaged in Survival Sex*, Urban Institute Research Report, February 2015. http://www.urban.org/research/publication/surviving-streets-new-york-experiences-lgbtq-youth-ymsm-and-ywsw-engaged-survival-sex/view/full_report (last visited August 25, 2016).

12. Rachel G. Moran, Opinion, "Buying Sex Should Not Be Legal," *NY TIMES*, August 28, 2015, at A19.

Chapter 8

Trauma in Sex-Trafficked Children

By Melissa L. Breger[1]

Every minute, two children are sexually enslaved across the globe.[2] The psychological and physical trauma endured by these children is incalculable and often untold. Even if these children eventually escape their traffickers, they continue to suffer from the severe traumatic psychological and physical effects of being trafficked, and they are in need of rehabilitation and reintegration services. One trafficked child may be "sold" up to 30 times a day, subjecting the child each time to sexual assault that is often accompanied by physical violence. The child is typically relocated to new cities and states in order to prevent his or her detection or escape, and to provide "fresh faces" to "customers." Arguably, each and every time a child victim is sold to a "customer," that child experiences yet another assault on the body, the mind, and the soul.

Practitioners and judges should be aware of the short and long-term rehabilitation needs of trafficked children. Until resources are available to create and implement specialized rehabilitation services to care for every child victim of sex trafficking, practitioners and judges should be considering alternatives within their own jurisdictions, such as therapeutic foster homes.

The trauma of repeated sexual assaults is linked to a heightened prevalence of dissociative and post-traumatic symptoms. Studies have found that a

171

significant number of sex-trafficked children fit the psychological profile of an individual suffering from Post-Traumatic Stress Disorder (PTSD).[3] This is not dissimilar from the rate of PTSD suffered by sexually abused children, which studies estimate occurs in the majority of survivors.[4] Because there are poignant similarities between the traumas experienced by other vulnerable populations of children, especially those who have endured child sexual abuse or family violence, sex-trafficked children should be placed where those vulnerable children are often placed: in our foster care system, preferably therapeutic foster care.

8.1 The Epidemic of Child Sex Trafficking

Internationally, it is estimated that the human trafficking industry generates $32 billion in profits each year. Some sources suggest that between 600,000 to 800,000 children are trafficked and exploited by the global sex industry every year, while others argue that the number is actually two to three million children per year. In some parts of the globe, a human slave costs a mere $90. Unlike finite commodities that can only be sold once, human victims can be sold and re-sold multiple times, making human victims a more profitable "commodity" than drugs or weapons.

Focusing on recovery and rehabilitation is of paramount importance when addressing children who have been sex trafficked because the psychological, physical, and emotional traumas affect victims in deep, complex ways that are not easily addressed, healed, or mitigated.

Both the United Nations and the United States Department of State agree that although rehabilitation of child victims of sex trafficking is critical, it remains challenging. The Department of State has set forth what it calls the "Three R's" platform to restore trafficking victims: Rescue, Rehabilitate, and Reintegrate.[5] This approach recognizes that rescuing child victims from a cycle of exploitation is only the first step—rehabilitating the physical and mental traumas faced by these victims and then reintegrating them into society are key steps on a victim's journey to recovery. The United Nations Protocol to Prevent, Suppress, and Punish Trafficking in Persons, a 2011 Directive from the European Union, and the Council of Europe Convention, similarly conclude that victim care and support are essential to rehabilitation.[6] "[A]ppropriate housing; legal advice in the victim's language; medical, psychological and material assistance; and employment, educational, and training opportunities" are some of the services that should be provided to trafficking victims to help aid in their recovery.[7] Additionally, child victims' special needs must be taken into account when considering the rehabilitative services best suited to assist in their recovery.

There are successful and long-standing rescue and rehabilitation programs and non-governmental organizations (NGOs) that are specifically tailored to sex-trafficked children in New York City, Los Angeles, Europe, Israel, and Asia, just to name a few.[8] Yet, funding and access to such highly specialized programs — particularly in rural or remote places — can be limited or not possible.

Because there is the salient nexus between the inherent sexual violence of trafficking and the sexual violence prevalent in family violence and childhood sexual abuse, we should adapt current infrastructures and services provided for child victims of sexual violence, as the first step to work toward rehabilitation of sex-trafficked children.

8.2 The Therapeutic Foster Care Model in the United States

The United States has a state governmental program already in place that can be modified to assist trafficked children — specifically, a sophisticated and long-running foster care system. Within that system, there are specialized options for children with special needs in what is called Therapeutic Foster Care (TFC). Therapeutic Foster Care provides a higher level of intense, specialized care for the child being served. The therapeutic foster family is provided extensive training on the needs of the child and offered additional supportive services not typically available to other types of foster homes and foster parents. Therapeutic foster parents are also teamed with various mental health professionals, who are trained to assist special needs youth.

In general, foster care in the United States is provided through the social services system and offers temporary care to children whose parents cannot care for them. Foster care systems, while often funded in part federally, are generally run within the state system. Almost all foster care systems include general foster care, kinship care, specialized foster care, and therapeutic foster care, along with group homes and other organized group living situations.

The foster care system began in the United States in the late 19th century, when Americans became aware of the deplorable conditions that orphans were experiencing in institutional housing, colloquially referred to as orphanages. As a solution to this problem, a system of "free foster homes" was developed. Foster homes were intended to provide full-time services and homes to children who were unable to remain with their birth families.

Foster homes and the foster care system are based upon a trauma-informed level of care, and it is presumed that children entering foster care have experienced some level of trauma or significant neglect. Not all children who have been routed to foster care experience exactly the same type of trauma. There are two types of trauma commonly experienced by children within the foster care system: acute trauma and complex trauma.[9] Acute trauma is caused by a single traumatic event. Complex trauma is the result of multiple traumatic incidents and experiences by an individual. Though acute trauma can certainly have long-lasting effects upon an individual, the effects of complex trauma, especially on children, are even more devastating.[10]

Foster parents, especially therapeutic foster parents, need to understand trauma effects. In fact, the success of the foster care system is dependent on the strengths of the foster parents who care for these children. As author Margaret Zukoski explains, "Foster parents are the backbone of the foster care system."[11] Even after certification, foster parents are typically required to take a certain number of training hours related to youth and children on a yearly basis.

Ultimately, the premise of the foster care system is that when it is not safe for children to reside with their own birth families, the ideal setting for most children is in a family-like setting. A foster family cares for the child temporarily with the ultimate goal that the child will return to the birth family. If the courts find it is not safe for the child(ren) to reunite with the birth family, or it is not possible to reunite with the birth family, the foster parents are often given the option to adopt the children in their homes.

TFC is a family-based form of treatment for children who need a higher level of care. Typically, these homes are tailored to children with emotional challenges and can be less costly than other forms of treatment, such as residential group treatment. States differ in the nomenclature (some refer to therapeutic homes as specialized homes or some other title) and states also differ in the delivery and set-up of therapeutic foster homes. Generally speaking, however:

> Youth who cannot live at home are placed in a foster home in which foster parents are trained to provide a structured environment for learning, social, and emotional skills. Youth in the program are monitored at home, in school, and in leisure activity; program personnel work closely with foster parents, and may collaborate with teachers, probation officers, employers, and others in the youth's environment to ensure prosocial learning and behavior.12

As one author describes it, the TFC approach "has been conceived to combine all of the best, family-centered features of traditional foster care with the most current and vigorous youth treatment methods available."[13] Another author explains that TFC programs generally have seven primary features. These include:

1. Care that is provided in a family setting
2. A focus on children who have special needs, who would otherwise be placed in more restrictive settings
3. A commitment to individualized and community-based treatment

4. Special and ongoing support and training for foster care parents, who are considered to be members of the treatment team
5. Restriction on the number of foster children placed in the family, generally limiting placement to one or two children
6. Limiting caseworker's caseloads to 10–15 children
7. Higher reimbursement for foster parents.[14]

TFC is typically a foster home with a family-like setting, but one that includes highly trained foster parents working with mental health professionals. When these models were initially devised, they were targeted towards children with behavioral disturbances. Yet, in the preface of the seminal book trilogy about TFC,[15] the authors state that they aim to "both motivate and guide professionals in the development of state-of-the-art therapeutic foster care programs for not only disturbed and conduct-disordered youngsters, but also for youngsters and oldsters with other problems."[16] The TFC model was created to be replicated and expanded.

When we are addressing sex-trafficked children, TFC programs might be a closer fit than traditional standard foster care programs to start the healing process. The goal of TFC and the desired outcome is for the child to achieve permanency within a family-based living situation where the child is safe, has his or her needs met, and has the opportunity to grow and achieve his or her potential. Children are placed in a therapeutic foster home, while collaborative treatment is provided by a team of professionals and caregivers, typically consisting of a mental health counselor, a psychiatrist or a psychologist, the foster parents, and the agency caseworker. Individual therapy can be provided to the child in order to focus on healing issues from any sexual, emotional, and physical abuse, as well as issues of loss and separation. Therapeutic foster parents are given intensive training on helping children cope with trauma, coupled with supportive supervision by trained professionals to help children work on traumatic issues. The collaborative team fosters an atmosphere where the child can acknowledge feelings, develop self-esteem, and practice open communication. Ideally, these services would be linked to NGOs that are already focused upon child sex trafficking.

Studies that examined TFC homes found that even where the child's stay with the therapeutic foster family was short-lived, if the quality of the connection was strong, the foster child still experienced significant benefits.[17] Because child victims of sex trafficking have endured immense trauma and have such specialized recovery needs, and because therapeutic foster homes are designed to provide a heightened level of care and support to treat such trauma, it follows that this intensive, home-like setting would likewise greatly benefit children rescued from sex trafficking.

With a therapeutic foster parent, sex-trafficked children can experience physical safety, emotional safety, patience, and consistency. In terms of physical safety, foster parents can teach children how to avoid placing themselves in positions of danger going forward, and help children work through challenging behaviors that may be a reaction to the trauma. In terms of emotional safety, therapeutic foster parents can model healthy relationships and interactions. In their new environment, children can feel secure in the care of their therapeutic foster parents, free from chaos, violence, and abuse. Furthermore, the foster parents can act as role models and help these children learn independent living skills. In terms of consistency, therapeutic foster parents, like any other foster parents, would typically have the option of adopting their foster children or serving as their permanent guardians, if the child requests such permanency.

One way that the TFC model has been described underscores why it is appropriate for sex-trafficked youth who have been rescued. Consider this definition of TFC: "A model of care and treatment . . . to meet the needs of children who require the structure that characterizes an institutional program but who could benefit from the richness and normalizing influence of a family environment."[18] Psychological research shows that a stable adult figure is key in healing the wounds of traumatized children and ensuring that the children are not re-traumatized.[19] Consistent and healthy adult role models and support systems also dramatically reduce the long-term effects of childhood violence,[20] allowing these children to grow into well-adjusted adults.

Child victims of sex trafficking may distort their view of their traffickers ,seeing them as parental figures or guardians who are taking care of their physical and emotional needs. This belief on the part of the child victim informs their understanding of relationships, authority, and family. Trafficked children need to be re-taught healthy relationships, and thus the foster child-foster parent relationship can make a unique impact on a child's life.

8.3 How Sex-Trafficked Children and Abused Children Are Similar in the Trauma Endured and Rehabilitation Needed

It is important to note that child victims of sex trafficking and child victims of family violence and of sexual abuse are often one and the same.[21] In other words, sexually abused children often become victims of sex trafficking, and sex-trafficked children are sexually abused by various perpetrators.[22] Additionally, a child victim may experience that his or her trafficker may come from within their own family. It is not uncommon that family members may be the traffickers themselves and the trafficking may, in fact, be part of the sexual, physical, or psychological abuse children experience.

There are significant similarities in trauma between children who have witnessed or experienced family violence or childhood sexual abuse, and those children who have been trafficked for purposes of prostitution. These similarities include the way in which the perpetrator establishes and exerts his or her control over the child victim, as well as the ways in which the child victim's trauma may manifest.

Scholars, practitioners, and survivors have also documented and drawn similarities between the relationships that victims of family violence and sex trafficking have with their abusers and perpetrators. These similarities include the perpetrator's isolation of the victim from the victim's family and friends, while normalizing threats and intimidation, and emotional, physical, and sexual abuse. When the abuse is of a child living in a home with a parent who has hurt the child and perhaps the other parent as well, severe trauma typically will ensue. Tactics of power, control, and violence used by the perpetrators of family/sexual violence and traffickers are notably very similar.[23] Perpetrators of violence seek to dominate their victims by asserting power and control over them. Asserting power and control over a victim often times involves a multifaceted approach; child sex abusers, batterers, and traffickers all use various tactics to exert and maintain dominance over their victims.

One foundational tactic frequently used by child abusers, batterers, and traffickers alike is isolation, which may be accomplished by persuading the victim to refrain from disclosing the abuse. When the victim is a child, this tactic has the added effect of fostering within the child victim a sense of hopelessness and helplessness, encouraging dependence on the perpetrator. Another tactic used by both child abusers and child traffickers to reinforce the child victim's subjugation and decrease the likelihood of the victim's escape is to control the child victim's finances and movement (sometimes in the form of transportation).[24] The psychological effects of these tactics on the child victim are so profound that even if the child victim is able to escape the abuser or trafficker, they too often return to the perpetrator.

Additionally, abusers and traffickers commonly use both physical and psychological violence to maintain power and control. As addressed above, sex-trafficked children may be raped up to 30 times a day and moved to new locales so that the buyers can have so-called "variety" with fresh faces. Both the buyers and the traffickers routinely employ violence as a means to control their victims.

Because a substantially large percentage of sex-trafficked children suffer from PTSD,[25] it is important that any treatment model implemented to help these children is capable of identifying and treating the disorder. PTSD is prevalent among child victims of both sexual abuse and sex trafficking. In today's psychological and social science literature, PTSD is commonly associated with both rape trauma and family violence. The symptoms of PTSD are serious and may include severe depression, anxiety, phobias, hyper-vigilance, suicidal ideation, and suicide attempts.[26]

Studies comparing the experiences of child victims of sexual abuse in relation to victims of other types of trauma have highlighted a heightened prevalence of dissociative and PTSD symptoms in victims of sexual violence and abuse.[27] For example, one study found that child victims of rape, torture, and molestation are more likely to sustain a chronic, life-long PTSD diagnosis.[28] Other research has revealed that three of the most prominent features of PTSD have been found in both child victims of sex trafficking and child victims of sexual abuse, including (1) intrusive re-experiencing of the traumatic event; (2) numbing and avoidance; and (3) hyper-arousal, such as being hyper-vigilant, easily startled, and unable to sleep.[29] To cope with these symptoms, it is not uncommon for children of both sex trafficking and sexual abuse to self-medicate with drugs or alcohol, or to detach, disassociate, become numb, or have temporary mental lapses.[30]

Trauma affects each child uniquely, but when comparing sex-trafficked children and sexually abused children, much can be learned from the similarities in the physical and psychological effects of their victimization. Many of these children experience what is termed as complex trauma or poly-victimization, discussed earlier, which can be described as multiple forms of maltreatment.[31] Because 70% of youth who are already in foster care are characterized as experiencing multiple forms of maltreatment,[32] and child victims of sex trafficking are abused by multiple individuals and endure physical, psychological, and emotional abuse, the parallels can easily be drawn between the already existing foster care population and child victims of sex trafficking.

Medically, children who have been sexually trafficked face many of the same physical health obstacles as a result of their victimization as do children who have been sexually abused. These health issues include sexually transmitted diseases, exhaustion, unwanted pregnancy, miscarriages, and bodily injury such as broken bones and improperly mended injuries.[33]

Psychologically, both survivors of abuse and sexual enslavement often suffer from depression, obsessive-compulsive disorder, suicidal ideation, and self-harm or self-mutilation. Children who witness or experience violence or sexual abuse can also experience anxiety manifested by social withdrawal, behaviors indicative of "acting out," bedwetting, and elimination disorders. Arguably, this is true of many children undergoing repetitive trauma, including trafficked children.

In order to accommodate trafficking survivors in the current therapeutic foster care system, foster parents need to be carefully selected, trained, and prepared. Part of this preparedness is raising awareness about the issues of child sex trafficking. Along with the usual challenges of preparing foster caregivers, many people are uninformed or poorly informed about the issue of sex trafficking, its dynamics, and its effects on victims.

In addition to techniques or skills that can be taught to foster parents taking in child victims of sex trafficking, the perceptions and feelings of the foster family itself will have an impact on the child victim's healing. Empathy is a human response that benefits any child in need. In the case of the trafficked child, it is crucial. Research suggests that training techniques such as training videos or small group training sessions may help foster parents empathize with a child who has endured sex trafficking.[34]

While not unique to sex-trafficked children, the combination of behaviors exhibited post-rescue is generally related to trauma. Among the common behaviors exhibited are numbing, denial, flooding, isolating, somatic complaints, eating disorders, irritability, excessive fear, inability to articulate needs, dependency issues, and aggression.[35]

Potential foster parents might fear that a child victim of sex trafficking could be hyper- or over-sexualized or may sexually abuse other children in the home. Some researchers have noted that trafficking victims often convert their feelings of powerlessness to feelings of being powerful by playing the role of seducer.[36] In this role, these children may not envision themselves as needing a nurturing home, but instead they may desire to control their own situation. It is not uncommon for these children to be hyper- or over-sexualized, presenting a danger of sexual abuse to other children in the home.[37] Yet, potential foster parents' concerns that a foster child will be hyper-sexual is not unique to situations involving child victims of sex trafficking: Hyper-sexualization is also a common concern of foster parents who are thinking about fostering any sexually traumatized child. Thus, there may be no distinction between the two groups in this regard. That said, concerns that child victims of sex trauma might exhibit hyper-sexual or seductive behavior within foster homes should be treated seriously and sensitively when considering whether or not to place a child victim of any sexual trauma within a home where other vulnerable children are placed.

Even though the two sets of children (sex-trafficked children and sexually abused children) exhibit similar behavior as a result of their trauma, they may be perceived differently by both foster parents and society at large. Perhaps while children who have been sexually abused are seen as victims and in need of protection, children who are prostituted could be viewed with disdain.[38] As addressed earlier, to ensure this mindset does not prevent foster families from taking in trafficked children, we must provide foster parents with appropriate education and awareness of the effects of sexual trauma in general.

Child victims of sexual trafficking may also experience significant difficulty in adjusting to structured programs with parental figures. "The trafficked child has often led a chaotic and unsystematic life (for example, being moved every few weeks), or been subject to a rigid and destructive order."[39] Notably, "[t]he trafficked child has usually been displaced by very personal experiences, and, because she often attaches to her trafficker, she is not always convinced that what has happened to her is disordered. The trafficked child has often been betrayed by family, and certainly by adults she trusted."[40] Yet this is not so distinct from a child who has been betrayed by his or her family through sexual abuse. Sexually abused children and trafficked children share a common type of trauma, a type of suffering, and both need a similar kind of healing. They both certainly need empathy, safety, shelter, consistency, medical care, and fundamental components to living.

8.4 Potential Obstacles to Healing Sex-Trafficked Children in Therapeutic Foster Homes

A. Children's Needs are Not Uniform

Despite the significant correlations between victims of sex trafficking and victims of family or sexual abuse, there are also some differences between the groups that need to be addressed when considering sex-trafficked children accessing foster care services.

For one, children who were trafficked into another country have quite literally been displaced without anything to aid them in the cultural transition inherent in moving from one culture to another.[41] Language barriers remain, as do issues of culture shock or disconnectedness due to a lack of familiarity with people, food, or customs. This disconnectedness can make these children feel additional isolation above and beyond traumas associated with their abuse. Further, the fear of deportation often experienced by being undocumented may cause foreign-born trafficking victims to be fearful of seeking medical and legal assistance, which exacerbates isolation and prevents them from accessing needed services. Because of the numerous cultural barriers that may be present, any services offered to these children need to be culturally competent and culturally sensitive. In this regard, parents in a therapeutic foster home must be provided with specialized training and education about trafficking prior to the child's placement in their home.

In a similar vein, "the *subculture* of human trafficking should be considered. Foster parents/institutions should be fully briefed on the criminal and clandestine nature of trafficking. Victims of human trafficking are often conditioned to an 'underworld' mentality. Their understanding of survival and relationships derives from this."[42]

For many child victims of sex trafficking, the future looks bleak. Odanadi, an agency in India that works to rehabilitate victims of sexual trafficking, estimates it takes a minimum of three to four years to rehabilitate trafficked children.[43] A report for the National Center for Missing and Exploited Children stated that 71% of trafficked children have suicidal ideations.[44] Similarly, Dr. Kate Transchel of California State University, Chico, found that even after being rescued, a high number of trafficked children will attempt suicide.[45]

Furthermore, individual psychotherapy, while common in some parts of the world, particularly as part of a therapeutic foster care setting, may be disarming for children who are not familiar with such treatment. A trafficking victim's country of origin may reject so-called Western-style methods of therapy, such as individualized psychotherapy or group therapy, and see such services as foreign, shameful, culturally inappropriate, or even stigmatizing.[46]

Similarly, group therapy is a commonly used form of therapy in conjunction with rehabilitative services for victims of family or sexual abuse.[47] Though peer support groups can have success in helping survivors of childhood violence, some researchers argue that group therapy can be counterproductive as an early intervention tool for some survivors of sex trafficking. Because sex traffickers often create an environment of competition and loyalty among their victims by using favoritism to divide them, group therapy situations can sometimes be unproductive.[48]

Researchers have discovered that to combat the above-mentioned barriers, it may be best to instead utilize creative therapy such as art, music, or dance to assist youth who have been sex-trafficked.[49] Such therapy has proven to be especially successful with younger children. Some programs—like the Indian agency for sex-trafficked survivors, Odanadi—find that both counseling programs and activities geared toward the self-esteem of the victims are helpful.[50] Survivors of sex trafficking at Odanadi are exposed to "various therapies, like dance, theater [and] psychiatric counseling and [are] encourage[d] . . . to think positive."[51] Another unique and successful treatment model comes out of Sanctuary for Families in New York City, where trafficking survivors are offered cooking and nutrition classes to encourage independent living and self-care skills while also providing therapeutic services.[52] Important services offered in recovery may include those that promote the development of independent living skills and that help survivors overcome economic and educational disadvantages caused by years of being enslaved.

Rescue is not always embraced wholeheartedly. As one successful agency combating sex trafficking, Love146, explains, rescues may not always be "welcomed" due to the fact that a "'rescue' can be an incredibly disorienting experience for a victim."[53] Many young victims who are exploited commercially fear or mistrust law enforcement and strangers.[54] "One girl was told by her rescuers, 'We have a safe place for you with help and services,' to which she responded '[l]ast time someone said that it didn't turn out so well.'"[55] When rescued, many trafficking victims feel anxious because they are being removed from something that "has become familiar and predictable" to them.[56] This anxiety grows if the child does not fully comprehend or accept that he or she is indeed a victim of trafficking. In other words, many children will not self-identify as sex-trafficked. This may be the result of fear instilled by the relationship with the trafficker or a warped sense of self that may arise as a defense mechanism to ensure self-preservation.[57] Often these children experience what is termed "trauma-bonding"—similar to what we think of as Stockholm Syndrome, where the victims become bonded to their traffickers.58 Some victims identify themselves as consensual participants in the sex trade after years of being trafficked. The sex trade may have led the children to feel powerful instead of powerless, and, therefore, there is a resistance to accessing help. Some children see themselves as adults based upon certain cultural beliefs they may hold. Overall, because of their sexual misuse by their traffickers, many sex-trafficked children have skewed ideas about love, relationships, and sexuality.

Additionally, it is often incredibly difficult for child victims to truly escape their traffickers, as this narrative explains:

> Janine F., a legal permanent resident, ran away from an abusive family situation in New York when she was 17. An acquaintance invited her to California and paid for her bus ticket. On arriving in California, she was forced into prostitution. After six months she was arrested and held in the custody of child protective services for a week before being sent back to New York on a bus. However, not wanting to return home, Janine F. got off the bus when it stopped in Phoenix. She was at the bus station when the same person who had trafficked her to California pulled up in a car. He said, "You should have known better than to try to get away from me." In Phoenix, he again forced her into prostitution.[59]

Janine F. is not alone in her experiences; other child trafficking victims have faced similar situations. Janine's story underscores why safety planning and anonymity are so crucial.

> Safety planning . . . requires that the child as well as foster care-givers understand the dangers often inherent in trafficking. The child needs to be aware of issues affected by three factors: her contact with traffickers, her contact with her family, and the content of what she communicates to whatever outside contacts she has.[60]

At times, victims may desire to reestablish a relationship with the traffickers. Each child victim may view his or her trafficker in a different light, with varying degrees of insight:

> [T]he child's relationship and perception of the traffickers has ranged from total identification ("they were nice enough to me, I was paying off my smuggling debt and doing work that was fine to do") to full comprehension of the injustice ("I hate them and I want to tell them that"). These perceptions are based on a variety of factors including: the length of time involved altogether and the duration of mistreatment; the child's connection to the traffickers, e.g. relatives, or boyfriends, or strangers; the skill of the trafficker in manipulating the child's perceptions; the child's pre-trafficking profile, and the child's conditioning to accept treatment, which we would consider cruel, as standard for herself.[61]

Traffickers often persuade their victims that they are safer to stay than to leave, or make the victims afraid to leave.[62] Moreover, some victims may be allowed to leave for short periods of time, giving them the illusion that they are not truly victims or being held captive.[63] Trafficked children have complicated relationships with their traffickers. They are accustomed to dependence upon their traffickers at the same time they are being abused. For children who have run away from family homes, their exploiters could be promising or even providing some level of structure that the children were not finding at home.

B. Critiques of the Overall Foster Care System

Of course, any governmental system that serves as a substitute parent for children who have been neglected and abused cannot serve as a panacea for all of society's ills. Some critics argue that the United States foster care system is already overburdened and unable to assist more children effectively.[64] Other critics explain that the foster care system itself serves as a major pipeline to child sexual trafficking in the United States, as many traffickers specifically target foster children because of their vulnerability and "need for love, affirmation, and protection."[65] It could be argued, however, that any dysfunction of our current foster care system is due to underlying societal problems that cause our children to be placed in the foster care system at the outset, and even perhaps to underlying institutional biases that dictate which children are placed into foster care at all. A critique of the overall foster care system should not be used as a bar to exploring the possibilities of placing sex-trafficked youth into an already robust and established system of care. Furthermore, this Chapter is recommending a particular kind of foster care, therapeutic foster care, which addresses many of the issues that plague the system in general, such as ongoing training and support for foster parents.

There is no question that foster children too often become runaway children, who then become prone and vulnerable to child sex traffickers and other criminals. Yet, it is difficult to argue against a therapeutic foster care model that could benefit tremendously from budget increases and more finely tuned training and support. The foster care system is not a miracle cure-all for an epidemic as widespread as child sexual slavery. Yet we cannot overlook the years of research and experience that have been employed to build the foster care system, and specifically the Therapeutic Care Model.

8.5 Conclusion

In sum, practitioners and judges should draw from existing systems, like therapeutic foster care, to rehabilitate sex-trafficked children on an immediate basis. Therapeutic foster parents could be paired with NGOs and other specialized agencies to assist particularly with the unique challenges of sex-trafficked children. Therapeutic foster care is a well-established model of care built on sensitivity and particular care to children with emotional issues.

The similarities between the traumatic effects of familial child abuse and the traumatic effects of child sex trafficking are striking. Therapeutic foster care with a trauma-centered approach in a home-like setting can be beneficial to all children who have been traumatized. While the current foster care system is certainly not without its flaws, practitioners and judges can borrow from our preexisting programs to begin the rehabilitation process for sex-trafficked children. The Therapeutic Foster Care model is a widely established model of care that is flexible enough to meet the numerous and complicated issues associated with the treatment, cultural, and protection needs of child trafficking survivors. Most importantly, awareness of the special needs of this population will aid any practitioner or judge who encounters these most vulnerable victims.

Endnotes

1. A longer, more comprehensive version of this Chapter was published in the West Virginia Law Review at 118 W. Va. L. Rev. 1131 (2016). Thank you to the wonderful editors of the West Virginia Law Review for permission to reformulate the piece into a book chapter. This paper was presented in earlier iterations—most notably at the United Nations in New York City in April 2014. I owe thanks to many people who have helped me envision this piece over the years. I dedicate this Chapter to all of them and also to my own children and family.

2. In terms of trafficking globally, some sources suggest that at least one million children are trafficked and exploited by the global sex industry every year, while others argue that the number is actually two to three million children per year. See Clayton et al., Inst. Med. & Nat'l Research Council, "Confronting Commercial Sexual Exploitation and Sex Trafficking of Minors in the United States" (2013).

3. Office for Victims of Crime Training & Tech. Assistance Ctr., Human Trafficking (2012) (http://www.ncdsv.org/images/OVCTTAC_HumanTraffickingResourcePaper_2012.pdf).

4. *See* Julie Kaplow et al., *Pathways to PTSD, Part II: Sexually Abused Children*, 162 Am. J. Psychiatry 1305, 1305 (2005).

5. Trafficking in Persons Report (2009).

6. Palermo Protocol, at art. 6(3); May Li, *Did Indiana Deliver in Its Fight Against Human Trafficking? A Comparative Analysis Between Indiana's Human Trafficking Laws and the International Legal Framework*, 23 Ind. Int'l & Comp. L. Rev. 277, 315 (2013).

7. G.A. Res. 54/263, Optional Protocol to the Convention on the Rights of the Child on the Sale of Children, Child Prostitution and Child Pornography, art. 8 (Jan. 18, 2002).

8. Examples, by no means an exhaustive list, include: CAST in Los Angeles, GEMS in New York City, My Life My Choice in Boston, Covenant House in New York City, Eyes Wide Open in Albany, NY, and Love146 in Connecticut.

9. *See* John Briere, Stacey Kaltman & Bonnie L. Green, *Accumulated Childhood Trauma and Symptom Complexity*, 21 J. Traumatic Stress 223, 223–26.

10. For children, the introduction of traumatic experiences into the developmental process typically impedes growth and development, especially when the child lacks a consistent and loving caregiver. Unfortunately, for many children who are the victims of complex trauma, there is not only a lack of such a caregiver, but for those children who are trafficked, caregivers are also typically placed in the role of the abuser. *See id.* at 8–9.

11. Laura M. Mauro, "Child Placement: Policy and Issues," in *Young Children and Foster Care* at 261, 278.

12. Hahn et al., *supra.*

13. John Carenen, *Son-Up, Son-Down,* iii (1990).

14. Uta M. Walter et al., "Best Practices in Therapeutic Foster Care: Review of National Literature and Local Practices in the State of Kansas" (2003).

15. *See* "Therapeutic Foster Care: Critical Issues."

16. *Id.* at vi.

17. Southerland et al., *supra* at 60–61.

18. Brad Bryant & Robert D. Snodgrass, "Therapeutic Foster Care: Past and Present," in *Troubled Youth in Treatment Homes: A Handbook of Therapeutic Foster Care* 1 (Pamela Meadowcroft & Barbara A. Trout (eds), 1990).

19. *See* Sara Younge, "Treating Child Traumatic Stress: Bearing Witness to Healing," CW360, Winter 2013, at 31.

20. For a corollary to prostituted women, see Ulla-Carin Hedin & Sven-Axel Mansson, *The Importance of Supportive Relationships in Leaving Prostitution,* 2 J. Trauma Practice 223 (2004).

21. *See* Clayton et al., *supra* at 80 (citing various studies where large percentages of juveniles involved in the sex trade or prostitution reported that a significant contributing factor for their entrance into the trade was sexual abuse).

22. *Id.*

23. Amy Barasch & Barbara C. Kryszko, "The Nexus Between Domestic Violence and Trafficking for Commercial Sexual Exploitation," in *Lawyer's Manual on Human Trafficking.*

24. Ryan Dalton, *Abolishing Child Sex Trafficking on the Internet: Imposing Criminal Culpability on Digital Facilitators,* 43 U. Mem. L. Rev. 1097, 1105 (2013).

25. Dean G. Kilpatrick & Benjamin E. Saunders, Med. Univ. S.C., "Prevalence and Consequences of Child Victimization: Results from the National Survey of Adolescents, Final Report," 27–28 (1997).

27. Children, especially young female children, are at the highest risk of developing PTSD.

28. A study conducted with children in the foster care system found that the rates of PTSD diagnosis were 39.7% for rape, 45.2% for being tortured or a victim of terrorists, and 32.8% for molestation. Amy M. Salazar et al., *Trauma Exposure and PTSD Among Older Adolescents in Foster Care*, 48 Soc. Psychiatry & Psychiatric Epidemiology 545, 547 (2012).

29. Lev-Wiesel, *supra*.

30. *See generally* Colin A. Ross & Naomi Halpern, *Trauma Model Therapy: A Treatment Approach for Trauma, Dissociation and Complex Comorbidity* (2009).

31. Lisa Goldblatt, Regina Musicaro & Joseph Spinazzola, "The Commercial Sexual Exploitation of Girls & Young Women," Webinar PowerPoint Presentation for the National Child Traumatic Stress Network (Sept. 12, 2013).

32. *Id.*

33. Trafficking in Person Report (2007).

34. Mindy Loiselle et al., *Care for Trafficked Children*, Bridging Refugee Youth Child. Servs. 3 (Apr. 2006).

35. U.S. Dep't of Health & Human Servs.," Guidance to States and Services on Addressing Human Trafficking of Children and Youth in the United States," 6 (2013).

36. Nat'l Child Traumatic Stress Network.

37. *Focal Point Complex Trauma.*

38. *See id.*

39. Loiselle et al., *supra* at 4.

40. *Id.*

41. Linda A. Piwowarczyk, *Our Responsibility to Unaccompanied and Separated Children in the United States: A Helping Hand*, 15 B.U. Pub. Int. L.J. 263, 281 (2006).

42. Many would argue that homeless youth who have engaged in "survival sex" also experience similar traumas and restrictions. Again, many of these children may have emerged from the foster care system, or have run away or been "thrown away." There is still an obligation to care for these homeless youth found on the streets.

43. Pritha Sen, *Combating Human Trafficking Through Social Policing,* 6 (Dec. 16, 2006) (unpublished manuscript).

44. Klain, *supra* at 8.

45. Transchel, *supra* at 13.

46 "Western-style therapy" is the traditional psychotherapist-patient counselling services that we see commonly in the United States (as opposed to meditation, acupuncture, mind over matter, seen more commonly in non-Western cultural contexts).

47. Caroline W. Jacobus, *Legislative Responses to Discrimination in Women's Health Care: A Report Prepared for the Commission to Study Sex Discrimination in the Statutes,* 16 Women's Rts. L. Rep. 153, 223 (1995).

48. Hopper & Hidalgo, *supra* at 196–97.

49. See Office of Juvenile Justice & Delinquency Prevention, "Commercial Sexual Exploitation of Children/Sex Trafficking," 10 (2014).

50. Neuroscience suggests that expressive therapies are quite helpful for traumatized youth.

51. Sen, *supra.*

52. See Erica Pearson, "Survivors of Sex Trafficking Learn Cooking and Nutrition Skills at Workshop," *N.Y. Daily News* (May 12, 2014).

53. *Common Myths*, Love146.

54. *Id.*

55. *Id.*

56. *Id.*

57. Raghavan & Doychak, *supra* at 583–86.

58. NCTSN Webinar, *supra*.

59. Harlan, *supra* at 1141–42.

60. Loiselle et al., *supra* at 4.

61. *Id.*

62. *Id.*

63. *Id.* at 4–5.

64. "Foster Care," Am. Acad. of Child & Adolescent Psychiatry.

65. Factsheet: "Foster Care and Human Trafficking," CAS Res. & Educ. (http://www.casre.org/our_children/fcht/).

Chapter 9

The Human Rights Argument in Human Trafficking: Duty to Identify Victims

By Julia Muraszkiewicz

9.1 Introduction

In the course of human trafficking, victims are subjected to heinous experiences that degrade and humiliate them, and impact their physiological and psychological wellbeing. Consequently, the offense has been described as a grave violation of human rights. European policy makers have embraced this notion, which is reflected in numerous legislations, case law, and national or regional Action Plans. It is important to look at the human rights obligation of identifying trafficked persons, because it is the gateway to all other matters—including protection, assistance, and even prosecution of perpetrators. Identification is here understood as the official identification process undertaken by competent national authorities as nominated in the national system of a country.

The history of human rights materialises in the legal regime as a vertical relationship between the State and its citizens, where the framework is designed to control and limit the State in its actions towards the people. "The essence of human rights law is that it makes the State accountable for failing to protect rights which it has the power and obligation to protect, such as the prohibition on slavery."[1] Donnelly, a scholar of human rights known for his conceptual frameworks on understanding international human rights as an operative part of international life, perceives human rights as a framework that protects our dignity: "We have human rights not to the requisites for health but to those things 'needed' for a life of dignity, for a life worthy of a human being, a life that cannot be enjoyed without these rights."[2]

Recognition of the significance of human rights has paved the way for the codification of these values within various international conventions and in domestic law. Codifying human rights is particularly important, as it shows that states have established a certain standard as to how persons have to be treated. The obligation to identify victims of human trafficking has now found a home in the human rights framework.

9.2 The Challenges of Identifying Victims of Trafficking

The nature of the crime of human trafficking is that the people who are trafficked end up being victims of a series of offences that reduce their dignity, are degrading, and at times inhumane. Human trafficking is a "brutalizing experience that destroys most aspects of the life of the trafficked person—health, self-confidence, family life."[3] These abuse imperatives demand that those who are victims receive a level of assistance and a chance of rehabilitation, or else they may forever continue to be sufferers and endure secondary victimisation.

Identification of trafficked persons is thus necessary to secure their safety, and rights, and to ensure that they have access to appropriate assistance. As summarised by the OSCE (Organisation for Security and Cooperation in Europe):

> A human rights approach requires early identification of and assistance to trafficking victims. Because trafficking in persons is such a complex phenomenon, the process of making a final identification of victims can be prolonged; thus initial identification of presumed victims is crucial. Failure to identify victims at an early stage can result in inadequate protection of victims and the violation of their rights, which in turn may obstruct effective prosecution of the crime.[4]

Human trafficking is, first and foremost, a human right discourse; the viola-tions of rights are both a cause and a consequence of the crime. According to the UN Recommended Principles and Guidelines on Human Rights and Human Trafficking: "The human rights of trafficked persons shall be at the centre of all efforts to prevent and combat trafficking and to protect, assist and provide redress to victims."

The document then goes on to say that a "failure to identify a trafficked per-son correctly is likely to result in a further denial of that person's rights. States are therefore under an obligation to ensure that such identification can and does take place."

The basic understanding of human trafficking as a breach of human rights should inform every aspect of investigation and work with trafficked persons, including identification. Yet, the Anti-Trafficking Monitoring Group in the U.K. highlighted that:

"Whilst the positive obligation to investigate trafficking has been es-tablished in law, there is still a discrepancy between the number of po-tential trafficked persons identified and the number of prosecutions of traffickers... The most worrying finding of the research was that a sig-nificant number of victims continue to be prosecuted for offences they have committed as a direct consequence of their trafficking."[5]

Arguably, most countries persistently fail to fulfill their human rights obliga-tions in respect of identifying human trafficking victims.

The nature of human trafficking is such that victims will be reluctant to come forward and self-report the crime. The victim may not recognise his or her status. Equally, she or he may have developed a relationship with the exploiter, and thus be unlikely to approach the authorities. It is also possible that the vic-tims will not wish to make contact with the authorities out of fear (fear of the authority and fear of the trafficker).

Many victims are too frightened to report their abuse: They could be worried about their immigration status, anxious about exposing them-selves to criminal charges, fearful of reprisals from their abusers, and/or just simply being too traumatized by the experience to cooperate with the authorities.[6]

The European Migration Network Study (March 2014) identified the following factors as obstacles to self-identification:[7]

- Lack of awareness that [she or he] has been a victim of this particular crime
- Mistrust [or] fear of the police and asylum authorities
- Fear of being identified as irregular and returned to the country of origin, to face (possible) stigmatisation by society
- Lack of country of destination language skills
- Lack of information on legal rights
- A first claim may have been rejected due to it being false, making it legally problematic for the applicant to make a new claim.

As such, much responsibility rests on the identification process. The issue of identifying trafficked victims is separate from that of identifying the traffickers, and is even separate from the overall prosecution. It is first and foremost about protecting victims.

States, through international, regional, and national legislative frameworks, now recognize that victims of human trafficking are entitled to protection. Notwithstanding, "in many countries, victims of trafficking are never identified and, as a result, are simply invisible."[8] Victims can become misidentified as criminals (e.g., if they were trafficked for the purpose of cannabis cultivation or theft) or irregular migrants, and thus subsequently deported. Without identification, any rights granted to victims are "purely theoretical and illusory."[9]

An interesting addition to the discourse on identification concerns the role of the media. The TRACE (Trafficking as a Criminal Enterprise) project—a two-year, EU-funded research project on the business of human trafficking—found that news stories are frequently couched in narratives that do little to challenge existing myths about trafficked persons. Indeed, the overrepresentation of sexual exploitation in human trafficking may prevent people from recognizing other forms of exploitation. As matters currently stand, the public does not see the full spectrum of the problem. The news media have created a specific framework within which they shape the way people think about human trafficking, and this does not account for exploitation beyond the sex industry.

9.3 European Frameworks for Victim Identification

The European continent has two regional frameworks, both of which contribute to human rights related discourse: the Council of Europe (C.o.E.) and the European Union (E.U.). Instruments from both the C.o.E. and the E.U. have addressed human trafficking and identification; each framework is presented below.

A. The European Union

The 2011 Directive on Preventing and Combating Trafficking in Human Beings and Protecting its Victims (Directive), repealed a Framework Decision of 2002 (Council Framework Decision 2002/629/JHA). The Directive focuses on measures to assist and support victims, as well as on prosecution and prevention. The E.U.'s 28 Member States were required to take the necessary measures to comply with the Directive by April 2013. The Directive is not a guide or recommendation but has legally binding force. Article 288 of the Treaty on the Functioning of the European Union states that Directives are "binding, as to the result to be achieved, upon each Member State to which it is addressed, but shall leave to the national authorities the choice of form and methods."[10] This, however, offers Member States wide discretion on how to transpose a Directive into national law.

On the whole, the 2011 E.U. Directive on Human Trafficking is perceived as a positive step in the protection of victims. It includes elaborate provisions on victim protection, reflecting a victim-centred approach.[11]

Article 11(4) states that: "Member States shall take the necessary measures to establish appropriate mechanisms aimed at the early identification of, assistance to and support for victims, in cooperation with relevant support organisations."

Criticism can be directed at the high discretion left to Member States, the lack of clarity as to the meaning of "early," and no guidelines as to who should be charged with identification. Similar questions arise with respect to the obligations placed by the Council of Europe, discussed below.

B. The Council of Europe

The Council of Europe originated in the aftermath of WWII (1949). It is a regional intergovernmental organization, with 47 Member States, aiming at promoting human rights, democracy, and rule of law. The population within the remit of the Council of Europe counts 800 million, and so the influence of the Council and its documents is not to be ignored. The focus of this section lies in the European Convention on Human Rights (ECHR)—the key instrument of protection in Europe. The ECHR has also established the European Court of Human Rights (ECtHR), which produces numerous judgments on a diverge range of human rights issues. Article 4 of The European Convention on Human Rights states:

Prohibition of slavery and forced labour
1. No one shall be held in slavery or servitude.
2. No one shall be required to perform forced or compulsory labour.

The provision does not provide for a specific definition of slavery, servitude, or forced labor. Rather, the conceptual understanding of the Article is interpreted through reference to other documents, such as the 1926 League of Nations Slavery Convention and the ILO Forced Labour Convention, 1930 (No. 29),[12] or by analysing case law coming out of the ECtHR. The absence of a provision on human trafficking in the human rights convention is not surprising; the definition on human trafficking would not be globally agreed upon until 50 years later.

For some scholars and law practitioners, especially the legal purists amongst us, the use of the ECHR with regard to cases of human trafficking may be problematic. Human trafficking and slavery are not synonymous. In some instances, human trafficking will consist of slavery or forced and compulsory labour, but not always.[13] Human trafficking is a crime of process that requires an action, a means, and a purpose, while slavery is a crime of status. This raises the question: Can human trafficking still be seen within the remits of human rights obligations?

The ECtHR, whether rightly or not, has held that human trafficking falls within the scope of Article 4 of the European Convention on Human Rights. The Court found human trafficking to be akin to slavery, arguing that, "trafficking in human beings, by its very nature and aim of exploitation, is based on the exercise of powers attaching to the right of ownership." In other words, "the Court based its reasoning on the following line of thought: [I]f trafficking goes against the very principles of Article 4, the legal standards that are applied to Article 4 can also be used to assess the alleged crime of human trafficking."[14]

In turn, the Court has developed a number of human rights obligations with respect to, amongst other things, victim identification. These echo the provisions of the Council of Europe Convention on Action against Trafficking in Human Beings.

The Convention was adopted on 3 May 2005 and entered into force on 1 February 2008. The Explanatory Report to the Human Trafficking Convention states that the document aims to achieve "a proper balance between matters concerning human rights and prosecution."[15] Article 4(a) of the CoE Convention adopts the same definition of trafficking as Article 3(a) of the UN Protocol. However, the Europe Convention on Action against Trafficking in Human Beings definition is seemingly broader, for it applies to all forms of human trafficking, whether national or transnational, whether or not connected to organised crime.

While the UN Protocol is silent on the issue of victim identification, Article 10 of the CoE Convention puts an obligation on States with respect to victim identification. Article 10 (1) – (2) states:

1. Each Party shall provide its competent authorities with persons who are trained and qualified in preventing and combating trafficking in human beings, in identifying and helping victims, including children, and shall ensure that the different authorities collaborate with each other as well as with relevant support organisations, so that victims can be identified in a procedure duly taking into account the special situation of women and child victims and, in appropriate cases, issued with residence permits under the conditions provided for in Article 14 of the present Convention.

2. Each Party shall adopt such legislative or other measures as may be necessary to identify victims as appropriate in collaboration with other Parties and relevant support organisations. Each Party shall ensure that, if the competent authorities have reasonable grounds to believe that a person has been victim of trafficking in human beings, that person shall not be removed from its territory until the identification process as victim of an offence provided for in Article 18 of this Convention has been completed by the competent authorities and shall likewise ensure that that person receives the assistance provided for in Article 12, paragraphs 1 and 2.

In summary, and similarly to the E.U. system, there needs to be a method at the national level for identifying persons who have been or are being trafficked. Regrettably, the Article does not require the adoption of national legislation, and party states are afforded discretion in terms of the legal and procedural aspects of this provision. There is no blanket approach to fulfilling these obligations. What works in some countries may not be appropriate in others. The United Kingdom, for example, has responded to its obligations by creating the National Referral Mechanism (NRM).

Importantly, the Trafficking Convention allows states to decide which national body is liable for victim identification. In many states, this task is entrusted to the immigration or police authorities. This, unsurprisingly, raises concerns as to objectivity:

Many victims of human trafficking have breached the national legislation regulating the conditions under which migrants can enter, stay and labour on the territory of the host state. When immigration authorities have the exclusive mandate to formally identify victims of human trafficking, victim identification can be reduced to identification of undocumented migrants for the purposes of their removal. As a result, the rationale behind having a specific procedure for identifying abused migrants is lost.[16]

Article 10 raises further concerns: There is no guidance as to what ought to trigger victim identification, what is reasonably expected of state authorities in terms of due diligence, and no obligation in regard to time scales. As to the issue of timing, because receiving assistance relies on a successful identification, the process should be carried out quickly and accurately, and should be irrespective of criminal proceedings. Unfortunately, these shortcomings are not discussed or explained by the E.U. legislator of the C.o.E. However, Stoyanova—a leading European scholar on case law relating to human trafficking and slavery in the European Court of Human Rights—perceives these ambiguities as gateways for positive interpretation, describing them as "opening opportunities for more advantageous interpretations based on its object and purpose and in the light of human rights standards."[17] As will be shown below, the European Court of Human Rights has not shied away from such advantageous interpretations.

As to other relevant provisions in the CoE Convention, these have been well-summarized by Turner:

Article 12 is concerned with the assistance to victims. Following on from Article 10, Article 13 introduces a recovery and reflection period, of at least 30 days, when there are reasonable grounds to believe that the person concerned is a victim of human trafficking. Such a period shall be sufficient for the person concerned to recover and escape the influence of traffickers and/or to make an informed decision on cooperating with the competent authorities. During this period, it shall not be possible to enforce any expulsion order against them. Article 26 of the CoE Convention, which is labelled as a "non-punishment provision," recommends not imposing penalties on victims for their involvement in unlawful activities, to the extent that they have been compelled to do so.[18]

In the U.K., victims are referred to the NRM through a first respondent, and the application is examined by one of the Competent Authorities. The following bodies are recognized as first respondents: Police forces, U.K. Border Force, Home Office, Immigration and Visas, Gangmasters Licensing Authority, Local Authorities, Health and Social Care Trusts (Northern Ireland), Salvation Army, Poppy Project, Migrant Help, Medaille Trust, Kalayaan, Barnardos, Unseen, TARA Project (Scotland), NSPCC (CTAC), BAWSO, New Pathways, and Refugee Council.

Referral is voluntary and can happen only if the potential victim gives their written consent. In the case of children, their consent is not required. In the U.K., the two Competent Authorities are: (i) The U.K. Human Trafficking Centre (UKHTC), which looks at forms from the police, local authorities, and NGOs; and (ii) The Home Office Visas and Immigration (UKVI), which deals with referrals recognized as being part of immigration procedures. Once a referral has been made, the Competent Authority will assess and make a decision on whether an individual is a human trafficking victim. If a positive assessment is mades such a person receives a letter confirming the status.

9.4 Case studies

Although the body of case law coming out of the ECtHR on human trafficking is relatively scarce, the cases that have appeared before the Court allow us to further determine how the basic understanding of trafficking as a breach of fundamental human rights should inform responsibilities with regard to identification. Three cases directly relating to the issue of identification have been chosen for discussion below; the legal authorities in all three cases missed opportunities to identify the trafficked person.

A. *Rantsev v. Cyprus and Russia*

1. The facts

The case of *Rantsev v. Cyprus and Russia* concerned a Russian citizen, Oxana Rantseva, who died in March 2001 in Cyprus.[19] In the words of Prof. Allain—a leading legal expert on issues of slavery and trafficking—the Russian woman "stopped off a plane in Cyprus in 2001 and less than a fortnight later was dead."[20] The judgment has become a key reference point when talking about states' human rights obligations with regard to exploitative practices such as slavery and forced labor.

The facts of the case are as follows: Ms. Rantseva was a 21-year-old woman from Russia. She had been brought to Cyprus on an artiste visa (an artiste was defined by the state as: any alien who wishes to enter Cyprus in order to work in a cabaret, musical-dancing place, or other night entertainment place and has attained the age of 18 years), applied for by the owners of a cabaret where she was supposedly to work as a dancer. Notably, it is accepted that these "artistes" were in practice mostly working as sex workers.

She started work on March 16th but after three days she escaped. On March 28th she was seen at a club in Limassol, and her previous employer, Mr. Athanasiou, was informed. With the assistance of another, Mr. Athanasiou took Ms. Rantseva to a police station where she was put into custody. Mr. Athanasiou's aim was that she would be detained and extradited, so that he could employ someone else. However, because her immigration status was not irregular, the police noted that they could not do anything and contacted the employer to pick her up. Mr. Athanasiou collected Ms. Rantseva and took charge of all her documents. It is important to note that the police did not question Ms. Rantseva or make an enquiry into the background of her case. They were not alerted that her employers held her documents or that she had run away from the cabaret.

Mr. Athanasiou then took the Russian girl to an apartment of his employee and placed her in a room, allegedly against her will. At 6.30 A.M., Ms. Rantseva was found dead on the street below. There was a bed sheet tied to the balcony of the 5th floor apartment.

A second autopsy of the body concluded that without a doubt the injuries on Ms. Rantseva's body "happened while she was alive" and transpired "within a very short time period, one after another," just before she died.[21] Ms. Rantseva's father, Nikolay Rantsev, made an application to the European Court of Human Rights under Articles Two (right to life), Three (prohibition on torture or inhumane and degrading treatment or punishment), Four (slavery, servitude and compulsory labor), Five (right to liberty and security of the person) and Eight (right to privacy and family life) of the ECHR. The father argued that:

1. Cyprus had not sufficiently investigated the circumstances of the death;
2. Cyprus Police did not provide sufficient protection whilst Ms. Rantseva was alive;
3. Cyprus authorities did not take sufficient steps to punish those responsible for Ms. Rantseva's death and ill-treatment;
4. Russian authorities did not investigate his daughter's alleged trafficking and subsequent death; and
5. Russia did not take steps to protect his daughter from trafficking.

2. Lessons learned

In this case, the European Court of Human Rights found that human trafficking can be interpreted with reference to Article 4 of the ECHR, and that Ms. Rantsev was a victim of human trafficking. Consequently, and as summarised by Stoyanova, the ECtHR enumerated states' obligations under Article 4 to include:

1. Adopting criminal law measures to punish traffickers
2. Putting in place appropriate legal and administrative frameworks, which include "adequate measures regulating businesses often used as a cover for human trafficking," and ensuring that "a State's immigration rules [...] address relevant concerns relating to encouragement, facilitation or tolerance of trafficking"
3. Taking protective operational measures when it is demonstrated that "the State authorities were aware, or ought to have been aware, of circumstances giving rise to a credible suspicion that an identified individual has been, or was at real and immediate risk of being, trafficked or exploited"
4. Investigating situations of trafficking
5. Cooperating in cross-border trafficking cases with the relevant authorities of other States concerned.[22]

From the Court's ruling, it can be understood that human trafficking is a breach of fundamental human rights, and that this ethos should inform all aspects of fighting the crime—including identification of victims. The European Court of Human Rights held that:

> The duty to penalize and prosecute trafficking is only one aspect of member States' general undertaking to combat trafficking. The extent of the positive obligations arising under Article 4 must be considered within this broader context.[23]

That broader context includes the need for victims of trafficking to be identified. Indeed, the Court continued that if it can be demonstrated that the State authorities were aware or ought to have been aware of circumstances giving rise to a credible suspicion that an identified individual had been or was at real and immediate risk of being trafficked, there will be a violation of Article 4 of the Convention if authorities do not remove the individual from the trafficking situation or risk.[24]

The phrase, "ought to have been aware," places a positive duty on States to identify victims such as Ms. Rantsev. In other words, violation will arise if a State ought to have been aware of a person's status as a victim of human trafficking, but it failed to formally identify that person as such.

However, the Court did not explicitly elaborate on what exactly "ought to have been aware" means. Central to this is the question of how much is expected of States. It is imaginable that the Court meant that all public servants who are likely to come into contact with (potential) victims of human trafficking ought to be able to carry out identification, including acting on any reasonable suspicion that a person might have been trafficked. Indeed, the Court recalled the Palermo Protocol[25]—Article 20—which emphasizes that states need to provide or strengthen training for law enforcement, immigration and other relevant officials in the prevention of human trafficking.[26]

The facts of the *Rantsev* case testify to the lack of training amongst the Cypriot police. According to the Court, the police had had enough indicators to arouse suspicion that Ms. Rantsev was a human trafficking victim. It thus follows that state authorities are required to investigate when there is suspicion of human trafficking. These measures can be justified in terms of protecting victims. The obligations of state authorities thus go beyond criminal law. Notwithstanding this, the Court did state that obligations must, however, be "interpreted in a way which does not impose an impossible or disproportionate burden on the authorities."[27]

Cyprus was also found not to use established routes for mutual legal assistance. In other words, Cyprus should have used international cooperation to full potential.

Recommendations

- When there is a credible suspicion that an identified individual had been, or was at, real and immediate risk of being trafficked, authorities need to remove the individual from the trafficking situation or risk.
- The relevant bodies determining the status of a (potential) victim should consider all information available.
- States need to provide or strengthen training on human trafficking, including the process of identification. The same should be directed at law enforcement, immigration, and other relevant officials engaged in the prevention of human trafficking.
- Law enforcement bodies should rely on intensified transnational cooperation.

B. *C.N. v. the United Kingdom*

1. The facts

In *C.N. v. The United Kingdom*, the applicant was a Ugandan national, who travelled to the U.K. on September 2, 2002 to escape sexual abuse.

According to the applicant's account, a relative (P.S.) and a Mr. Abdul arranged for her false travel documents. On arrival to the U.K., P.S. took C.N.'s documents and never returned them. Subsequently, she lived in various houses, arranged by P.S. During that time, she experienced threats and felt controlled:

> In January 2003 P.S. introduced the applicant to a man called M. who ran a business providing carers and security personnel for profit. The applicant attended a short carers' training course and thereafter did some overnight shifts as a carer and as a security guard in a number of locations. The applicant asserted that on each occasion payment was made by the client to [Mohammed], who transferred a share of the money to P.S.'s bank account in the apparent belief that he would pass it on to her. However, she claimed that she did not receive any payment for the work that she did.[28]

In early 2003, the applicant began to work as a live-in carer for an elderly Iraqi couple (Mr. and Mrs. K.); she was always on call and found the job very demanding. On one Sunday every month, she was given a couple of hours leave but on these occasions she would usually be collected by Mohammed and driven to P.S.'s house for the afternoon. She accepted that after a couple of years she would be permitted to take public transport, but said she was warned that it was not safe and that she should not speak with anyone.

Again, the applicant received no significant payment for her labour and all money was sent directly to Mohammed by cheque. A percentage of that money was passed by Mohammed to P.S. on the apparent understanding that it would be paid to the applicant. However, the applicant received no significant payment for her labour. At times, Mr. and Mrs. K. would give her second-hand clothes or a small sum of money.

When in 2006 Mr. and Mrs. K. left to Egypt, the applicant stayed in the house of P.S. under the care of his partner.

> On 18 August 2006 the applicant left the house. She went to a local bank, where she asked someone to call the police. Before the police arrived, she collapsed and was taken to St Mary's Hospital, where she was diagnosed as HIV positive. She was also suffering from psychosis, including auditory hallucinations.[29]

The authorities thus first became aware of the applicant's claim after she collapsed at the bank in August 2006.

> On 21 September 2006 she made an application for asylum, in the course of which she complained, inter alia, that she had been forced

to work for the K. family without remuneration. Furthermore, in April 2007 the applicant's solicitor wrote to the police and asked that they investigate her case. She was interviewed by the Human Trafficking Team on 21 June 2007 and gave a detailed statement in which she set out her domestic servitude complaints.[30]

The police undertook some inquiries, but concluded that there was no evidence of trafficking. In contrast, the POPPY project (operated by Eaves for Women, then a government-funded project providing housing and support for human trafficking victims) concluded that the applicant had been subjected to five of the six indicators of forced labour.

In particular, her movement had been restricted to the workplace, her wages were withheld to pay a debt she did not know about, her salary was withheld for four years, her passport was retained, and she was subjected to threats of denunciation to the authorities.[31]

Notwithstanding, the Police determined that the applicant was not trafficked into the U.K., that she willingly worked, and that she had asked that all money go to her relative.

The European Court of Human Rights found that the investigation into the applicant's complaints of domestic servitude were ineffective due to the absence of specific legislation criminalizing such treatment. Accordingly, the Court held that there was a violation of Article 4 of the Convention. The court awarded the applicant 8,000 EUR in respect of non-pecuniary damage.

2. Lessons learned

The police's focus in the case of C.N. was not on the control that she was subjected to, but on how she had breached immigration. Indeed, the police believed that the fact that C.N.'s wages were paid to her relative was a tactic to conceal her irregular presence in the country.[32] The lack of wages was not an indicator of human trafficking, but instead was used as evidence against C.N. The applicant complained that there was a failure by the national authorities to properly investigate her complaints of abuses of domestic servitude. In this case, again, the Court held that:

In order for a positive obligation to take operational measures to arise in the circumstances of a particular case, it must be demonstrated that the State authorities were aware, or ought to have been aware that an identified individual had been, or was at real and immediate risk of being subjected to such treatment.[33]

The Court also added that "[a] requirement of promptness and reasonable expedition is implicit in all cases but where the possibility of removing the individual from the harmful situation is available, the investigation must be undertaken as a matter of urgency."[34]

While the Court's remarks go to the heart of the obligation to conduct criminal investigations, they can be interpreted as creating an obligation of identification. Indeed, acknowledging the prominence of victim protection, the purpose of an investigation is not only the identification of the traffickers but also of the victim. The court found that the applicant's complaint was not implausible, and that there was sufficient evidence for authorities to find her to be a victim.

C.N. v. The United Kingdom can be applauded for its appreciation that domestic servitude involves overt and subtle forms of coercion. The Court held that:

> A thorough investigation into complaints of such conduct therefore requires an understanding of the many subtle ways an individual can dall under the control of another.[35]

Thus, the positive obligation of victim identification extends to also having appropriate knowledge of the different forms of human trafficking, and for relative authorities to understand the nuances of the crime and the control it exerts over persons. In this case, the Court also considered that due to the absence of a specific offence of domestic servitude (at the time), the domestic authorities were unable to give due weight to signs of domestic servitude. In particular, the Court was concerned by the fact that during the course of the investigation into the applicant's complaints, no attempt appears to have been made to interview P.S. despite the gravity of the offence he was alleged to have committed.

Recommendations
- Formal identification should be carried out as soon as possible.
- Those responsible for identification should be aware of people's vulnerabilities and the nuances of the different forms of human trafficking.
- All persons identified by the (potential) victim as part of the trafficking process should be interviewed.
- States should ensure that specific legislation criminalizing different forms of human trafficking is present.

C. *L.E. v. Greece*

1. The facts

L.E. v. Greece was ruled on in January 2016.[36]

The facts of the case are as follows: L.E. was a Nigerian national who came to Greece in 2004, accompanied by K.A., who had promised the applicant that she would work in bars and nightclubs. To facilitate the deal, L.E. promised not to tell the police, and was indebted to K.A. for 40,000 Euro. A voodoo priest secured the debt.

Once in Greece, K.A. took control of the applicant's passport and forced her into prostitution for two years. In the course of the two years, the applicant was arrested for breaching prostitution laws, but all cases against her resulted in acquittals. Importantly, she had come into contact with state authorities.

In April 2006, the applicant was detained and pending expulsion as her migration status was irregular. In November 2006, she filed a criminal grievance against K.A. and his wife D.J., accusing them of compelling her into sex work. L.E. also asserted that she was a human trafficking victim. The prosecutor in the Athens Criminal Court overruled this claim. Importantly, in doing so it did not consider testimony provided by an NGO (Nea Zoi). In 2007, the applicant requested a re-examination of her complaint, which was successful. In August 2007, the prosecutor recognized that the applicant was a human trafficking victim, and her imminent deportation was suspended.

2. Lessons learned

Given Greece's national legislation criminalizing human trafficking and its accession to numerous international and regional anti-human trafficking instruments, the ECtHR was satisfied that the country had not violated its positive obligation to adopt an effective legal and regulatory framework. However, "The Court preferred to analyze the deficiencies in the national procedure for identification of victims of human trafficking through the lens of the positive obligation to take protective operational measures."[37]

Of particular importance is the fact that the applicant had "been required to wait more than nine months after informing the authorities of her situation before the justice system granted her that status."[38] The Court held that nine months was an unreasonable amount of time—thus somewhat correcting the shortcoming of the Trafficking Convention by giving indication as to the time scales in which identification should be carried out.

The Court's ruling affirms the position that identification and a formal awarding of victim status to trafficked persons is a human rights positive obligation. Moreover:

Greece was also found to have failed to conduct an effective investigation; the national court proceedings were also found to be deficient. There were various aspects that were unsatisfactory: [T]he testimony provided by the director of Nea Zoi, who was in continuing contact with the applicant and reported that she was a victim of trafficking, was not initially included in the record; after the inclusion of this testimony, the competent authorities did not initiate a renewal of the proceedings, rather it was the applicant who had to do this; there were long periods of inactivity; the police did not search other addresses mentioned by L.E. where the alleged perpetrator might have been; the police did not try to gather additional information.[39]

Overall the investigation was poor, for which Greece was found to be accountable.

The obligation to carry out identification and efficient investigation appears to extend to carrying out thorough and efficient interviews with potential victims. It would appear that in the case of L.E., the authorities did not pay attention to what the applicant was saying.

Thus, interviews with victims should be aimed at exploring the following issues:

1. The practices of exploitation
2. The means of control employed by those in contact with the victim
3. The circumstances that led to the recruitment of the victim
4. Any travel that the victim undertook
5. The nature of the relationship between victims, traffickers, and others involved in trafficking and exploitation
6. The victim's living arrangements
7. The victim's autonomy
8. Victims' understanding of their situation and ways of coping.

The Court placed emphasis on the lack of consideration of the statement from the director of the NGO assisting the applicant. Consequently, we can ascertain that the positive duty to identify victims of human trafficking requires careful consideration of all available information, from a diverge range of sources.

Often, community organisations and NGOs are better placed than other bodies in identifying trafficked persons. First, such organisations may be the first body to come into direct contact with the trafficked person (e.g., a victim may turn up at a homeless shelter or a soup kitchen). Secondly, due to their direct contact with victims, their independence, their victim-focused approach, and often a strong human rights background, they may be better placed to gain the trust of vulnerable persons. Trafficked persons may have concerns over their immigration status, and they may fear deportation and fear the traffickers; this, in turn, translates into mistrust and reluctance to approach law enforcement personnel. Victims may prefer to give their account in a safe and comfortable environment, such as a safe house.

Recommendations
- Identification procedures should be carried out with due diligence.
- States should have appropriate national mechanisms for identifying trafficked persons.
- Law authorities should acknowledge the importance of civil society organisations in addressing cases of human trafficking.

9.5 Other Solutions to Identification

Case law indicates that human trafficking should be at the forefront of law enforcement work; frontline Police and immigration officers should receive training on trafficking and identification of victims. However, irregular migrants may either fear deportation if they were to contact authorities, or they may fear reprisal from their traffickers, or both. As such, they may not come forth and identify themselves as victims. Operative systems, therefore, cannot rely on victims to do the identifying; rather, States need efficient mechanisms in place that provide for the maximum opportunities of victim identification.

Likewise, numerous other stakeholders can play a significant role in victim identification. Guidance on human trafficking and identification should, therefore, also be available to:

- Municipality authorities: e.g., those endowed with monitoring housing regulations or health and safety in a work place
- National tax and revenue authorities (e.g., the Internal Revenue Service)
- Landlords renting properties
- Labour inspectorate (or equivalent) and trade unions
- Civil society organisations.

Importantly, these bodies should first come to understand that human trafficking is not outside their domain, and should act if they spot signs of exploitation. In addition, the above-mentioned units, together with law enforcement, should cooperate to recognise and identify human trafficking cases so as to allow for early involvement. To allow for maximum cooperation, a central intelligence unit should be available to all of them and the cooperation itself should be formalised. This is because "sometimes cooperation and information exchange is to a large extent dependant on personal contacts between people from the inspectorate and the police, which must be considered a weak point; when people leave or are replaced by another person the cooperation will stop."[40] However, any data collection, management, and sharing must adhere to data protection and privacy regulations.

In addition, governments should monitor their efforts. If facts and statistics illustrate that an approach is ineffective, the government must find new or additional tools. Moreover, it would appear rational to expect governments to monitor what approaches are used in other countries and, if need be, to transcend best practices. Thus, for example, if the use of technology to identify victims of human trafficking is found to be an effective measure in one or more nations, this should be applied by other governments.

9.6 Conclusion

The need for identification in the regulatory framework has a human rights function. When a victim is not identified, but should have been, she or he can argue that the national system is lacking and results in a violation of their human rights. The same is manifested in the trafficked person's lack of access to assistance, possible prosecution or penalization, or, in the worst-case scenario, re-trafficking. Consequently, a victim can build a case that there was a failure by the government. In turn, the government should change national legislation, so that it has adequate frameworks.

Endnotes

1. Piotrowicz, *The legal nature of trafficking in human beings*, International Human Rights Law Review, 4, (2009) at 192.

2. J, Donnelly, *Universal Human Rights in Theory and Practice*, 17 (1989).

3. J. Bhabha, *Child migration & human rights in a global age*, 111 (2014).

4. OSCE (2011), "Trafficking in Human Beings: Identification of Potential and Presumed Victims. A Community Policing Approach." Vienna: OSCE, 26.

5. Anti-Trafficking Monitoring Group, "In the Dock. Examining the UK's Criminal Justice response to human trafficking" (2013).

6. Turner, I. (2015), *Human Rights, Positive Obligations, and Measures to Prevent Human Trafficking in the United Kingdom*, Journal of Human Trafficking 1, 296-317 at 302.

7. The European Migration Network, "Identification of victims of trafficking in human beings in international protection and forced return procedures" (2014).

8. A. Gallagher, *The International Law of Human Trafficking*, 278, (2010).

9. Council of Europe, "Explanatory Report on the Convention on Action against Trafficking in Human Beings," ETS 197, 16.V.2005 at par 131.

10. Consolidated Version of the Treaty on the Functioning of the European Union art. 288, 2008 O.J. C 115/47.

11. Letschert, & Rijken, *Rights of Victims of Crime: Tensions Between an Integrated Approach and a Limited Legal Basis for Harmonisation*, New Journal of European Criminal Law 4(3), (2013) p. 250.

12. League of Nations, Convention to Suppress the Slave Trade and Slavery, 25 September 1926, 60 LNTS 253, Registered No. 1414; ILO Forced Labour Convention, 1930 (No. 29).

13. Muraszkiewicz, J. "Modern slavery—but let us remember the trafficked," LSE Human Rights Blog, 2015, retrieved on 12 March 2016 (http://blogs.lse.ac.uk/humanrights/2016/01/18/modern-slavery-but-let-us-remember-the-trafficked/).

14. Vijeyarasa, R. and Villarino, J. (2012). *Modern-Day Slavery? A Judicial Catchall for Trafficking, Slavery and Labour Exploitation: A Critique of Tang and Rantsev*. 8 Journal of International Law and International Relations, 36-61, p. 53.

15. Council of Europe, *Explanatory Report on the Convention on Action against Trafficking in Human Beings*, ETS 197, 16 May 2005, at para. 29.

16. Stoyanova, V. (2015) *Human Trafficking and Slavery Reconsidered. Conceptual Limits and States' Positive Obligations*, 540.

17. *Id.* at 333.

18. *Rantsev v Cyprus and Russia* App No. 25965/04 (ECtHR 7 January 2010), para. 280.

19. Allain, J. (2010). *Rantsev v Cyprus and Russia: The European Court of Human Rights and Trafficking as Slavery*, Human Rights Law Review, 10(3), 546-557 at 546.

20. *Rantsev v. Cyprus and Russia*, Application no. 25965/04, European Court of Human Rights, 7 January 2010, para. 45.

21. Stoyanova, V., *Dancing on the Borders of Article 4: Human Trafficking and the European Court of Human Rights in the Rantsev case*, Netherlands Quarterly of Human Rights (2012) 30(2), 163–194 at 174.

22. *Rantsev v. Cyprus and Russia*, Application no. 25965/04, European Court of Human Rights, 7 January 2010, para. 284. United Nations Economic and Social Council, "Recommended Principles and Guidelines on Human Rights and Human Trafficking: Report of the United Nations High Commissioner for Human Rights to the Economic and Social Council," E/2002/68. Add 1 (2002).

23. *Id.* at para. 285.

24. United Nations Protocol To Prevent, Suppress And Punish Trafficking In Persons, Especially Women and Children, Supplementing The United Nations Convention Against Transnational Organized Crime, UN 2000, Came Into Force 25 December 2003 (Here Forth Palermo Protocol).

25. *Rantsev v. Cyprus and Russia*, Application no. 25965/04, European Court of Human Rights, 7 January 2010, para. 295.

26. *Id.* at para. 286.

27. *C.N. v. the United Kingdom*, Application no.4239/08, European Court of Human Rights, 13 November 2012, para. 8.

28. *Id.* at para. 12.

29. *Id.* at para. 72.

30. *Id.* at para. 20.

31. *Id.* at para. 25.

32. *Id.* at para. 67.

33. *Id.* at para. 69.

34. *Id.* at para. 80.

35. *L.E. v. Greece*, Application no.71545/12, European Court of Human Rights, 21 January 2016.

36. Stoyanova, V. (2016). "L.E. v. Greece: Human Trafficking and States' Positive Obligations" [Online] Retrieved 6 March 2016, from https://strasbourgobservers.com/2016/02/02/l-e-v-greece-human-trafficking-and-states-positive-obligations/.

37. European Commission, "Together against trafficking in human beings."

38. Stoyanova, V. (2016). "L.E. v. Greece: Human Trafficking and States' Positive Obligations."

39. Rijken, C. (2013). *Trafficking in Human Beings for Labour Exploitation: Cooperation in an Integrated Approach.* European Journal Of Crime, Criminal Law And Criminal Justice, 21(1), 9-35 at 25.

Chapter 10

Gender Issues in Human Trafficking:

Empowering Women and Girls Through Awareness and Law

By Felicity Gerry, QC, and Catarina Sjölin, LL.M.

Synopsis
10.1 The Effect of Human Trafficking on Women and Girls
10.2 Protection and Empowerment
10.3 The Scope of the Labour Problem
10.4 Lessons from Outside the U.S.
10.5 U.S. Action and Strategies
10.6 Suggestions for a Solution
10.7 A Holistic Approach
    A. The Istanbul Convention
    B. Response by the Private Sector
10.8 Conclusion
Endnotes

This chapter focuses on women and girls because human trafficking dispropor-tionately involves females, and the effect on them—and society in general—is far-reaching. With some focus on the approaches of the U.K. and the U.S., this chapter considers existing international obligations and where and why they fail, and provides suggestions for how the situation can and should be improved. Achieving gender equality will be ever more elusive if the gender issues in both criminal and commercial enterprises are not tackled in a holistic and strategic manner, and in a way that can have global effect.

It is important in human trafficking to understand the complex factors at work that drive the varied practices coming under this banner, as well as those factors making people more vulnerable to it. There will be specific factors that act as a push from or a pull to a particular place.[1] When considering the broad range of human trafficking that particularly affects females, we need to differentiate trafficking for work (whether criminal or commercial) from trafficking for other gender-based reasons (sexual exploitation or forced marriage, for example), because of the different drivers at work.

However, we must also remember the important commonalities. Trafficking for work may often not be simply down to poverty and lack of education; instead, relative poverty, together with some education, is often more likely to place a female at risk.[2] Enabling safe migration, while also focusing on positive education and work options (including the provision of small-scale finance) has been shown to be effective.[3] The role of a safe environment—where the rights of females are protected and that protection is enforced—is more often seen as important in relation to the second category of trafficking, where significant risk factors include gender inequality, the burden of familial and societal expectations, pressure based on prevailing discriminatory social norms and harmful religious narratives, a desire to control female sexuality, poverty, lack of education and opportunity, and a failure to enforce laws and policies against such practices.[4] It is, however, vitally important in relation to trafficking for work too, as women who are not safe struggle to be truly economically active.[5]

The UN Protocol to Prevent, Suppress and Punish Trafficking in Persons, especially Women and Children[6] (the Trafficking Protocol) defines human trafficking as the recruitment, transport, transfer, harbouring or receipt of persons for exploitation where this is done by threat or use of force, coercion, abduction, fraud, deception, abuse of power or making payments to a person in control of the trafficked person. This may, but does not need to, involve the traffickers making financial gain. There may even be a belief that the purpose of the trafficking is for the trafficked person's own good, to lift family members out of poverty or to create individual opportunity, albeit after some period of servitude.

Numerous international and regional instruments comprehensively prohibit human trafficking, but there remains a failure to comprehensively prevent exploitation of women and girls in this context. The Global Gender Gap Index examines the gap between men and women in four fundamental categories (sub-indexes): Economic Participation and Opportunity, Educational Attainment, Health and Survival, and Political Empowerment. The United States was ranked 28th out of 145 countries in the 2015 Global Gender Gap Report published by the World Economic Forum.[7] It is important to examine the gender issues that exist in the context of human trafficking, which can arise in both a criminal and corporate setting, as well as the effect that human exploitation has on the opportunities of woman and girls.

The U.S. has signed, but not ratified, The United Nations Convention for the Elimination of Discrimination Against Women[8] (CEDAW), and therefore does not comply with the optional protocol to CEDAW, which carries reporting provisions. Essentially, this means that countries that have agreed to work towards the elimination of discrimination against women within the meaning of the Convention have developed the obligation of "due diligence," which is not followed in the U.S. The consequence is that the documents produced by those countries that do commit to UN reporting mechanisms are not available for analysis or evaluation. It is a significant lacuna that must impact on the ability to assess the U.S. response to human trafficking where it affects the empowerment of women and girls. In 2002, the Senate Foreign Relations Committee voted 12-7 to approve the treaty, but it was never sent to the full Senate for advice and consent to ratification.

In addition, the Istanbul Convention on Preventing and Combating Violence against Women and Domestic Violence[9] (the Istanbul Convention) is open to all countries. It has also not been signed and ratified by the U.S. It is:

Based on the understanding that violence against women is a form of gender-based violence that is committed against women because they are women. It is the obligation of the state to fully address it in all its forms and to take measures to prevent violence against women, protect its victims and prosecute the perpetrators. Failure to do so would make it the responsibility of the state.

It is a reasonable conclusion that the failure to implement international and well-researched instruments that are designed to protect and empower women and girls means that the U.S. falls short of what is necessary to combat human trafficking. It remains difficult, in particular, to assess implementation in the absence of agreed basic global principles and mechanisms. Investment in training, awareness, intervention, and protection remain ad hoc and state-by-state, making the enforcement of rights opaque, and risking the U.S. responses falling woefully short of what is necessary to protect women and girls.[10]

10.1 The Effect of Human Trafficking on Women and Girls

Females are disproportionately affected by human trafficking. Women and girls make up about 55 percent of all forced labour victims, and they represent the vast majority of victims exploited for commercial sex work.[11] The negative health consequences of sexual exploitation are well-documented, and include long-term physical, mental, and emotional harm. The economic disempowerment of sexual exploitation is inherent; the victim will work but receive no or little economic benefit, while others are enriched. Tackling human trafficking as a gender issue therefore becomes an imperative, particularly in a world that currently suffers significant dislocation of people at risk of exploitation.

10.2 Protection and Empowerment

Women and girls who are trafficked are often trapped in peril and poverty. The negative effects of trafficking upon women are also likely to negatively affect the next generationm who will grow up in poverty, violence, and ignorance. Tackling trafficking of women—not just signing up to international instruments, but implementing them effectively—can thus have a disproportionately positive effect through not just empowering women, but also protecting the next generation from poverty, violence, exploitation, and trafficking.

It is not just in understanding the causes of trafficking that there is a dangerous temptation to divide into categories, but also in understanding the nature of the trafficking and its effects. For instance, too often domestic violence is seen separately from commercial exploitation of women, despite the obvious overlaps, e.g., the woman persuaded by a partner into travelling abroad who finds herself forced into prostitution. A focus on sexual exploitation in legal terms often results in a failure to recognise the now-accepted serious health effects of sexual exploitation. A focus on health alone fails to tackle the root cause—sexual exploitation.

The reality is that trafficking and exploitation can be domestic, intimate, or as a result of the actions of strangers. Women who are trafficked are less able to access work opportunities, although they are often generating income for others: A high degree of criminal income is generated by modern slavery—particularly in the context of the sex trade.[12] An estimated \$105 billion is generated annually.[13]

When law and policy is designed to tackle only domestic or only commercial exploitation of women and girls, it inevitably fails. When attitudes to females in a society are not considered and, if necessary, challenged meaningfully as part of implementation of legal approaches, well-meaning laws are unlikely to succeed. Further, national boundaries are meaningless to those who traffic persons. Legal approaches similarly must be transnational to succeed.

10.3 The Scope of the Labour Problem

At the international level, a number of instruments are aimed at tackling the various manifestations of human trafficking. The International Labour Office (ILO) has provided the Forced Labour Convention (1930)[14] and the Worst Forms of Child Labour Convention (1999).[15] The ILO Committee of Experts on the Application of Conventions and Recommendations (CEACR) has provided guidance on the scope of the definition of forced labour, stressing that it encompasses trafficking in persons for the purposes of labour and sexual exploitation as defined by the Palermo Protocol.[16] This guidance supplements the UN Convention against Transnational Organised Crime (2000),[17] criminalising trafficking in persons whether it occurs within countries or across borders, and whether or not conducted by organised crime networks.[18] Slavery and mistreatment has been the subject of international treaties since the Legaue of Nations Slavery Convention in 1926,[19] and more recently, the UN Supplementary Convention on the Abolition of Slavery (1956)[20] and the Convention against Torture (1985).[21] Children generally are covered by the UN Conventions on the Rights of the Child (1989)[22] and women are covered by CEDAW.

10.4 Lessons From Outside the U.S.

At the regional level in Europe, human trafficking is addressed by the Council of Europe's Convention on Action against Trafficking in Human Beings[23] and Chapter 4 of the European Convention on Human Rights, together with the European Union's Directive on Preventing and Combating Trafficking in Human Beings and Protecting its Victims.[24] The Council of Europe also produced the Istanbul Convention mentioned above. Trafficking for sexual exploitation is criminalized in the U.K. by the Sexual Offences Act 2003. Slavery, servitude, compulsory and forced labour as well as trafficking are the subject of offences under the Modern Slavery Act 2015, and employing an illegal worker is also a crime (Immigration, Asylum and Nationality Act 2006).

10.5 U.S. Action and Strategies

Awareness and legislative reactions can also be seen in the U.S. USAID has committed to work alongside lawmakers to "increase United States implementation of the U.S. Strategy to Prevent and Respond to Gender-Based Violence Globally," as well as "supporting projects aimed at keeping adolescent girls in school and public outreach campaigns."[25] There are laws and regulations in the U.S. that provide for prevention, victim protection and prosecution of perpetrators of human trafficking, slavery, servitude, and forced labour, but they are by no means comprehensive.[26] Practitioners will need to be familiar with the relevant provisions.

The Trafficking Victims Protection Act 2000 (TVPA) and its reauthorizations work at the federal, and in some respects the international, level despite problems and gaps. The TVPA created important federal offences of human trafficking, and also allowed for restitution to victims and their resettlement in the U.S., creating the T visa. There was also a focus on information gathering and co-operation in the creation of the Office to Monitor and Combat Trafficking in Persons and the Interagency Task Force to Monitor and Combat Trafficking.

The 2003 Reauthorization Act broadened the focus, enabling victims to sue their traffickers, and strengthening the protection of victims against deportation. Importantly, in criminal terms, it added human trafficking to the list of crimes that can be charged under the Racketeering Influenced Corrupt Organisations Act (RICO), enabling prosecution of those who lead a trafficking organisation, rather than just the foot soldiers. The 2005 Reauthorization looked internationally, and the 2008 Act improved prevention strategies as well as improving the criminal scheme. The 2013 Reauthorization act against child marriage again attempts to improve the federal criminal scheme's interaction with the state and local level.

A T visa introduced in 2000 is available to some victims who assist in the prosecution of their traffickers, and allows the victim, spouse, children and parents to remain in the United States as long as strict criteria are satisfied. There is a low cap on the total number of visas per year (5,000), but that number has never been reached; in 2015 only 508 T visas were issued.[27] The low numbers of victims identified can be attributed to many different factors, including the stringent criteria.[28] One important obstacle is a lack of access to necessary legal services, and it is here that an understanding by lawyers of the issues involved can be of significant benefit.[29]

The U.S. has signed but not ratified many international human-rights-based treaties, including those relating to children. The degree of legal authority or relevance that a treaty may have in U.S. courts depends in large part on whether the U.S. has taken action to implement the relevant principles through its domestic process. This means that human rights law can be difficult to enforce in the U.S. If it is ratified through treaties or as customary law, then it will take precedence over conflicting state laws, since international law is part of the federal law.

International law applies to states through the Supremacy Clause of the U.S. Constitution. Unless ratification includes the clear intent that the treaty be directly enforceable by the courts (i.e., "self-executing"), or unless Congress passes implementing legislation, the treaty is not judicially enforceable. It follows that in the U.S., human rights law can be difficult to enforce directly in the courts, and the sorts of protective measures outlined herein can be difficult to achieve.

However, human-rights-based arguments in pleadings and briefs can add value to judicial interpretation and through the citation. For U.S. practitioners, there is a handbook prepared by the Center for Human Rights and Humanitarian Law at Washington College of Law that sets out how human-rights-based arguments can be presented in the U.S., particularly by legal aid attorneys.[30]

We have only selected a few examples, but it is clear that while legislative efforts have been made at state and federal level, there is a risk that a lack of harmonisation will create a lacuna that can be exploited by traffickers. What is important is the interrelationship between legislation and community engagement.[31] Communities must be equipped to deal with the complex problems that lead to and are caused by human trafficking.[32]

In the end, what is needed is a visible comprehensive commitment to tackling human trafficking, whether for work or in areas such as child marriage or forced marriage, through a well-resourced, coordinated, and evaluated action plan with a systematic framework to effectively monitor progress, which together will enable the government to fulfil its responsibilities to women and girls. These systems exist in the international instruments that the U.S. has not endorsed, and therefore the risk is that the evaluation also fails. The losers of such global disharmony are most likely to be the women and girls who are trafficked and exploited, particularly when moved from one location to another, frustrating any task force by creating cross-border difficulties that are not solved when the approaches differ.

10.6 Suggestions for a Solution

By its intrinsic nature, trafficking in human beings is a hidden crime, where criminal individuals or organisations quickly adapt and advance their modus operandi in order to respond to law enforcement strategies, often acting under the guise of legitimate operations.[33] The criminalisation of practices is not sufficient to protect those at risk or to catch and deal with those who offend. Indeed, simply treating the issue as one of criminal law can be counterproductive. Thus, the U.S. TVPA and its reauthorizations are welcome in their attempt to provide prevention and protection as well as criminalisation, but such a scheme fails unless there is a thorough understanding of drivers and effects of trafficking, leading to a genuinely holistic, rather than piecemeal, approach. Effective implementation also requires additional non-legal measures, particularly in the context of honor-based violence, where women and children are abused in order to sustain male dominance within the social system.

10.7 A Holistic Approach

Currently, we have international norms in relation to aspects of human trafficking and other forms of sexual exploitation of females, but they lack legal backing, making them ineffective—a point made strongly and repeatedly by the outgoing UN Special Rapporteur on Violence against Women, Rashida Manjoo.[34] International communiqués and even agreements are welcome, but fail to have an impact at the personal level because they are not of direct effect.

Examining the extent to which States can be held responsible for human rights violations by individuals, Patricia Wheeler observed in 2004 that: "If it can be demonstrated that legislation at national level is an essential part of the 'effective measures' required to put a stop to the practice of [female genital mutilation]... States which fail to adopt appropriate legislation will be in breach of their obligations under The Convention [on the Rights of the Child]."[35] When nationally enforceable laws are created, the focus, as in the U.K., is on criminalization at the national level. Wheeler recognized that most organizations were asserting in 2004 that the answer was to legislate. She gave an example of where an excision was prevented by intervention of the authorities where legislation gave the police and health professionals the legitimacy to intervene. International conventions can be useful if a four-pronged approach is taken: adoption of uniform definitions, agreed rules for the extra-territorial effect of a state's laws, planned implementation that goes beyond simple criminalization, and the statutory sphere and corporations taking responsibility for adopting and enforcing these standards.

Agreed definitions make enforcement of legislation across national boundaries possible; human trafficking is no respecter of state boundaries, and it profits from the territorial limits of national laws. The good that can come out of a transnational harmonisation of law and policy in this context is that all nations can focus on common rules on the basis of their common interests. Improvements in one country can therefore directly influence another country that has not yet made such progress.

A. The Istanbul Convention

An important step forward toward a less-piecemeal approach toward tackling the problem of women and girls being trafficked would be the immediate global ratification and implementation of the Istanbul Convention. By doing this, the global community would deal with some important aspects of trafficking, but importantly, they would do so in a way that would create a blueprint for tackling trafficking more widely.

The Istanbul Convention has four fundamental themes: prevention, protection, prosecution, and monitoring. Crucially, the Istanbul Convention requires governments that agree to be bound by the Convention not only to make laws, but also to ensure that the laws are enforced. This is to be done by implementing the following:

- Training professionals who are in close contact with victims
- Regularly running awareness-raising campaigns

- Taking steps to include in teaching materials issues such as gender equality and non-violent conflict resolution in interpersonal relationships
- Setting up treatment programs for perpetrators of domestic violence and for sex offenders
- Working closely with NGOs
- Involving the media and the private sector in eradicating gender stereotypes and in promoting mutual respect.

Global harmonisation by ratification of the Istanbul Convention would demonstrate a commitment to a rights-based mechanism. The document already sets out a great deal of what needs to be done in relation to human trafficking and other violence to and exploitation of women. The Convention also includes within the Chapters data collection, integration of policies, prevention, protection, and support, before it lays out the substantive law. The Convention requires implementation by ratifying States in a manner that prioritizes the advance protection of victims through short- and long-term early intervention and through prevention initiatives against harmful practices. It also requires specific training for frontline health, education, and welfare practitioners, accompanied by community engagement initiatives, to enable such practitioners to speak to community leaders about the law and human rights concerns.

B. Response by the Private Sector

Tackling global exploitation does not stop with governments, NGOs or the criminal justice system. Corporate and financial entities must also be engaged, particularly to tackle trafficking for work. There are now international "super corporations" with economies dwarfing those of many countries.[36] Corporate enterprises in legitimate global markets now widely seek good practical advice in the move toward corporate responsibility. It is, in the long run, in the interests of global corporations to have uniformity in law and policy in the States in which they do business. They and their competitors are then on a level playing field, so that turning a blind eye to trafficking and exploitation cannot be a choice to cut costs. The difficulties and costs of complying with numerous different regimes would be curtailed. More than this, empowering women to be more economically active also means a greater number of economically active consumers of the wares and services offered by global corporations. An economically virtuous circle can thus be created.

More than simply creating profit for large corporations, greater economic activity on the part of women has positive effects on the women themselves. As noted earlier, relative poverty can be a risk factor for trafficking. Poverty in itself can curtail women's work opportunities, limiting them to certain jobs or to certain geographical areas due to their fears of sexual violence if they go beyond these parameters.[37] It can, in particular, force them towards poorly paid occupations like sex work, which carry greater risks of victimisation by sexual violence[38] and trafficking. Such violence can be domestic (from family or intimate partners) or commercial (from customers or those controlling the sex worker). Once the woman achieves better-paid, higher-status work, this tends to act as a protection from sexual violence, particularly domestic violence.[39] Better-paid work will still not be protective, though, if there remains impunity around violence to women. Again, we return to the need for effective implementation to accompany laws that protect women from sexual violence, if trafficking of women is to be tackled.

10.8 Conclusion

It is with a holistic approach that progress can be made at an international level to tackle trafficking and other practises disproportionately affecting women and girls globally. In the meantime, awareness of the gender issues involved in human trafficking is a powerful weapon to improve social and legal responses in any country or state committed to addressing gender issues in order to empower women and girls.

Endnotes

1. UN Inter-Agency Project on Human Trafficking, "Human Trafficking Background Information" (http://www.no-trafficking.org/resources_background_risks.html); see also The Asian Foundation, "Human Trafficking in Mongolia: Risks, Vulnerability and Trauma" (The Asia Foundation, Ulaanbaatar, 2006).

2. ICRW, "Child Marriage and Poverty," from *Too Young to Wed: Advocacy Toolkit: Education & Change Toward Ending Child Marriage* (ICRW: Washington, D.C., 2006) p4. and WHO Female genital mutilation, online at http://www.who.int/mediacentre/factsheets/fs241/en/ accessed 20 January 2016.

3. *See* note 1 above.

4. F. Gerry, J. Muraszkiewicz, & N. Vavoula, *The role of technology in the fight against human trafficking: Reflections on privacy and data protection concerns* (forthcoming – accepted by Computer Law and Security Review); M. Hester, C. Khatidja, et al, "Forced marriage: The risk factors and the ef-

fect of raising the minimum age for a sponsor, and of leave to enter the UK as a spouse or fiancé(e) (School for Policy Studies: University of Bristol, 2008). UN Women, "Causes, protective and risk factors."

5. F. Gerry and C. Sjölin, "Achieving the G20 gender equality target by tackling sexual exploitation through legal uniformity, extra territoriality and corporate responsibility" conference paper delivered at 4th International Conference on Law, Regulation and Public Policy, June 2015 (published in the conference proceedings DOI: 10.5176/2251-3809_LRRP15.43).

6. United Nations Convention against Transnational Organised Crime, Protocol to Prevent, Suppress and Punish Trafficking in Persons, Especially Women and Children, supplementing the United Nations Convention against Transnational Organised Crime (signed 15 November 2000, entered into force 15 November 2003) 2237 UNTS 319; Doc A/55/383.

7. World Economic Forum, "The Global Gender Gap Report 2015" (World Economic Forum: Geneva, 2016) available online at http://reports.weforum.org/global-gender-gap-report-2015/.

8. United Nations, Convention on the Elimination of All Forms of Discrimination Against Women (signed 18 December 1979, entered into force 3 September 1981) 1249 UNTS 13.

9. Council of Europe, Convention on Preventing and Combating Violence against Women and Domestic Violence (signed 11 May 2011, entered into force 1 August 2014) CETS 210.

10. C. Thomas, "Forced and early marriage: A focus on central and Eastern Europe and former Soviet Union Countries with selected laws from other countries," prepared for the Expert Group Meeting on group practices in legislation to address harmful practices against women, Addis Ababa 25-28 May 2009 available online at http://www.un.org/womenwatch/daw/vaw/vegms-gplahpaw#expert accessed 8 March 2016.

11. International Labour Office, *Profits and Poverty: The economics of forced labour* (2014) p7.

12. Polaris Project, "Human Trafficking: An Overview" (online).

13. International Labour Office, *Profits and Poverty: The economics of forced labour*.

14. International Labour Organisation, Forced Labour Convention, C029 (adopted 28 June 1930, entered into force 1 May 1932).

15. International Labour Organisation, Worst Forms of Child Labour Convention, C182 (adopted 17 June 1999, entered into force 19 November 2000).

16. International Labour Office, International Labour Conference, 102nd Session, 2013 Report of the Committee of Experts on the Application of Conventions and Recommendations (International Labour Office, Geneva, 2013).

17. United Nations, Convention against Transnational Organised Crime, (signed 15 November 2000, entered into force 29 September 2003) 2225 UNTS 209.

18. *Id.*

19. League of Nations, Slavery, Servitude, Forced Labour and Similar Institutions and Practices Convention (adopted 25 September 1926, entered into force 9 March 1927) 60 LNTS 253.

20. United Nations, Supplementary Convention on the Abolition of Slavery, the Slave Trade, and Institutions and Practices Similar to Slavery (signed 7 September 1956, entered into force 30 April 1957) 266 UNTS 3.

21. United Nations, Convention against Torture and Other Cruel, Inhuman or Degrading Treatment or Punishment (signed 10 December 1984, entered into force 26 June 1987) 1465 UNTS 85.

22. United Nations, Convention on the Rights of the Child (signed 20 November 1989, entered into force 2 September 1989) 1577 UNTS 3.

23. Council of Europe, Council of Europe Convention on Action against Trafficking in Human Beings (signed 16 May 2005, entered into force 1 February 2008) CETS 197.

24. European Union: Council of the European Union, Directive 2011/36/EU of the European Parliament and of the Council of 5 April 2011 on preventing and combating trafficking in human beings and protecting its victims, and replacing Council Framework Decision 2002/629/JHA, 15 April 2011, OJ L. 101/1-101/11; 15.4.2011, 2011/36/EU.

25. "Child, Early, and Forced Marriage: United States Government's Response" (https://www.usaid.gov/news-information/fact-sheets/child-early-and-forced-marriage-usg-response).

26. See useful discussion in Edwards, *Traffic in Human Beings: At the Intersection of Criminal Justice, Human Rights, Asylum/Migration and Labor* (2007) Denver Journal of Law and Policy 36(1) 9.

27. Report of the Visa Office 2015 Table XVI(A) available online a https://travel.state.gov/content/visas/en/law-and-policy/statistics/annual-reports/report-of-the-visa-office-2015.html (accessed 22 March 2016).

28. R. Kandathil, *Global Sex Trafficking and the Trafficking Victims Protection Act of 2000: Legislative Responses to the Problem of Modern Slavery* (2005) Michigan Journal of Gender and Law 12(1) 86.

29. Fight Slavery Now, "Trafficking Victims Protection Act" online at http://fightslaverynow.org/why-fight-there-are-27-million-reasons/the-law-and-trafficking/trafficking-victims-protection-act/trafficking-victims-protection-act/ accessed 22 March 2016.

30. Local Human Rights Lawyering Project, "Human Rights in the U.S. Handbook for Legal Aid Attorneys" (Washington College of Law, American University: 2013).

31. World Health Organization, "Female Genital Mutilation: Programmes to Date: What works and What Doesn't" (WHO Geneva: 1999).

32. R. Kandathil, *Global Sex Trafficking and the Trafficking Victims Protection Act of 2000: Legislative Responses to the Problem of Modern Slavery* (2005) Michigan Journal of Gender and Law 12(1) 86.

33. F. Gerry, J. Muraszkiewicz, & N. Vavoula, *The role of technology in the fight against human trafficking: Reflections on privacy and data protection concerns* (forthcoming – accepted by Computer Law and Security Review).

34. United Nations, "Violence against women—A pervasive human rights violation calls for a binding standard of accountability at the international level,"

35. Wheeler, *Eliminating FGM: The role of the law* (2004) 11 The International Journal of Children's Rights 257- 271.

36. Global Policy Forum, "Comparison of the World's 25 Largest Corporations with the GDP of Selected Countries" (based on data from *Fortune* magazine and The World Bank.

37. World Health Organisation, "World Report on Violence and Health" (WHO, Geneva, 2002) Chapters 4 and 6.

38. The links between sex work and violence are well known and thoroughly documented. For example, the paper by S. Church, M. Henderson, & M. Barnard, "Violence by clients towards female prostitutes in different work settings: Questionnaire survey" BMJ 2001: 322:524, found that half of all prostitutes working outside had been the subject of violence from clients in the preceding 12 months (ignoring violence from pimps and/or intimate partners).

39. Dalal, *Does economic empowerment protect women from intimate partner violence?* J. Inj. Violence Res. 2011 Jan; 3(1): 35–44.

Part IV
Additional Legal Applications for Trafficking Laws

Chapter 11

Human Trafficking and Cults

By Robin Boyle Laisure

Human trafficking and cults have much in common. This chapter will compare common characteristics of human traffickers and cult leaders. (For a more in-depth explanation of cults, please see author's article in the *Oregon Review of International Law*.[1]) To begin this comparison, the statutory construction of human trafficking laws will be explored. These laws may be used by prosecutors to capture cult leaders.

Because cults are undocumented and are not calculated by the U.S. census, it is difficult to estimate how many are in the United States today. Estimates range from 2,500 to 8,000 cults, with membership ranging from a few individuals to tens of thousands in any given cult.[2] According to the International Cultic Studies Association (ICSA), an organization that monitors cults and provides education and counseling, approximately 2.5 million Americans have joined cultic groups since the 1970s.[3]

This chapter focuses on cults that harm its members or outsiders. Some cults are benign, others destructive. Benign cults appear not to inflict physical or emotional trauma to their members. In contrast, destructive cults do harm their members and are characterized by exploitative, manipulative, and controlling interpersonal dynamics. Destructive cults are the focus of this chapter.

Cults continue to evade our justice system here in the United States and abroad. This chapter seeks to offer a fresh legal framework that could aid in the capture and prosecution of cult leaders.

11.1 Cults: An Overview

Destructive cults have common traits. Cults share three characteristics: "(1) a charismatic leader who increasingly becomes an object of worship as the general principles that may have originally sustained the group lose their power; (2) a process . . . call[ed] coercive persuasion or thought reform; (3) economic, sexual, and other exploitation of group members by the leader and the ruling coterie."[4] The leader often tells a unique story about the foundation of the organization that elevates this group or religion above all others. The leader claims to have been selected by some supreme being, and he or she frequently preaches that followers will find salvation after death, if they follow the teachings. Only this leader has a true understanding of the religion and, thus, all information must flow through the leader.

In contrast with more traditional religious affiliations, destructive cults often fail to disclose to recruits what the organization is about. The late Herbert Rosedale, Esq.[5] would ask his audience whether they have ever joined a church. Often some members would nod their heads. And then he would ask them if they knew that they were joining a church when they decided to participate. As a bottom line distinction between what is a religious organization versus a cult, the difference often comes down to the narrow question of whether the adherent knew what kind of group he or she was joining at the outset. Fraudulent inducement is also common among human traffickers in luring their victims into their trafficking rings.

A. Four Processes of Indoctrination

Cults indoctrinate their members through mind or thought control, as former "Moonie" Steven Hassan explains.[6] In addition, cults use the following to indoctrinate members: behavior control, emotional control, and information control. Ultimately, the individual loses his or her freedom of choice.

Thought control or mind control is described as follows:

> [A] system which disrupts an individual's identity. An identity is made up of elements such as beliefs, behavior, thought processes, and emotions that constitute a definite pattern. Under the influence of mind control, a person's authentic original identity given at birth, and as later formed by family, education, friendships, and most importantly that person's own free choices, becomes replaced with another identity, often one that they would not have chosen for themself without tremendous social pressure.[7]

Depending upon the group, to exert undue influence or mind control, cult leaders may also rely on other techniques, including deception in recruitment; fear; physical, sexual, and verbal abuse; and isolation.

Why does one join a cult? Often, the new recruit knows little about the organization when joining. It is common practice in cultic groups to use deceptive pretenses to lure in followers. Typically, one would not join these groups if it were advertised as a cult. Once inside the cult, the individual undergoes a process that results in a loss of freedom of choice. Unfortunately, it is this aspect of cults that provide obstacles to our judicial system's ability to provide a remedy. Courts have not accepted mind control as an element of traditional crimes.[8]

To inculcate an adherent, cults prey on people's fears. Their leaders preach that should members leave, they will die by accident or fate (health or otherwise). Adherents are forewarned that deserters will be denied salvation.

Sexual and physical abuse, prevalent in destructive cults, reinforces undue influence, fear, and paranoia among followers. Often, beatings are publicly displayed for other members to see as a lesson of what would happen should they be disobedient. Atrocities shape the adherents' minds to submission and control by the destructive cult. The individual is no longer the former self, but a different self.

Three other aspects of control by cult leaders over their followers are **behavior, emotions, and information**. Destructive cults may control behavior by assigning specific tasks for followers to do. Often, followers must ask permission for basic daily occurrences, such as obtaining bus fare. Restriction on freedom of movement is also common among traffickers and their victims.

To conform behavior and channel emotions, cult leaders use guilt and fear. Harm can occur on the outside because involvement with the authorities—who are portrayed as being associated with "the devil" or evil in general—will result in the follower's eternal life in hell. The leaders themselves can punish followers if they do not follow their rules.

Destructive cult leaders often control information. Many cults restrict access to news events of the outside world. Members may have limited information about what is happening within their own organization. If the cult is located in a remote geographical setting, then isolation from the public and the media can be acute. However, even where cults exist in urban areas, members may be restricted from interacting with outsiders. Thus, there is physical as well as psychological isolation.

The ultimate result of undue influence is that the victim loses freedom of choice. The cult member has a new identity. These kinds of controls are common in human trafficking. Cult leaders rely upon a belief system, such as to higher supreme being, to prey on adherents, whereas traffickers or pimps will induce a young girl by flattery or threaten a young man that the trafficker will reveal an LGBTQ identity to the man's family. The victims of both the cult leaders and the human trafficker become dependent upon their exploiter.

B. Five Types of Cults

A common misconception is that the term "cult" refers only to religious organizations. Although religious cults are the most notorious, there are also political, terrorist, psychotherapy, educational, and commercial cults.

Religious cults are centralized around a religious dogma. "Doomsday cults" are focused on the end of the world.[9] Other cults have ongoing ideology and spirituality. At the core of religious cults is the preaching of their spiritual leader who often claims to have unique knowledge or some connection to the after-world.

Rather than using religion as their tenet, **political cults** have an ideology built upon a belief that the political system must be changed. The Workers Democratic Union (WDU) was described as a small political cult led by a charismatic woman. The WDU was a feminist, Marxist-Leninist party with women leading its upper ranks. After twelve years of existence, one hundred members of WDU met in San Francisco and voted to expel their leader, Doreen Baxter, and dissolve the organization. Baxter was accused of corruption and abuse.[10]

Since the September 11, 2001, attacks on America's soil, cult researchers have drawn parallels between **terrorist groups** with an ideological premise, such as Al Qaeda, and religious cults.[11] Al Qaeda had a charismatic, self-appointed leader in Osama bin Laden, and followers were so devoted to their cause they were willing to commit suicide and mass murder as part of the September 11th attacks. This arguably indicates Al Qaeda's leaders' extreme undue influence over its followers. Thus, Al Qaeda can be characterized as a religious cultic terrorist group.

One of the distinctions between a political cult operating as a terrorist organization and a "traditional" cult is that the terrorist group is centered on the destruction of others outside its group, whereas a religious cult is destructive to its own members.

Followers of **psychotherapy cults** espouse that their followers' devotion leads to greater intellectual enlightenment in a pseudo-analytic setting. These groups are profit-motivated centers run by the unskilled who do more harm than good.

An example is the Sullivan Institute in Manhattan, New York, which was a community of middle-class artists and professionals who lived together in the 1970s and '80s, and engaged in unorthodox psychoanalytic therapy.[12] The collective included an estimated 200 members who lived in three buildings on the Upper West Side and ran a political theater group in the East Village. Children were separated from parents. A former Sullivanian explained that the basic tenet of the teachings was that the nuclear family was the "root of all evil." Pyschotherapy cults can cause harm to the members' psyches.

Commercial cults recruit with a promise of profit for the individual. Often the leaders build their organization around pyramid schemes that depend upon recruitment of people to sell and purchase magazine subscriptions or any other goods. Their technique could be door-to-door sales or word-of-mouth. The destructive nature of this category of cults is in the leaders' treatment of the salespeople. The salespeople are often manipulated through fear, guilt, and sometimes physical and sexual abuse into selling products to the public to create revenue for the cult.

C. Cults and the Law

Court cases reveal two legal impediments to prosecuting cult leaders and defending vulnerable adherents. First, U.S. law strongly protects religion.[13] Second, U.S. evidence rules generally impair prosecutors' ability to introduce evidence of brainwashing and coercion.

1. U.S. law strongly protects religion

In the United States, every person has the right to freely believe in and practice the religion of his or her choice.[14] Furthermore, any religious group has the right to persuade and attract new members to its ranks. This Constitutional right to freedom of religion has, at times, been misinterpreted.[15]

Although the First Amendment, which describes the freedom of religion, is laudable in its conception, deference to this constitutional right has impeded legal intervention when cults tilt towards destructiveness.[16]

As an illustration, former members of the Unification Church brought an action against the Church for fraud, false imprisonment, and intentional infliction of emotional distress. Although the court was sympathetic to claims of fraudulent inducement to join the Church, the court stopped short of granting the plaintiffs a remedy. In considering (in dicta) whether to criminalize brainwashing, the court found such a solution too "coercive" because it "could result in the jailing of church members" and "would clearly impose a greater burden on religion than would civil tort liability for fraud."[17]

2. U.S. evidence rules impair ability to introduce evidence of brainwashing and coercion

In 1993, the United States Supreme Court established a set of criteria for federal courts to follow when considering whether to admit expert testimony during a trial known as the *Daubert* test.[18] The *Daubert* test did not relax the rules on expert testimony. Put another way, if someone lower on the cult ladder were being prosecuted, then the standards of *Daubert* would cause an undue influence defense to fail. From the defense side, the most challenging element of the *Daubert* test would be establishing that the expert testimony on brainwashing meets the criterion of general acceptance in the scientific community.

The prosecution cannot rely on a psychological coercion theory to support its case either. *United States v. Kozminski* set the standard for many years to come.[19] In that case, the defendants were charged with holding two mentally-challenged farm workers in involuntary servitude. The Government relied primarily upon the theory that defendants used psychological coercion to keep the men on the farm. The court held that the Government could not prove a violation of the defendants' constitutional rights based on this mental coercion alone; it also had to prove that defendants used or threatened to use physical or legal coercion, which the prosecution could not do.[20]

In 1993, Congress passed the federal Religious Freedom Restoration Act (RFRA).[21] By passing RFRA, Congress made it more difficult to prosecute behavior claimed to be a religious practice. Under it, courts were obligated to apply a more rigorous test (known as the "compelling interest" test) against the government when it defended laws such as a religious ritual restriction.

Eventually, the U.S. Supreme Court struck down RFRA, but Congress enacted the Religious Land Use and Institutionalized Persons Act of 2000 (RLUIPA) to amend and retain parts of the former legislation. RLUIPA focuses on land-use laws and makes it easier for religious landowners to get approval for zoning law changes, for example.[22]

On the civil side in the United States, former cult members have initiated suits based upon the wrongs done to them. Recognizing the difficulty of asserting undue influence, plaintiffs base these lawsuits upon grounds of lost wages, conversion of property and money, and psychological harm caused by the group's programs.[23]

The law does not go far enough to deal with cults that are so highly destructive. In the Jonestown tragedy, over 900 people were killed. There were group suicides at the "Branch Davidian" compound in Waco, Texas, in 1992 and at "Heaven's Gate" in the 1990s. The "Order of the Solar Temple," geographically dispersed from Canada, to Switzerland and France, killed a total of seventy-four people in brutal and ritual deaths between 1994 and 1997. In 2000, more than 400 members of "The Movement for the Restoration of the 10 Commandments" were brutally murdered. Another 300 or more were burned to death in a locked church building in Uganda.

Our current legal system seems inept with respect to prosecution of cult leaders. As I wrote in an article for the *Cultic Studies Journal* back in 1998, "[t]here are no [U.S.] state or federal laws that prohibit cults."[24] In that article, I described criminal statutes pertaining to rape, the Violence Against Women Act, and anti-stalking laws. Today, trafficking laws provide an additional avenue for prosecution.

11.2 Human Trafficking

It is difficult to calculate the number of people trafficked around the world, but it is estimated that approximately 27 million people around the globe are victims of human trafficking. Victims could be in any country and in any state of America. Traffickers and their victims continue to elude authorities. Less than one percent, or one victim for every 2000, has been identified.

A. Laws Prohibiting Human Trafficking

1. International laws

How is human trafficking defined? An accepted international definition of human trafficking is broad and is provided in the Protocol to Prevent, Suppress and Punish Trafficking in Persons, Especially Women and Children:

[T]he recruitment, transportation, transfer, harbouring or receipt of persons, by means of the threat or use of force or other forms of coercion, of abduction, of fraud, of deception, of the abuse of power or of a position of vulnerability or of the giving or receiving of payments or benefits to achieve the consent of a person having control over another person, for the purpose of exploitation.[25]

The Protocol defines "exploitation" as "the prostitution of others or other forms of sexual exploitation, forced labour or services, slavery or practices similar to slavery, servitude or the removal of organs."[26]

Human trafficking goes beyond sex trafficking. Other categories of trafficking, as our international and federal laws provide, are the following: workplace labor, domestic servitude, debt servitude, and child soldiering. Also criminalized are acts involving child sexual exploitation, forced marriage, servile forms of marriage, child marriage, and forced prostitution.

2. Protections for trafficking victims under international law

Trafficking victims have rights under international law. Further protections are given to child victims of trafficking, such as rules and obligations specified in the Convention on the Rights of the Child, which provides that "the best interests of the child are to be at all times paramount." (The Convention on the Rights of the Child has not been ratified by the United States, despite it being the most widely ratified human rights treaty in history.[27]) According to the Convention, children trafficked from other countries are to be given the same legal protections as nationals, including rights to privacy and physical and moral integrity. Privacy rights are particularly important to trafficked victims to prevent further humiliation and harm.

3. Legal effect of the international treaties

What is the effect of international treaties? Countries (referred to as "States") that are signatories to the treaties are obligated to conform their national legislation to those of the international law, staying consistent with the standards of the international treaty. Designated international courts all have enforcement power making signatories accountable. There are related treaties that can be used to combat and prevent trafficking.

Also significant, human rights treaties contain substantive reference to trafficking. International community organizations recognize the need to prevent and combat trafficking and provide protections to victims.

Decisions from legal cases of international tribunals can serve as a source of legal authority by U.S courts. The European Court of Human Rights affirmed that States are required to "take such steps as are necessary and available in order to secure relevant evidence, whether or not it is located in the territory of the investigating State," and that "in addition to the obligation to conduct a domestic investigation into events occurring on their own territories, member States are also subject to a duty in cross-border trafficking cases to cooperate effectively with the relevant authorities of other States concerned in the investigation of events which occurred outside their territories."[28]

There are influential documents that do not have enforcement power, but nevertheless help form the international legal framework. Examples include the guidelines on child trafficking issued by the United Nations Children's Fund (UNICEF) and those on trafficking and asylum issued by the Office of the United Nations High Commissioner for Refugees (UNHCR). These guidelines can serve as persuasive authority for legislation and models for best practices in combating trafficking.

4. U.S. laws prohibiting human trafficking

In 2000, the U.S. Congress passed the Victims of Trafficking and Violence Protection Act (TVPA). The goals of the federal legislation in the United States are similar to those of the international laws. The purpose of the TVPA was to "combat trafficking in persons." Since 2000, the TVPA was reauthorized by Congress four times. Like international law, there are essentially two categories of crimes affected by this legislation: sex trafficking and labor trafficking.

In addition to the federal statute, the Obama Administration, announcing a plan to coordinate U.S. federal agencies, denounced trafficking by stating that "[h]uman trafficking is a denial of our common humanity and an affront to our ideals as Americans."[29] The Obama Administration declared human trafficking to be "a crime that involves the exploitation of a person for the purpose of compelled labor or a commercial sex act." The aim of the federal legislation was tri-fold: prevention, protection, and prosecution. The Obama Administration adds to the so-called "3 p's" a fourth goal: partnership.

On the federal level, prosecution for trafficking is coordinated by the Human Trafficking Prosecution Unit of the Department of Justice's (DOJ) Civil Rights Division. The DOJ provides technical assistance to and coordinates with the U.S. Attorney's Offices. Individual U.S. states have also enacted their own statutes for protecting trafficked persons.

Worldwide, it is estimated that approximately 4,000 traffickers are convicted every year, but only 138 were convicted federally in the United States, and this was from the sex industry.[30] The United States is missing a large percentage of labor traffickers.

5. How U.S. federal law is changing

The federal trafficking statutes can be used to expand the remedies available to cult victims and to prosecutors seeking to hold cult leaders accountable for their criminal acts. Remedies are no longer limited to those of the federal case of *Kozminski*, as discussed above, because courts have expanded the breadth of what constitutes forced labor in reliance upon the TVPA. Section 1589 of the TVPA provides:

(a) Whoever knowingly provides or obtains the labor or services of a person by any one of, or by any combination of, the following means...

...

(3) by means of the abuse or threatened abuse of law or legal process; or

(4) by means of any scheme, plan, or pattern intended to cause the person to believe that, if that person did not perform such labor or services, that person or another person would suffer serious harm or physical restraint.[31]

For instance, teachers who came from the Philippines to work in the United States filed actions against a teacher-recruiting service alleging fraud and violations of the TVPA and other criminal laws.[32] Plaintiffs argued that they paid steep recruitment fees in order to teach in the United States and that they were induced by fraud and verbal threats. The defendants argued that the human trafficking statutes did not apply to teachers, and, instead, were meant only to apply to those in the sex trade or other forms of nonprofessional labor. The court disagreed. In relying upon the TVPA, the court reasoned that the "TVPA not only protects victims from the most heinous human trafficking crimes, but also various additional types of fraud and extortion leading to forced labor."

In another case, *Menocal v. GEO Group, Inc.*, detainees at a for-profit immigration detention facility brought an action against the facility for their meager compensation in the Voluntary Work Program.[33] They were performing menial jobs without compensation and were held under threat of solitary confinement. Citing the TVPA (among other statutes), the plaintiffs alleged that by requiring them to perform manual labor under threats, defendants knowingly provided or obtained the "labor or services of a person . . . by means of force, threats of force, physical restraint, or threats of physical restraint." Defendants argued that the TVPA was intended to apply to trafficking persons for labor and/or sex. In holding for the plaintiffs, the court reasoned that the language at issue under the TVPA is "broader than the language at issue in *Kozminski*" and other cases.[34]

In synthesizing case holdings, courts are employing an expansive view of the rights of victims under the TVPA to seek justice. The evolving case law pertaining to the U.S. federal trafficking statutes opens the door for potential litigation strategy in cases seeking justice for the ills of cults.

B. Cults Compared with Human Trafficking Rings

Cultic organizations and trafficking rings have much in common, and thus prosecution of elusive cult leaders could proceed similarly. Much like cult adherents, trafficked victims are threatened by their traffickers with serious consequences should they escape and seek help. Not all trafficked persons live in isolation, but, much like those living under the undue influence exhibited in cults, trafficked persons are fearful of reaching out for help.

1. Physical force, threats, malnourishment

Both cult leaders and traffickers use actual physical assaults, including beatings, stabbings, burnings, and sexual abuse, to maintain control over their victims. Traffickers are known to threaten harm as well, both by making direct threats to the victim and his or her family, and by inflicting harm on others in the victim's presence. Malnourishment is common among both trafficked persons and cult members. Traffickers withhold food as a form of punishment. For example, some trafficked factory workers have reported subsisting on broth and rice for a year, and domestic workers have had nutritional meals withheld entirely. Similarly, cult adherents are, at times, pressured to forgo nutrition.

2. Psychological coercion and surveillance

Traffickers and cult leaders often use psychological coercion. The victims in both situations are psychologically restrained by bonding and dependency. Persons lured to their traffickers through fake romantic relationships have continued to remain loyal, despite the illegality of trafficking. Cults also use false pretenses to lure adherents.

One result of psychological coercion is that victims may say things or exhibit behaviors that, perpetrators can argue, signal their consent to their circumstances. In trafficking cases, international human rights law has recognized that one cannot consent to having his or her freedom taken away. Thus, the prosecution can use these laws to attack a victim's expressions of consent, especially if the victim's freedom was obviously restricted (for example, through locked doors or shackles). In the religious cult, while the courts had previously provided deference to freedoms of religious belief, now the trafficking statutes may provide relief.

Much like cult adherents, trafficked persons are under surveillance. Traffickers watch their captives through video cameras in massage parlors, through human watch as armed guards around a work site, and by other means.

3. Labor and profit motives

Both traffickers and cult leaders are known to exploit their victims for profit. Labor traffickers, for example, may force their victims to endure up to eighteen-hour workdays, often under grueling conditions, only to have their earnings taken by the trafficker at the end of the day. Sex traffickers force their victims to engage in sexual activities for the trafficker's income. Harsh conditions can be inflicted as punishment for those who are noncompliant with the rules. Traffickers may overcharge a person for something (such as passage to the United States), such that the person is left with a debt to the trafficker that is impossible to pay down and requires the person to remain under the trafficker's control.

Similarly, cults need to survive somehow and leaders often rely upon the labor of followers, including the children. Some cults run businesses as a means of income, such as the pyramid schemes described above. Other cults do not run a single enterprise, but have members obtain work on the outside and then contribute their wages to the cults. Also, some cults insist that members who perform poorly or who violate rules are obliged to contribute money to the cult as a form of punishment, which would likely come from savings accounts. Cult victims may have turned over mortgages and life savings to their ringleaders, such that they do not feel they can afford to leave the group.

When the dogma of cults is stripped away, it is clear that their leaders run a business like traffickers—whether it is a church in a U.S. rural or urban town, a Jonestown in a developing country that housed a 1,000 people, or an overcrowded apartment in Manhattan. Cults are organizations that must be managed; their members are fed and sheltered, they often have jobs, and they provide some form of education for their young. The devotee, in some way, contributes to the economic functioning of the cult. As one former cultist expressed:

> I now understand that I was used as a tool to serve the leader's need for increased membership and therefore increased income. I was in a community that valued spirituality over materialism with double standards. As "co-workers," most of us lived very modestly, giving whatever we could to support the leader's lifestyle.[35]

4. Fraudulent recruitment

The tactics of traffickers are much like those of cult recruiters. Both use fraud as a recruitment tool to deceive their target. Some traffickers lure victims in with the pretense of a friendship, romance, or mentorship, but the end result could be a prostitution ring. Some traffickers promise jobs and assistance with emigration to another town or country; sometimes traffickers even seal their alleged agreement in writing or by verbal contract. Traffickers use traditional forms of publicity such as ads in the newspaper or other promotions and word-of-mouth. What trafficked victims are not told, however, is that traffickers may have created false identifications for them that can later be used to coerce the victims (who fear the trafficker will report the false identification to authorities). Trafficked victims are also not told that their traffickers may withhold their true passports once they have emigrated. And, of course, trafficked persons are not told of the abuse they are likely to face if they are being trafficked for labor or sex, for example.

Just as traffickers have posed as boyfriend, girlfriends, or parental figures to entice persons into their ring, cults may use flirtation and sex as lures. For instance, in the cult known as "Children of God," recruiters attracted new members using a technique called "flirty fishing."[36] Flirty fishing involved using young members as prostitutes to entice others to join the group.

Both traffickers and cult leaders rely on the Internet to fraudulently recruit members. The Internet is the "latest hot spot for promoting global trafficking and recruitment of women and children."[37] It is especially used to advertise "businesses" offering women and girls as brides for marriage; these "businesses" are actually sex trafficking operations in disguise. Analogously, some cults have used the Internet to attract followers. Members of Heaven's Gate, for example, lured followers by broadcasting their apocalyptic doctrine over the Internet.[38] The doctrine advised listeners to leave the earth via a spacecraft behind the comet Hale-Bopp.

5. Isolation

Both traffickers and cultic organizations use physical and psychological isolation as a tactic for controlling their victims. Traffickers restrict communication between their victims and victims' families, and they physically segregate their victims in living and working quarters that are away from mass society. Cult researchers believe that some destructive cults continue to exist in isolated communities, likely depriving children and adults of their basic human rights. Often, cults are physically set apart from society; they may be geographically separated in a rural area or, if located inside an urban area, the adherents live in close proximity to one another and are coached not to interact with non-member neighbors. Cult members are often told not to associate with nonmembers, particularly family members who are not part of the cult. This isolation distances the member from the outside world and makes it easier for him or her to be controlled.

6. Shaming tactics

Both traffickers and cults may gain control of their victims by shaming. Trafficked individuals are threatened with exposure back home of the forced sex acts they have performed or the lack of money they have produced. Taking advantage of the pride of the individual, traffickers exploit this vulnerability by threatening to shame them at home. Traffickers have resorted to blackmail, threatening to send videos or photographs home. Similarly, cults have publicly humiliated their members to set examples of behavior.

11.3 Using Human Trafficking Strategies to Combat Destructive Cults

Despite legislation, a high number of trafficking victims go undetected and evade authorities, as do cults victims and their leaders. Critics complain that not enough resources have been expended to prosecute human traffickers, rendering the laws ineffective. Significant resources and effort should be devoted to preventing and combating both human trafficking and cults.

A. Applying Criminal Trafficking Statutes to Prosecute Cult Leaders

Depending upon the criminal acts perpetrated by the cult leader, various statutory sections of the trafficking laws would conceivably be violated. For instance, cults that rely on sex to recruit new members may be committing illegal "commercial sex acts," which are defined in the anti-trafficking statute as "any sex act on account of which anything of value is given to or received by any person." The phrase "**anything of value**" could translate to the cult context if that phrase is read as encompassing a broad range of benefits brought to a cult through sexual exploitation of its adherents to recruit new members. As explained above, "flirty fishing" used by destructive cults to attract recruits could be prosecuted.

The provisions that protect children from sex trafficking provide, in relevant part, that a person may not "knowingly. . . . (2) benefit[] financially or by receiving anything of value, from participation in a venture which has engaged in an act described in violation of paragraph (1)," which, in turn, prohibits transporting, and also recruiting, enticing, or harboring a minor.[39] This language is also broad enough that it could be used to prosecute cults. Specifically, it could be used to prosecute a leader that receives "**benefits**" (which includes not just money but "anything of value") from the transport of minors.

Anti-trafficking laws can also be used to prosecute cults in situations where cult leaders inflict "**threats of serious harm** to or physical restraint against" any person or threaten to engage the "legal process." The statutory definition of "abuse or threatened abuse of law or legal process" is very broad and encompasses both the "use" and "threatened use" of "law or legal process"—in any conceivable category: administrative, civil, or criminal. It is meant to protect victims when traffickers are abusing the legal process "for any purpose of which the law was not designed" or to "exert pressure." The statutory definition of "serious harm" is broad and encompasses "any harm," including physical, psychological, and other nonphysical harms.

Alternatively, if the victim is a minor and was "caused to **engage in a commercial sex act**," the cult leader can also be punished.[40] Under federal statutes, the trafficking of a minor for commercial sex does not require a showing of force, fraud, or coercion. Courts, and the statute, provide a broad interpretation of the word "commercial." Thus, if a cult leader advanced or benefited from the child's exploitation in any way, that could satisfy the element.

In passing the anti-trafficking laws, Congress recognized that "[t]raffickers often make **representations** to other victims that physical harm may occur to them or others should the victim escape or attempt to escape" and that "such representations can have the same coercive effects on victims."[41] Using that sentiment and the statute (in particular, the "psychological harm" language), cult prosecutors could encourage courts to expand the restrictive common law regarding mind control that is currently available.

Finally, prosecutors could utilize the portions of the anti-trafficking laws related to prohibiting certain businesses to prosecute cults. As noted, cults, like trafficking rings, are businesses. Whether cult leaders run a commercial enterprise in which followers directly sell to the public, or they coerce their followers into donating their labor and money to the organization, the group runs as a business. Given the expansive language in the trafficking statutes, a creative prosecutor would not have trouble explaining how a cult functioned as a business, how the adherents were an integral part of that business, and how the leader exploited the adherents for labor, sex, or both through that business.

B. Suggestions for Expanding Resources to Identify and Support Cult Victims

1. Violence against women

Under international law, states are obligated to investigate and prosecute violence against women.[42] Victims of any international crime, including human trafficking, have the right to seek and obtain reparations. Given the different treatment that women receive in cults (often harsher than what their fellow male members receive), these services should be provided to women who leave cults.

Such services could be modeled after those already being provided to women who have overcome other forms of trauma, such as domestic abuse. For example, in U.S. states such as New York, programs are developing to provide counseling and other assistance to trafficked women.[43] Those who have been in prostitution rings have protections, under state law, from being prosecuted for crimes they were forced to commit. In 2007, the New York legislature passed a statute that establishes an interagency task force, including the Division of Criminal Justice Services and the Office for Temporary and Disability Assistance. Currently, eight other state agencies participate in the task force. Charges of the unified taskforce include the collection of data on the nature of human trafficking, and the identification of programs for victims. The resources being spent developing these programs could be shared with programs supporting former cult members, if cults are held accountable under the justice system.

In 2015, the interagency task force was extended by law as part of the Women's Equality Act. The task force is accepting referrals from social and legal service providers. This resource may be able to assist former cult members who are seeking help in adjusting to life outside the cult.

2. Training programs

Training programs educating attendees about trafficking prevention are now being offered abroad and in the United States, and they should continue to be developed. They should also be expanded to include information about destructive cults. Educators, hospital administrators, and others who are in frequent contact with immigrants and other populations vulnerable to trafficking should be trained to recognize the signs of trafficking. Specifically, training in the professional fields of "health, education, immigration, labor and employment, social service, and corporate sectors"[44] is needed. In the United States, the Department of Justice provides funding for human trafficking task forces, which pool together resources from law enforcement, prosecutorial offices, women's services, housing shelters, public health agencies, and other agencies.

Trafficking task forces should become familiar with International Cultic Studies Association (ICSA)'s work with cultic groups. Formed in 1979, ICSA provides extensive counseling services and public education about cults. Although based in the United States, it has been holding conferences internationally. ICSA is "a global network of people concerned about psychological manipulation and abuse in cultic or high-demand groups, alternative movements, and other environments."[45] ICSA offers help to former members of cultic groups and their families. It also fosters research and publications through its academic journals, and its website includes an extensive library of articles and books.

Another resource for former cultic members and their families is Info Secte Cult in Montreal, Canada. "Info Secte Cult is a non-profit charitable organization founded in 1980 based in Montreal (Quebec, Canada) that offers help and information about cults, new religious movements and related groups and subjects."[46] Info Secte Cult, like ICSA, provides an online library.

3. Providing victims' rights to former cult members

As victims' rights continue to develop abroad and in the United States, they should be considered in the cult context as well. Under both international and U.S. law, trafficked victims are protected from being prosecuted for crimes they were forced to commit. In the international arena, the Recommended Principles and Guidelines advises that "trafficked persons [should not be] prosecuted for violations of immigration laws or for the activities they are involved in as a direct consequence of their situation as trafficked persons."[47] It is time that the same be recommended for victims of cults in recognition of the power of undue influence.

Victims of cults should have other legal protections already afforded to trafficked persons as well. For instance, international law provides that trafficked victims are entitled to participate in legal proceedings safely and to be fully informed about the legal process.[48] In the United States, some states have enacted trafficking statutes to protect victims in similar ways,[49] and protecting the rights of trafficked victims is a developing legislative concern.[50] For example, in New York, if a person is convicted of prostitution but has been coerced into the commercial act as a result of being trafficked, then he or she may file a post-judgment motion in state court to vacate the conviction where the charge was for "loitering for the purpose of engaging in a prostitution offense" or "prostitution."[51] Similarly, when cult adherents are charged with crimes that they were duped into committing because of the power of undue influence, they too should arguably be immune from punishment, depending upon the factual circumstances.

In New York, the rights of the trafficked victim were expanded in the case of *People v. L.G.*[52] In that case, the court held that a weapons conviction was the direct result of the victim's actions as a sex trafficking victim, and thus vacated the judgment of conviction for the weapons charge. At a young age, the victim had been forced into prostitution and finally escaped. She sought to have the weapons' conviction vacated so that she could rebuild her life. She argued before the court that while being trafficked, her pimp instructed her to carry a pocket-knife for her protection from violence on the street. Even though the weapons offense was not one of prostitution, the court reasoned that the defendant was a minor at the time of her arrest and under the coercive control of her trafficker.

Finally, in the United States, trafficking victims are gaining civil remedies, such as back wages. A similar remedy could be afforded to cult victims whose property and wages were turned over to a cult leader under fraudulent circumstances.

4. Helping to identify child victims

International law provides special measures for trafficked children to be afforded their true identity, and efforts are made to obtain correct information so that these children are correctly identified.[53] Some cults also strip their followers of their names and identities. Often, they are given new names. They are groomed differently and given different clothing than they wore when they were their former selves. When appropriate, children defecting from cults, or those gaining emancipation status, should be provided similar assistance to that received by trafficking victims.

C. A Case in Point

A case from Atlanta, Georgia, is one example of how trafficking laws were used to prosecute a leader who ran a commercial enterprise that could also be characterized as a "commercial cult."[54] The ringleader, Jimme Lee Jones, often referred to religious scripture, knowing that certain recruits would identify with religion. Jones also rigidly controlled the recruitment and operations of a modeling agency, exploiting the models and subjecting them to physical and sexual abuse and forced prostitution.[55] It could be categorized as a "commercial cult."

Rachel Thomas was a college student in Atlanta who was approached by Jones on campus, claiming to be a modeling agent. Two young women also approached Thomas, and they vouched for the man. They convinced Thomas to sign a modeling agency contract and fill out a W-4 tax form, which required that she reveal her permanent address where her parents lived; her current address, which she shared with roommates; and her social security number. Jones did obtain modeling jobs for Thomas, but she quickly saw him physically abusing another model, and she tried to back out. At that point, Jones threatened her and her family, saying, "I own you; you do what I tell you; I know where your parents live." Thomas felt trapped and scared for herself, her family, and her roommates. Thereafter, he verbally and physically coerced her to perform sex for money with "buyers," and he physically abused her.[56]

Thomas was under this man's control for at least a year. He coerced her to perform sex acts for clients and to continue modeling, while he served as her agent and got paid for her work. Knowing that she was raised in a Christian home, he quoted scripture to manipulate her into doing what he wanted, and he claimed to hear God's word. He also used her to recruit other women in similar ways that she was recruited.[57]

Eventually, law enforcement was tipped off about this man, and Thomas was brought to a station house to discuss the business. Thomas began reading literature about other cults and realized that this pimp was similar to cult leaders. The FBI arrested Jones and posted his capture on the evening news. In response to a telephone hotline, over seventy-five viewers provided information to the authorities within an hour. Authorities learned that Jones had visited all six colleges in the Atlanta area and had recruited women from each into this prostitution ring.[58]

Jones was sentenced to 15 years on charges of sex trafficking and violations of the federal Mann Act.[59] The Department of Justice issued a press release acknowledging that the case proved that "human trafficking can occur anytime, anywhere, and against any vulnerable victim, including U.S. citizens and college students."[60]

Thomas surmises that traffickers and cult leaders have similar traits.[61] In her case, the "agent" manipulated her into believing that God would be vengeful should she not comply with his demands. He used other tactics with other women; for example, he acted as a father figure to women with no fathers. With over 75 victims, this modeling ring could be categorized as a "commercial cult."

Whether it is a cult on our soil or abroad, human trafficking laws provide a framework, resources, and an international community to prevent and combat future tragedies. Recent court cases in the United States have shown courts' expanding views of the rights of trafficked victims to see restitution and freedom from their constricted employ.[62] These more recent cases, and the human trafficking statutes, can be the basis for future causes of action on behalf of cult victims and in the criminal prosecution of cult leaders.

Endnotes

1. Laisure, *Employing Trafficking Laws to Capture Elusive Leaders of Destructive Cults*, 17 Or. Rev. Int'l L. 205 (2016).

2. Landa, *Children and Cults: A Practical Guide*, 29 J. Fam. L. 591, 591 n.1 (1991).

3. *See* Rosedale et al., *On Using the Term "Cult,"* Int'l Cultic Stud. Ass'n (ICSA); Langone, *supra Prevalence*. ICSA provides guidance, counseling, and support to former cultic members and their families.

4. See Schwartz, *The Millennium is Here—and So are the Cults*, 18 Cultic Stud. J. 82, 83 (2001).

5. *People Profiles*, Int'l Cultic Sutd. Ass'n. Herb Rosedale was a practicing attorney and former President of American Family Foundation—name changed to International Cultic Studies Association (ICSA). Mr. Rosedale was of Counsel with Jenkens & Gilchrist Park Chapin, LLP, and was one of the nation's leading authorities on cults from the late 1970s until his death in 2003.

6.   S. Hassan, *Combating Cult Mind Control* 52–65 (25th Anniv. Ed. Freedom of Mind Press 2015). Formal title of the organization is "The Holy Spirit Association for the Unification of World Christianity." The organization is dubbed the "Moonies" after its leader Sun Myung Moon. According to Hassan, the Moonies is one of the more visible and destructive cults, both in the United States and worldwide.

7.   *Id.* at 109 (emphasis in original).

8.   *See* Scheflin, *Supporting Human Rights by Testifying Against Human Wrongs,* 6 Intl J. Cultic Stud. 69, 70–71 (2015).

9.   *See id.*

10.   *Id.*

11.   In contrast, Masoud Banisadr argues that some terrorist groups should be considered political cults in that they share the cult characteristics of a strong charismatic leader, a shared ideology, and isolation. Banisadr, *Terrorist Organizations are Cults*, 8 Cultic Stud. Rev. 154, 164 (2009). It is in isolation from wider society that makes a terrorist group dangerous. In order to combat terrorism, Banisadr suggests reducing isolation by forcing them to abide by the moral fabric of the larger society. *Id.*

12.   A. Siskind, *The Sullivanian Institute/Fourth Wall Community: The Relationship of Radical Individualism and Authoritarianism* (Praeger: Westport, Conn. 2003); reviewed by Shaw, 5 Cultic Stud. Rev. 333 (2006).

13.   American jurisprudence stems from the constitutional tenet of free exercise of religion. U.S. Const. amend. I.

14.   U.S. Const. amend. I; see also Brown, Note, *He Who Controls the Mind Controls the Body: False Imprisonment, Religious Cults, and the Destruction of Volitional Capacity*, 25 Val. U. L. Rev. 407, 410–11 (1991).

15.   *See* M. Hamilton, *God vs. the Gavel: The Perils of Extreme Religious Liberty* 18–21 (2d ed., Cambridge Univ. Press 2014).

16.   *See* Hassan, *supra*, at 316.

17.   *Id.* at 61, 252 Cal. Rptr. at 137 (Criminalizing brainwashing may not produce the best result, anyway. If the cult recruiter has also been subjected to

brainwashing, then perhaps the remedy does not fit the target).

18. *See* Scheflin, *supra*, at 71 (citing *Daubert v. Merrell Dow Pharmaceuticals, Inc.*, 509 U.S. 579 (1993)). The four-prong test is (a) Whether the expert's theory can be tested; (b) Whether the expert's theory has been supported by publication or peer review; (c) Whether the expert's theory has a known error rate; and (d) Whether the expert's theory is generally accepted in the relevant scientific community. *Id.*

19. *United States v. Kozminski*, 487 U.S. 931, 933 (1988), *superseded by statute*, Victims of Trafficking & Violence Protection Act of 2000, *infra*. The *Kozminski* court held: "Since the [lower court's] jury instructions encompassed means of coercion other than actual or threatened physical or legal coercion, the instructions may have caused respondents to be convicted for conduct that does not violate [the statutes]. The convictions must therefore be reversed." *Kozminksi*, 487 U.S. at 933. The *Kozminski* decision remained intact until the "TVPA expressly overturned the Supreme Court's narrow definition of 'involuntary servitude.'" Weiss, *Human Trafficking and Forced Labor: A Primer*, 31 ABA J. Lab. & Emp. L. 1, 31 (2015).

20. *Id.* at 944.

21. 42 U.S.C. § 2000bb, bb-1 (2012) [hereinafter RFRA].

22. Hamilton, *supra*, at 188.

23. *See* Hassan, *supra*.

24. Laisure, *supra*, at 1.

25. U.N. High Commissioner for Human Rights, *Protocol to Prevent, Suppress and Punish Trafficking in Persons, Especially Women and Children, Supplementing the United Nations Convention Against Transnational Organized Crime*, art. 3(a), U.N. Doc. 55/25 (Nov. 15, 2000), http://www.ohchr.org/EN/ProfessionalInterest/Pages/ProtocolTrafficking In ersons.aspx (last visited on May 10, 2016).

26. *Id.*

27. UNICEF, http://www.unicef.org/crc/index_73549.html (last visited July 12, 2016).

28. *Id.* at 13.

29. *Id.* at 5.

30. Trafficking in Persons Report, 2014

31. 18 U.S.C.A. Sec. 1589 (2015). Furthermore, section 1589 (c) (1) provides:

> The term "abuse or threatened abuse of law or legal process" means the use or threatened use of a law or legal process, whether administrative, civil, or criminal, in any manner or for any purpose for which the law was not designed, in order to exert pressure on another person to cause that person to take some action or refrain from taking some action.
>
> The term "serious harm" means any harm, whether physical or nonphysical, including psychological, financial, or reputational harm, that is sufficiently serious, under all the surrounding circumstances, to compel a reasonable person of the same background and in the same circumstances to perform or to continue performing labor or services in order to avoid incurring that harm.

32. *Nunag-Tanedo v. East Baton Rouge Parish School Bd*, 790 F. Supp. 2d 1134 (C.D. Cal. 2011).

33. *Menocal v. GEO Group, Inc.*, 113 F. Supp. 3d 1125 (D. Colo. July 6, 2015).

34. *Id.* at 1133.

35. Russell, *Touched: Disconfirming Pathogenic Beliefs of Thought Reform Through the Process of Acting*, 9 Int'l Cultic Sutd. Ass'n 106, 112 (2010) (recollecting Eckankar in Southern California).

36. Boeri et al., *Creativity and Cults from Sociological and Communication Perspectives: The Processes Involved in the Birth of a Secret Creative Self*, 9 Cultic Stud. Rev.173, 192 (2010); Arnold, *Human Trafficking as a Commercial Cult Mind Control Phenomenon*, vimeo (July 5, 2014) (vimeo. com/102628 104) (presenting on abuses in Children of God). Arnold is the Founder/Board President of Preventhumantrafficking.org.

37. Tiefenbrun, *The Saga of Susannah A U.S. Remedy for Sex Trafficking in Women: The Victims of Trafficking and Violence Protection Act of 2000*, 2002 Utah L. Rev. 107, 119 (2002).

38. Santamaria del Rio, *The Internet as a New Place for Sects*, 7 Cultic Stud. Rev. 20, 23 (2008).

39. *See Id.* § 1591(a)(1).

40. *See Id.* § 1591(a).

41. 22 U.S.C.A. § 7101(7) (Westlaw 2015).

42. *See* U.N. Facts Sheet No. 36, "Human Righst and Human Trafficking."

43. New York Social Services Law § 483-ee (West 2016) (effective October 2015, this statute established an interagency task force to assist trafficked persons).

44. *Id.*

45. *Id.*

46. *Id.*

47. *Id.* at 18. The Trafficking Protocol does not specifically address prosecution but makes a similar recommendation for countries to implement domestic legislation.

48. *See Id.* at 15.

49. Trafficking in Persons Report, 2014

50. *See, e.g.*, Runaway and Homeless Youth and Trafficking Prevention Act; 42 U.S.C.A. § 5701 (2016).

51. *Id.* § 230.00. "Loitering" for purpose of prostitution is a separate crime from that of prostitution.

52. *People v. L.G.*, 41 Misc. 3d 428, 972 N.Y.S.2d 418 (Crim. Ct. 2013).

53. *See* "U.N. Fact Sheet No. 36," *supra*, at 20 (citing UNICEF Guidelines). Often times, trafficked persons are given false names and documentation.

54. Department of Justice, "Georgia Man Sentenced to 15 Years on Sex Trafficking and Mann Act Charges" (Jan. 24, 2008); Rachel Thomas, Human

Trafficking as a Commercial Cult Mind-Control Phenomenon, vimeo (July 5, 2014), vimeo.com/102628104.

55. *See Id.*

56. *See Id.*

57. *See Id.*

58. *See Id.*

59. Department of Justice, *supra*; *see* 18 U.S.C. § 2421 (West 2016) (formerly § 398) makes it an offense to transport in interstate comer females for purposes of prostitution or for other immoral purposes.

60. *Id.*

61. Thomas, *supra*.

62. *See generally, State v. Jeffs*, 243 P.3d 1250 (Utah 2010); *Menocal v. GEO Group, Inc.*, 113 F. Suppl. 3d 1125 (D. Colo. 2015).

Appendix 1

Side-by-Side Sex Trafficking Penal Law Comparison

Sex Trafficking Statutes

Mental States

New York	California	Texas	Pennsylvania	Arizona	Ohio	Florida	Federal Law
N.Y. Penal Law § 230.34 (2007)	Cal. Penal Code § 236.1 (2012)	Tex. Penal Code Ann. § 20A.02 (2011)	18 Pa.C.S.A. § 3011 (2014)	Ariz. Rev. Stat. Ann. § 13-1307 (2010)	Ohio Rev. Code Ann. § 2905.32 (2014)	Fla. Stat. Ann. § 787.06 (2015)	18 U.S.C.A. § 2422 (2006)
A person is guilty of sex trafficking if he or she intentionally advances or profits from prostitution by:	Any person who deprives or violates the personal liberty of another with the intent to obtain forced labor or services, is guilty of human trafficking. "Forced labor or services" means labor or services that are performed or provided by a person and are obtained or maintained through force, fraud, duress, or coercion, or equivalent conduct that would	A person commits an offense if the person knowingly: (1)Traffics another person with the intent that the trafficked person engage in forced labor or services; (2) Receives a benefit from participating in a venture that involves an activity described by Subdivision (1), including by receiving labor or services the person knows are forced labor or services;	A person is guilty of human trafficking if the person; • Recruits, entices, solicits, harbors, transports, provides, obtains or maintains an individual if the person knows or recklessly disregards that the individual will be subject to involuntary servitude • Knowingly benefits financially or	It is unlawful for a person to knowingly traffic another person who is eight teen years of age or older with either of the following: • The intent to cause the other person to engage in any prostitution or sexually explicit performance by deception, force or coercion • The knowledge that the other person	No person shall knowingly recruit, lure, entice, isolate, harbor, transport, provide, obtain, or maintain, or knowingly attempt to recruit, lure, entice, isolate, harbor, transport, provide, obtain, or maintain, another person: • If the offender knows that the other person will be subjected to involuntary servitude or be compelled	Any person who knowingly, or in reckless disregard of the facts, engages in human trafficking, or attempts to engage in human trafficking, or benefits financially by receiving anything of value from participation in a venture that has subjected a person to human trafficking. • "Human trafficking" means transporting, soliciting,	The term "sex trafficking" means the knowing recruitment, harboring, transportation, provision, obtaining, patronizing, or soliciting of a person for the purpose of a commercial sex act. The term "severe forms of trafficking in persons" means-- (A) sex trafficking in which a commercial sex act is induced

New York	California	Texas	Pennsylvania	Arizona	Ohio	Florida	Federal Law
	reasonably over-bear the will of the person.	(3) Traffics another person and, through force, fraud, or coercion, causes the trafficked person to engage in conduct prohibited by: • Section 43.02 (Prostitution) • Section 43.03 (Promotion of Prostitution) • Section 43.04 (Aggravated Promotion of Prostitution) • Section 43.05 (Compelling Prostitution). "Traffic" means to entice, recruit, harbor, provide, or otherwise obtain another person by any means.	receives any-thing of value from any act that facilitates any activity described above.	will engage in any prostitution or sexu-ally explicit performance by deception, coercion or force.	to engage in sexual activity for hire.	recruiting, harboring, providing, enticing, maintaining, or obtaining another person for the purpose of exploitation of that person.	by force, fraud, or coercion, or in which the person induced to perform such act has not attained 18 years of age; or (B) the recruitment, harboring, transportation, provision, or obtaining of a person for labor or services, through the use of force, fraud, or coercion for the purpose of subjection to involuntary servitude, peonage, debt bondage, or slavery. (C) In a prosecution under subsection (a) in which the defendant had a

New York	California	Texas	Pennsylvania	Arizona	Ohio	Florida	Federal Law
							reasonable opportunity to observe the person so recruited, enticed, harbored, transported, provided, obtained, maintained, patronized, or solicited, the Government need not prove that the defendant knew, or recklessly disregarded the fact, that the person had not attained the age of 18 years.

Fraud Elements

New York	California	Texas	Pennsylvania	Arizona	Ohio	Florida	Federal Law
Making material false statements, misstatements, or omissions to induce or maintain the person to engage or continue to engage in prostitution.	"Deprivation or violation of the personal liberty of another" includes substantial and sustained restriction of another's liberty accomplished	"Forced labor or services" means labor or services, other than labor or services that constitute sexual conduct, that are performed or provided by	Fraud.		"Compelled" does not require that the compulsion be openly displayed or physically exerted. The element "compelled"	Enticing or luring any person by fraud or deceit.	

New York	California	Texas	Pennsylvania	Arizona	Ohio	Florida	Federal Law
	through fraud or deceit.	another person and obtained through an actor's use of fraud.			has been established if the state proves that the victim's will was overcome.		
Coercion Elements							
Unlawfully providing a person who is patronized with the intent to impair their judgment: • A narcotic drug or a narcotic preparation; • Concentrated cannabis; • Rohypnol.	"Coercion" includes any scheme, plan, or pattern intended to provide and facilitate the possession of any controlled substance to a person with the intent to impair the person's judgment.		Facilitating or controlling the individual's access to a controlled substance.	Facilitating or controlling another person's access to a controlled substance.	"Lowder described how Warren enabled her increasing drug addiction in exchange for working as a prostitute for him. Warren introduced Lowder to heroin and manipulated her physical dependence on the drug to accomplish his will. In fact, it was Lowder's desperation to make money to obtain heroin from Warren		

New York	California	Texas	Pennsylvania	Arizona	Ohio	Florida	Federal Law
					that led to the downfall of Warren's prostitution ring." *State v. Warren,* 45. N.E.3d 1050, 40 (Ohio Ct. App 2015)		
Withholding, destroying, or confiscating documents with intent to impair a person's freedom (passports, immigration documents, etc.).	"Duress" includes knowingly destroying, concealing, removing, confiscating, or possessing any actual or purported passport or immigration document of the victim, or a direct or implied threat to do so.		Engaging in unlawful conduct with respect to documents: • Cannot prevent or restrict or attempt to prevent or restrict, without lawful authority, the ability of an individual to move or travel, the person knowingly destroys, conceals, removes, confiscates	Coercion: • Knowingly destroying, concealing, removing, confiscating possessing or withholding another person's actual or purported passport or other immigration document, government issued identification document, government record or personal property.	No person, without privilege to do so, shall knowingly destroy, conceal, remove, confiscate, or possess any actual or purported government identification document or passport of another person in the course of a violation of, with intent to violate, or with intent to facilitate a violation of section 2905.32.	Destroying, concealing, removing, confiscating, withholding, or possessing any actual or purported passport, visa, or other immigration document, or any other actual or purported government identification document, of any person.	Whoever knowingly destroys, conceals, removes, confiscates, or possesses any actual or purported passport or other immigration document, or any other actual or purported government identification document, of another person- (1) in the course of a violation of section 1581, 1583, 1584,

New York	California	Texas	Pennsylvania	Arizona	Ohio	Florida	Federal Law
			or possesses an actual or purported: ○ Passport or other immigration document of an individual ○ Government identification document of an individual. 18 Pa. Stat. and Cons. Stat. Ann. § 3014.		Ohio Rev. Code Ann. § 2905.33.		1589, 1590, 1591, or 1594(a); (2) with intent to violate section 1581, 1583, 1584, 1589, 1590, or 1591; or (3) to prevent or restrict or to attempt to prevent or restrict, without lawful authority, the person's liberty to move or travel, in order to maintain the labor or services of that person, when the person is or has been a victim of a severe form of trafficking in persons, as defined in section 103 of the Traf-

New York	California	Texas	Pennsylvania	Arizona	Ohio	Florida	Federal Law
							ficking Victims Protection Act of 2000. 18 USC § 1592.
Requiring that prostitution be performed to retire, repay, or service a real or purported debt.	"Coercion" includes any scheme, plan, or pattern intended to cause debt bondage.		Debt coercion.	Extortion: • Causing or threatening to cause financial harm to any person.		Using lending or other credit methods to establish a debt by any person when services are pledged as a security for the debt, if the value of the labor or services as reasonably assessed is not applied toward the liquidation of the debt, the length and nature of the labor or services are not respectively limited and defined.	Debt bondage: The term "debt bondage" means the status or condition of a debtor arising from a pledge by the debtor of his or her personal services or of those of a person under his or her control as a security for debt, if the value of those services as reasonably assessed is not applied toward the liquidation of the debt or the length and nature of those

New York	California	Texas	Pennsylvania	Arizona	Ohio	Florida	Federal Law
							services are not respectively limited and defined.

Force / Physical Elements

New York	California	Texas	Pennsylvania	Arizona	Ohio	Florida	Federal Law
Using force or engaging in any scheme, plan or pattern to compel or induce the person to engage in or continue to engage in prostitution by means of instilling a fear in the person if the demand is not complied with, the actor or another will do one or more of the following: • Cause physical injury, serious physical injury, or death to a person;	"Coercion" includes any scheme, plan, or pattern intended to cause a person to believe that failure to perform an act would result in serious harm to or against any person.	Obtained through an actor's use of Force.	Causing or threatening to cause serious harm to any individual.	"Force" includes causing or threatening to cause serious harm to another person.	"Compelled" does not require that the compulsion be openly displayed or physically exerted. The element "compelled" has been established if the state proves that the victim's will was overcome by: • Force	Coercion means • Using or threatening to use physical force against any person	The term "coercion" means-- (A) threats of serious harm to or physical restraint against any person; (B) any scheme, plan, or pattern intended to cause a person to believe that failure to perform an act would result in serious harm to or physical restraint against any person; or

New York	California	Texas	Pennsylvania	Arizona	Ohio	Florida	Federal Law
• Cause damage to property, other than the property of the actor;			Taking or retaining the individual's personal property or real property as a means of coercion.				
• Engage in other conduct constituting a felony or unlawful imprisonment;	"Coercion" includes any scheme, plan, or pattern intended to cause a person to believe that failure to perform an act would result in physical restraint against any person.		Physically restraining or threatening to physically restrain another individual Kidnapping or attempting to kidnap any individual.	Force" includes physically restraining or threatening to physically restrain another person		Restraining, isolating, or confining or threatening to restrain, isolate, or confine any person without lawful authority and against her or his will.	The term "coercion" means-- (C) the abuse or threatened abuse of the legal process. The term "abuse or threatened abuse of the legal process" means the use or threatened use of a law or legal process, whether administrative, civil, or criminal, in any manner or for any purpose for which the law was not

New York	California	Texas	Pennsylvania	Arizona	Ohio	Florida	Federal Law
• Expose a secret or publicize an asserted fact, whether true or false, tending to subject some person to hatred, contempt or ridicule;					• Fear • Duress • Intimidation • Fraud		designed, in order to exert pressure on another person to cause that person to take some action or refrain from taking some action.
• Testify or provide information or withhold testimony or information with respect to another's legal claim or defense;	"Coercion" includes any scheme, plan, or pattern intended to cause a threatened abuse of the legal process.		Abusing or threatening to abuse the legal process.	Coercion • Abusing or threatening to abuse the law or the legal system			
	Deprivation or violation of the personal liberty of another includes substantial and sustained restriction of						

New York	California	Texas	Pennsylvania	Arizona	Ohio	Florida	Federal Law
	another's liberty accomplished through: • Fear • Duress • Menace • Threat of unlawful injury to the victim or to another person; Under circumstances where the person receiving or apprehending the threat reasonably believes that it is likely that the person making the threat would carry it out.						
• Use or abuse his or her position as a public servant by performing							

New York	California	Texas	Pennsylvania	Arizona	Ohio	Florida	Federal Law
some act within or related to his or her official duties, or by failing or refusing to perform an official duty, in such manner as to affect some person adversely;							
• Perform any other act which would not in itself materially benefit the actor but which is calculated to harm the person who is patronized materially with respect to his or her health, safety, or immigration status.			Extortion. Duress Using any scheme, plan or pattern intended to cause Duress				

Appendix 2

Side-by-Side Labor Trafficking Penal Law Comparison

New York	California	Texas	Pennsylvania	Arizona	Ohio	Florida	Federal Law
N.Y. Penal Law § 135.35 (McKinney 2016)	Cal. Penal Code § 236.1 (West 2012)	Tex. Penal Code Ann. § 20A.02 (West 2011)	18 Pa.C.S.A. § 3011 (West 2014)	Ariz. Rev. Stat. Ann. § 13-1308 (West 2010)	Ohio Rev. Code Ann. § 2905.32 (West 2014)	Fla. Stat. Ann. § 787.06 (West 2015)	18 U.S.C.A. § 1589
Labor Trafficking Statutes							
Mental States							
A person is guilty of labor trafficking if he or she compels or induces another to engage in labor or recruits, entices, harbors, or transports such other person by means of intentionally;	Any person who deprives or violates the personal liberty of another with the intent to obtain forced labor or services, is guilty of human trafficking. "Forced labor or services" means labor or services that are performed or provided by a person and are obtained or maintained through force, duress, fraud, or coercion, or equivalent conduct	A person commits an offense if the person knowingly: (1)Traffics another person with the intent that the trafficked person engage in forced labor or services (2)Receives a benefit from participating in a venture that involves an activity described by Subdivision (1), including by receiving labor or services the per-	A person is guilty of human trafficking if the person: • Recruits, entices, solicits, harbors, transports, provides, obtains or maintains an individual if the person knows or recklessly disregards that the individual will be subject to involuntary servitude • Knowingly benefits financially or receives any-	It is unlawful for a person to either: • Knowingly traffic another person with the intent to or knowledge that the other person will be subject to forced labor or services. • Knowingly benefit, financially or by receiving anything of value, from participation in a venture that has engaged in an act in viola-	No person shall knowingly recruit, lure, entice, isolate, harbor, transport, provide, obtain, or maintain, or knowingly attempt to recruit, lure, entice, isolate, harbor, transport, provide, obtain, or maintain, another person if any of the following applies: • The offender knows that the other person will be subjected to involuntary servitude.	Any person who knowingly, or in reckless disregard of the facts, engages in human trafficking, or attempts to engage in human trafficking, or benefits financially by receiving anything of value from participation in a venture that has subjected a person to human trafficking. • "Human trafficking" means transporting, soliciting, recruiting,	(A) Whoever knowingly provides or obtains the labor or services of a person by any one of, or by any combination of, the following means-- (B) Whoever knowingly benefits, financially or by receiving anything of value, from participation in a venture which has engaged in the providing or obtaining of labor or services by any of the means described in subsection

New York	California	Texas	Pennsylvania	Arizona	Ohio	Florida	Federal Law
	that would reasonably over-bear the will of the person.	son knows are forced labor or services. "Traffic" means to entice, recruit, harbor, provide, or otherwise obtain another person by any means.	thing of value from any act that facilitates any activity described above.	tion of § 13-1306, § 13-1307 or this section. "Traffic" means to entice, recruit, harbor, provide, transport or otherwise obtain another person by deception, coercion or force.		harboring, providing, enticing, maintaining, or obtaining another person for the purpose of exploitation of that person.	(a), knowing or in reckless disregard of the fact that the venture has engaged in the providing or obtaining of labor or services by any of such means, shall be punished as provided in subsection (d).
Debt Bondage / Financial Coercion							
Requiring that the labor be performed to retire, repay, or service a real or purported debt that the actor has caused by a systematic ongoing course of conduct with intent to defraud such person.	"Coercion" includes any scheme, plan, or pattern intended to cause debt bondage.		Debt coercion. Fraud.	Extortion. • Causing or threatening to cause financial harm to any person.		Enticing or luring any person by fraud or deceit. Using lending or other credit methods to establish a debt by any person when services are pledged as a security for the debt, if the value of the la-	By means of any scheme, plan, or pattern intended to cause the person to believe that, if that person did not perform such labor or services, that person or another person would suffer serious harm or physical restraint.

New York	California	Texas	Pennsylvania	Arizona	Ohio	Florida	Federal Law
						bor or services as reasonably assessed is not applied toward the liquidation of the debt, the length and nature of the labor or services are not respectively limited and defined.	The term "serious harm" means any harm, whether physical or non-physical, including psychological, *financial*, or reputational harm, that is sufficiently serious, under all the surrounding circumstances, to compel a reasonable person of the same background and in the same circumstances to perform or to continue performing labor or services in order to avoid incurring that harm.

New York	California	Texas	Pennsylvania	Arizona	Ohio	Florida	Federal Law
			Documentation / Immigration				
Withholding, destroying, or confiscating any actual or purported passport, immigration document, or any other actual or purported government identification document, of another person with intent to impair said person's freedom of movement.	"Duress" includes knowingly destroying, concealing, removing, confiscating, or possessing any actual or purported passport or immigration document of the victim, or a direct or implied threat to do so.	"Forced labor or services" means labor or services, other than labor or services that constitute sexual conduct, that are performed or provided by another person and obtained through an actor's use of force, fraud, or coercion.	Engaging in unlawful conduct with respect to documents: It is illegal to prevent or restrict or attempt to prevent or restrict, without lawful authority, the ability of an individual to move or travel, the person knowingly destroys, conceals, removes, confiscates or possesses an actual or purported: • Passport or other immigration document of an individual	Knowingly destroying, concealing, removing, confiscating, possessing or withholding another person's actual or purported passport or other immigration document, government issued identification document, government record or personal property.	No person, without privilege to do so, shall knowingly destroy, conceal, remove, confiscate, or possess any actual or purported government identification document or passport of another person in the course of a violation of, with intent to violate, or with intent to facilitate a violation of section 2905.32. Ohio Rev. Code Ann. § 2905.33 (West 2011).	Destroying, concealing, removing, confiscating, withholding, or possessing any actual or purported passport, visa, or other immigration document, or any other actual or purported government identification document, of any person.	Whoever knowingly destroys, conceals, removes, confiscates, or possesses any actual or purported passport or other immigration document, or any other actual or purported government identification document, of another person— (1) in the course of a violation of section 1581, 1583, 1584, 1589, 1590, 1591, or 1594(a); (2) with intent to violate section 1581, 1583, 1584, 1589, 1590, or 1591; or

New York	California	Texas	Pennsylvania	Arizona	Ohio	Florida	Federal Law
			• Govern-ment iden-tification document of an indi-vidu-al. 18 Pa. Stat. and Cons. Stat. Ann. § 3014 (West).				(3) to prevent or restrict or to attempt to prevent or restrict, without lawful authority, the person's liberty to move or travel, in order to maintain the labor or services of that person, when the person is or has been a victim of a severe form of trafficking in persons, as defined in section 103 of the Trafficking Victims Protection Act of 2000. 18 U.S.C.A. § 1592.

New York	California	Texas	Pennsylvania	Arizona	Ohio	Florida	Federal Law
			Force / Coercion Elements				
Using force or engaging in any scheme, plan or pattern to compel or induce such person to engage in or continue to engage in labor activity by means of instilling a fear in such person that, if the demand is not complied with, the actor or another will do one or more of the following: • Cause physical injury, serious physical injury, or death to a person;	"Coercion" includes any scheme, plan, or pattern intended to cause a person to believe that failure to perform an act would result in serious harm to or against any person.	"Forced labor or services" means labor or services, other than labor or services that constitute sexual conduct, that are performed or provided by another person and obtained through an actor's use of force.	Causing or threatening to cause serious harm to any individual.	Causing or threatening to cause serious physical injury to any person.	"Compelled" does not require that the compulsion be openly displayed or physically exerted. The element "compelled" has been established if the state proves that the victim's will was overcome by • Force	Using or threatening to use physical force against any person;	By means of force, threats of force, physical restraint, or threats of physical restraint to that person or another person;

New York	California	Texas	Pennsylvania	Arizona	Ohio	Florida	Federal Law
• Cause damage to property, other than the property of the actor;			Taking or retaining the individual's personal property or real property as a means of coercion.				
• Engage in other conduct constituting a felony or unlawful imprisonment in the second degree;	"Coercion" includes any scheme, plan, or pattern intended to cause a person to believe that failure to perform an act would physical restraint against any person.		Physically restraining or threatening to physically restrain another individual. Kidnapping or attempting to kidnap any individual.	Restraining or threatening to physically restrain another person.		Restraining, isolating, or confining or threatening to restrain, isolate, or confine any person without lawful authority and against her or his will.	By means of any scheme, plan, or pattern intended to cause the person to believe that, if that person did not perform such labor or services, that person or another person would suffer serious harm or physical restraint. The term "serious harm" means any harm, whether physical or nonphysical, including psychological, financial,

New York	California	Texas	Pennsylvania	Arizona	Ohio	Florida	Federal Law
							or reputational harm, that is sufficiently serious, under all the surrounding circumstances, to compel a reasonable person of the same background and in the same circumstances to perform or to continue performing labor or services in order to avoid incurring that harm.
• Accuse some person of a crime or cause criminal charges or deportation proceedings to be instituted against such person.	"Coercion" includes any scheme, plan, or pattern intended to cause a threatened abuse of the legal process.		Abusing or threatening to abuse the legal process.	Abusing or threatening to abuse the law or the legal system.	• Fear • Duress • Intimidation • Fraud		By means of the abuse or threatened abuse of law or legal process. Abuse or threatened abuse of law or legal process" means the use or threatened use of a law or legal process,

New York	California	Texas	Pennsylvania	Arizona	Ohio	Florida	Federal Law
							whether administrative, civil, or criminal, in any manner or for any purpose for which the law was not designed, in order to exert pressure on another person to cause that person to take some action or refrain from taking some action.
• Expose a secret or publicize an asserted fact, whether true or false, tending to subject some person to hatred, contempt or ridicule							

New York	California	Texas	Pennsylvania	Arizona	Ohio	Florida	Federal Law
• Testify or provide information or withhold testimony or information with respect to another's legal claim or defense.			Abusing or threatening to abuse the legal process.	Abusing or threatening to abuse the law or the legal system.			By means of the abuse or threatened abuse of law or legal process. "Abuse or threatened abuse of law or legal process" means the use or threatened use of a law or legal process, whether administrative, civil, or criminal, in any manner or for any purpose for which the law was not designed, in order to exert pressure on another person to cause that person to take some action or refrain from taking some action.

New York	California	Texas	Pennsylvania	Arizona	Ohio	Florida	Federal Law
• Use or abuse his or her position as a public servant by performing some act within or related to his or her official duties, or by failing or refusing to perform an official duty, in such manner as to affect some person adversely.			Extortion. Criminal coercion. Duress. Using any scheme, plan or pattern intended to cause duress.				
	"Coercion" includes any scheme, plan, or pattern intended to provide and facilitate the possession of any controlled substance to a person with the intent to impair the person's judgment.	While Texas does not have a provision, they have a catch all that states that traffic means to entice, recruit, harbor, provide, or otherwise obtain another person by any means. One case, *Dukes v.*	Facilitating or controlling the individual's access to a controlled substance.	Extortion: Facilitating or control-ling another person's access to a controlled substance.		Provides a controlled substance as outlined in Schedule I or Schedule II of s. 893.03 to any person for the purpose of exploitation of that person.	

New York	California	Texas	Pennsylvania	Arizona	Ohio	Florida	Federal Law
		State has expert testimony which establishes that the traffickers often target drug addicts because of their vulnerability and this is a means of trafficking them. Testimony from the victims indicates the trafficker would withhold drugs and not allow the women to buy drugs from anyone but him. There is no case where this was used for labor trafficking as of yet in Texas, only sex trafficking. *Dukes v. State,* (Tex. App 2016).			Ohio does not have a provision specifically relating to the control or facilitation of a controlled substance as one means of labor trafficking. However, in *State v. Warren,* 45. N.E.3d 1050, 40 (Ohio Ct. App 2015), the court uses the testimony of a victim that her trafficker manipulated her dependency on heroin as a means of controlling her and forcing her to continue to engage in prostitution. It is unsure if this would also apply to labor trafficking cases, even though they use the same statute.		

New York	California	Texas	Pennsylvania	Arizona	Ohio	Florida	Federal Law
			Facilitating or controlling the individual's access to a controlled substance.	Facilitating or controlling another person's access to a controlled substance.			
	California also applies a totality of the circumstances inquiry when determining trafficking cases: "The total circumstances, including the age of the victim, the relationship between the victim and the trafficker or agents of the trafficker, and any handicap or disability of the victim, shall be factors to consider in determining the presence of						

New York	California	Texas	Pennsylvania	Arizona	Ohio	Florida	Federal Law
	'deprivation or violation of the personal liberty of another, duress, and coercion' as described in this section".						

Appendix 3

Resources

This list is by no means exhaustive; rather, it is meant to be a point of reference to assist in reporting suspected human trafficking or obtaining assistance for victims.

Australia:

STOP THE TRAFFICK Australia
http://stopthetraffik.com.au/
PO BOX 1703 Castle Hill
NSW 1765
+61 438 040 959
australia@stopthetraffik.com.au

Anti-Slavery Australia
University of Technology Sydney
Email: antislavery@uts.edu.au
Phone: +61-2-9514 9660

Salvation Army
Locations throughout Australia
46 891 896 885 (NSW)
22 035 976 360 (QLD)
52 609 689 893 (Overseas Aid)
https://salvos.org.au/need-help/human-trafficking-and-slavery/

Australian Catholics Religious Against Trafficking
54 Beaconsfield Parade
Albert Park, VIC, 3206
03 9645 5986
Email: info@acrath.org.au

Australian Human Rights Commission
Level 3, 175 Pitt Street
Sydney, NSW 2000
GPO Box 5218
Sydney, NSW 2001
Telephone: 02 9284 9600
National Information Service: 1300 656 419
General enquiries and publications: 1300 369 711
TTY: 1800 620 241
Fax: 02 9284 9611

Hagar
Hagar specializes in working with women and children who have survived trafficking and severe abuse in Cambodia, Afghanistan, and Vietnam.
237 Cecil Street
South Melbourne, VIC 3205
admin@hagar.org.au
03 9257 2369

Uniting Care
National Office Canberra
PO Box 5218
Braddon, ACT 2612
mail@nat.unitingcare.org.au
02 6249 6717

Red Cross
155 Pelham Street
Carlton, VIC 3053
Mail PO Box 196
Carlton South VIC 3053
Phone 03 9345 1800
Fax 03 9341 7572
national_stpp@redcross.org.au

Law Council of Australia
19 Torrens Street
Braddon, ACT 2612
GPO Box 1989
Canberra, ACT 2601
Telephone: +61 2 6246 3788
Fax: +61 2 6248 0639
Email: mail@lawcouncil.asn.au

Australian Federal Police Human Trafficking Team
(dial from inside Australia) 131 AFP (237)

European Union:

Action for Trafficked Persons Network (ATN)
Red Cross EU Office
Rue de Trèves, 59-61
1000 Brussels
Belgium
Tel: +32 (0)2 235 06 80+32 (0)2 235 06 80
Fax: +32 (0)2 230 54 64

Netherlands:

STOP THE TRAFFIK Netherlands
Minahassastraat 1
1094 RS Amsterdam
The Netherlands
Email: info@stopthetraffik.nl
Tel: 020-4203952

United Kingdom:

National Crime Stoppers
www.crimestoppers-uk.org/give-information/give-information-online/
0800 555 111

Migrant Help

http://www.migranthelpuk.org/
Charlton House, Dour Street
Dover, CT16 1AT
01304 203 977
info@migranthelpuk.org

STOP THE TRAFFIK

Global Office Address
First Floor Millbank Tower
21-24 Millbank, Westminster,
London, SW1P 4QP
E-mail: info@stopthetraffik.org
Tel: +44 (0)207 921 4258

United States:

Polaris National Human Trafficking Resource Center

P.O. Box 65323
Washington, DC 20035
Tel: (202) 745-1001
www.traffickingresourcecenter.org
Hotline: 1-888-373-7888
"Be Free" Text: HELP or INFO to BeFree (2337333)
This hotline operates 24 hours a day, 7 days a week and is available to anonymously report any incident of human trafficking or to obtain assistance if you are a victim.

Freedom Network

A national alliance of experienced advocates advancing a human rights-based approach to human trafficking in the United States.
www.freedomnetworkusa.org
info@freedomnetworkusa.org

The Human Trafficking Pro Bono Legal Center

www.htprobono.org
info@htprobono.org
1030 15th Street, NW #104B
Washington, DC 20005

About the Authors

About the Editors

Nora M. Cronin is the Coordinator for Response to Human Trafficking and Unaccompanied Minors programs at the New York State Office of Temporary and Disability Assistance. Nora has also held the position of Senior Trial Attorney at the Kings County District Attorney's Office, and has been a consultant for the American Bar Association's Rule of Law Initiative in Panama. Before beginning her career as an attorney, Nora was a staff writer for the *Long Island Press*. Nora received her Bachelor of Arts in International Affairs and Philosophy *cum laude* from Mary Washington College and her law degree from St. John's University School of Law.

Kimberly Ellis, is a freelance legal editor and copywriter. She earned her Bachelor of Arts *cum laude* from Wellesley College, her law degree from the University of Arizona College of Law, and her Graduate Certificate in Writing, Editing, and Publishing from the University of Queensland. She co-authored *Forensic Science Today* (1st and 2nd editions), co-edited *Toxic Mold Litigation*, and wrote several chapters on legal ethics in the *High Court Case Summaries* series.

About the Contributors

Peter W. Blair, Jr. is originally from New York and attended the State University of New York at New Paltz where he received a bachelor's degree in both Political Science and Philosophy. Peter is currently in his second year at the University of Oregon School of Law focusing on environmental and human rights law.

Robin Boyle Laisure is Professor of Legal Writing at St. John's University School of Law, and is on the editorial board of ICSA's International Journal of Cultic Studies. She lectures on topics concerning cults and the law. In 2005, she received the Faculty Outstanding Achievement award from the President of St. John's University. Robin is a graduate of Fordham University School of Law (J.D.) and Vassar College (B.A.).

Melissa L. Breger has been teaching at the law school level since 1999, first at The University of Michigan Law School (her alma mater) and then at Albany Law School. Prior to teaching, Professor Breger dedicated her career to children, women, and families, with her formative years practicing in New York City in a number of capacities. She is the recipient of several teaching and service awards, both on a local level and on a national level. Professor Breger is the co-author of *New York Law of Domestic Violence*, a two-volume treatise published by Reuters-Thomson-West, as well as the author of numerous law review articles regarding issues of family law, children and juveniles, gender, and justice.

Nicole Campion is an Albany Law School student expected to graduate with her Juris Doctor in May 2017. She holds a Bachelor's Degree in Criminal Justice and a Bachelor's Degree in Spanish from the State University of New York's University at Albany, as well as a Master's Degree in Justice Studies from Southern New Hampshire University.

Felicity Gerry, QC is an international barrister with chambers in London and Leeds in the UK and Darwin in Australia. She is a Senior Lecturer in the School of Law at Charles Darwin University. She lectures on women and justice and transnational law, and has research projects on Women's Health and Law, Women in Prison, Indigenous Justice, Child Rights and Cyber Rights. She has made numerous media appearances providing legal commentary, including the documentary, *Saving Mary Jane*, about her client featured in this book.

Gonzalo Martinez de Vedia is a Senior Policy Associate with the Alliance to End Slavery and Trafficking (ATEST), in Washington, D.C. Previously, he served as a Human Trafficking Specialist for the Worker Justice Center of New York, and Policy Co-Chair for Freedom Network USA. He holds a B.A. *cum laude* from Cornell University, where he also completed the Strategic Corporate Research Program at the School of Industrial and Labor Relations.

Bryanne Perlanski is a Little Falls, New York native and is a recent graduate of Albany Law School. During law school, Bryanne gained experience with the

Albany County District Attorney's Office, The Legal Project, NYS Department of Corrections and Community Supervision, and the United States Attorney's Office for the Northern District of New York. She is a 2013 graduate of the State University of New York at Cortland, where she majored in Sociology and minored in Social Philosophy.

Fiona McLeod, SC is a Senior Counsel at the Victorian Bar (Australia) practicing in the areas of human rights, commercial law, common law, and administrative law. Fiona studied law at the University of Melbourne, and has completed a Masters of Public and International Law. She has won numerous awards, including the inaugural Anti-Slavery Australia Freedom Award and the Lawyers Weekly Women in Law Barrister Award. At time of publication, she was leading the Australian governmental legal team in the Royal Commission Into Institutional Child Sex Abuse.

Julia Muraszkiewicz is a research analyst with a strong background in human rights. She is completing her Ph.D. in law at Vrije University Brussels. Julia has experience in managing research activities for EU-funded projects, writing reports, undertaking dissemination activities and writing grants. In her spare time, Julia co-runs the Manchester Stop the Traffic group and volunteers at a safe house for victims of human trafficking.

Alan W. Scheflin is Professor Emeritus at Santa Clara University School of Law and a judicially recognized expert in federal and state courts on mind and behavior control, suggestion and suggestibility, memory, and hypnosis. He has won 18 awards from a variety of professional associations and holds a B.A. with honors from the University of Virginia, a J.D. with honors from George Washington University School of Law, an LL.M. from Harvard University, and an M.A. in counseling psychology from Santa Clara University.

Catarina Sjölin, LL.M. is a senior lecturer at Nottingham Trent University. She spent 15 years at the Bar, ultimately specializing in tough cases involving a wide range of serious violence, appearing on behalf of the defense or prosecution. She has an M.A. (Hons) in Law and an LL.M. from Cambridge University. She has written for *Counsel Magazine* and *Criminal Law and Justice Weekly*, and is co-author of the *Sexual Offences Handbook* with Felicity Gerry.

Niovi Vavoula, LL.M. is an attorney based in Greece and a member of the Athens Bar Association. She graduated from the Law School of the University of Athens, Greece, and earned an LL.M. in European Law at Queen Mary University of London. She has volunteered with the Legal Department of the Greek Council for Refugees and interned for the Greek Desk at EUROJUST. She assists with the European Criminal Law Academic Network (ECLAN) and the *New Journal of European Criminal Law* (NJECL).

Index

Terrorism Law: Materials, Cases, Comments, Seventh Edition

by Jeffrey F. Addicott, B.A., J.D., L.L.M., S.J.D.

An essential reference text on the War on Terror. As the first edition of Terrorism Law suggests, terrorism, like crime, can never be completely eradicated. Over the past few years, as previous editions were released, the United States has faced many changes and challenges pertaining to the War on Terror, and continues to do so today. Although it was realized at the time the war started that legal and policy challenges would exist, no one could have predicted exactly what events would occur. The seventh edition of Terrorism Law has been updated to include new developments in this war, including the Boston Marathon bombing, as well as some of our nation's and the world's biggest challenges while fighting it.

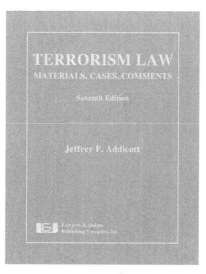

Topics include:
- What is terrorism?
- The Rule of Law: use of force
- Civil liberties and the War on Terror
- Addressing Terrorism since 9/11
- Interrogation techniques and what is torture
- Allegations of United States sanctioned torture
- Cyberterrorism
- Bioterrorism
- Civil litigation and the War on Terror

Product Code: 6028 • ISBN: 978-1-936360-17-8
Pages: 576 • Casebound • Size: 8.5″ × 11″

Terrorism Litigation: Cases and Materials, Second Edition

by David Strachman

Terrorism law is an emerging field which has brought the "war on terrorism" into the courtroom. This new area of law has several unique features and has attracted widespread attention from academia, the media, the bar, and public interest groups.

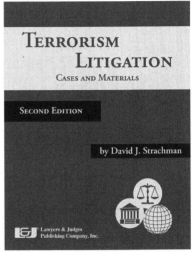

Terrorism Litigation, Second Edition, focuses on the law and practice of litigating claims of victims of international terrorism. Author David J. Strachman discusses the major landmark cases and explains applicable federal statutes. Strachman demonstrates the many differences between civil terrorism litigation, in which virtually all defendants are either rogue state sponsors of terrorism or designated terrorist organizations, and more common tort litigation which typically attempts to balance the conflicting claims of litigants.

This book is an essential reference for lawyers, law professors, political scientists and students. It also serves as a complete text for law school and undergraduate courses in terrorism law.

Topics Include:
- Historical attempts to bring terrorists to justice
- Alien Tort Claims Act of 1789
- Foreign Sovereign Immunities Act
- Antiterrorism and Effective Death Penalty Act of 1996
- Torture Victim Protection Act
- Terrorism Risk Insurance Act
- Acts of war
- Personal jurisdiction: states and non-states
- Punitive damages
- "Standard" terrorism damages
- Role of the U.S. government
- Payment of judgments

Product Code: 4462 • ISBN: 978-1-936360-10-9
Pages: 628 • Softbound • Size: 8.5″ × 11″